DRAFTED

RICK PARKER

Abrams ComicArts • New York

This book is dedicated to my partner in life and in love, Lisa Trusiani, and to our children, Grant and Grayson

Editor: Charles Kochman
Assistant Editor: Lydia Nguyen
Managing Editor: Ashley Albert
Designer: Josh Johnson
Design Manager: Pam Notarantonio
Production Manager: Alison Gervais

Cataloging-in-Publication Data has been applied for and may be obtained from the Library of Congress.

ISBN 978-1-4197-6159-1
eISBN 978-1-64700-660-0

This book was hand-drawn, hand-lettered, and digitally colored by Rick Parker.

Printed and bound in China
10 9 8 7 6 5 4 3 2 1

ABRAMS The Art of Books
195 Broadway, New York, NY 10007
abramsbooks.com

ACKNOWLEDGMENTS

First, I would like to thank my editor Charles Kochman and my agent, Judith Hansen. Charlie, Editor-in-Chief of Abrams ComicArts, provided brilliant insights and helped me shape the scope of *Drafted* to make it more personal and more historical. Judy Hansen believed in this book from the very beginning, and her expertise gave me confidence.

I hereby gratefully acknowledge the patience, love, and support of the people in my childhood, and the example they set for me. My grandmother, Nelle Cole Goodson, who by reading to me as a small child, instilled a love for comic strips and picture books. To my mother, Nell G. Parker, I give credit for valuing the arts and encouraging my creativity, and for all her love, and for making sure I had the best teachers in elementary school. I will never forget my second-grade teacher, Josephine Sutlive, who praised my crayon drawing of a sinking ship and held it up for the class to admire. My father, a pragmatic businessman, shocked me by handing over five hundred dollars for the Famous Artists correspondence course when I was a teenager. Two others in my early life proclaimed to all, "Ricky is going to be an artist when he grows up." Jerry Fillingim, a friend's older brother, asked me to draw a picture of the newly elected president, John F. Kennedy. Nina Williams, my grandmother's caretaker, watched as I covered the walls of my bedroom with drawings of monsters.

There are many artists and writers whom I never met but whose creations left an indelible impression. Thank you, J. R. Williams, Frank Willard, George McManus, Walt Disney, Rudyard Kipling, Edgar Allan Poe, Fritz Eichenberg, Victor Fleming, Bob Keeshan, John Gnagy, Alfred Hitchcock, Wally Wood, Hal Foster, Roy Crane, Ted Geisel, Harold Gray, Chester Gould, E. C. Segar, Charles Addams, Richard Taylor, Peter Arno, Chon Day, George Booth, B. Kliban, Henri Rousseau, Pablo Picasso, Andy Warhol, Jasper Johns, Claes Oldenburg, and H. C. Westermann.

I am deeply indebted to friends and fellow comics professionals. Among those who have influenced my career or inspired me are Harvey Kurtzman, Will Elder, Jack Davis, Archie Goodwin, Jim Salicrup, Mark Gruenwald, Mike Judge, Sid Jacobson, and Glenn Herdling.

I'm grateful to the following creators, for whom I have the utmost respect: Derf Backderf, Larry Hama, James Romberger, Louise Simonson, and Noah Van Sciver. They were all kind enough to read *Drafted* and write blurbs.

I'd like to recognize the contributions of the following people who read my manuscript: army veterans Carl Youmans and Randy Dunham, for guidance on military procedures; cousin Kathryn Hochman and my friend Ken Browd for proofreading.

Finally, I appreciate the enthusiasm of my friends and family who read early versions of the book and provided valuable feedback.

PRAISE FOR *DRAFTED*

"Rick Parker's remarkable graphic novel *Drafted* is a painfully honest, funny, and often troubling account of his time in the U.S. Army during the Vietnam War. It's a page-turning tale of a young rube sucked into the dysfunctional war machine, packed with details that can only come from enduring that experience firsthand. Engaging, insightful, and wonderfully drawn, *Drafted* is a fascinating read by a master storyteller."

—**Derf Backderf**, *My Friend Dahmer, Trashed,* and *Kent State*

"Rick Parker went through basic training a few years before I did, but man, everything in his graphic novel rings true and clear. This is observational graphic storytelling at its best. If you've never been in the service, this will be an eye-opener, and if you are a vet, this will trigger some long-forgotten memories."

—**Larry Hama**, *G.I. Joe, The 'Nam,* and Vietnam veteran

"Rick Parker's graphic novel is about an incredibly important part of the American experience, a subject that should appeal across party and ideological lines. He writes and draws as an everyman soldier, much like everyone's kid or sibling who went into service, but he happens to have the skill to render it viscerally as a comic. And in this endeavor, Parker brings all of his expertise to bear; all of his humor, empathy, and humanity, and his sense of right and wrong. *Drafted* is his magnum opus."

—**James Romberger**, *7 Miles a Second*

"Rick Parker's recall of his harrowing youth in the military is so clearly told that it will make your stomach sink while your eyes are glued to the page. I loved every minute of this book!"

—**Noah Van Sciver**, *Joseph Smith and the Mormons*

"I loved everything about this thoroughly engaging graphic memoir of a young artist coming of age in the 1960s, with the draft unavoidable and the Vietnam War looming large—a sensitive, funny evocation of cluelessness, vulnerability, and emerging focus as a fledgling recruit becomes a man in the U.S. Army."

—**Louise Simonson**, *New Mutants* and *Superman: The Man of Steel*

CONTENTS

PROLOGUE

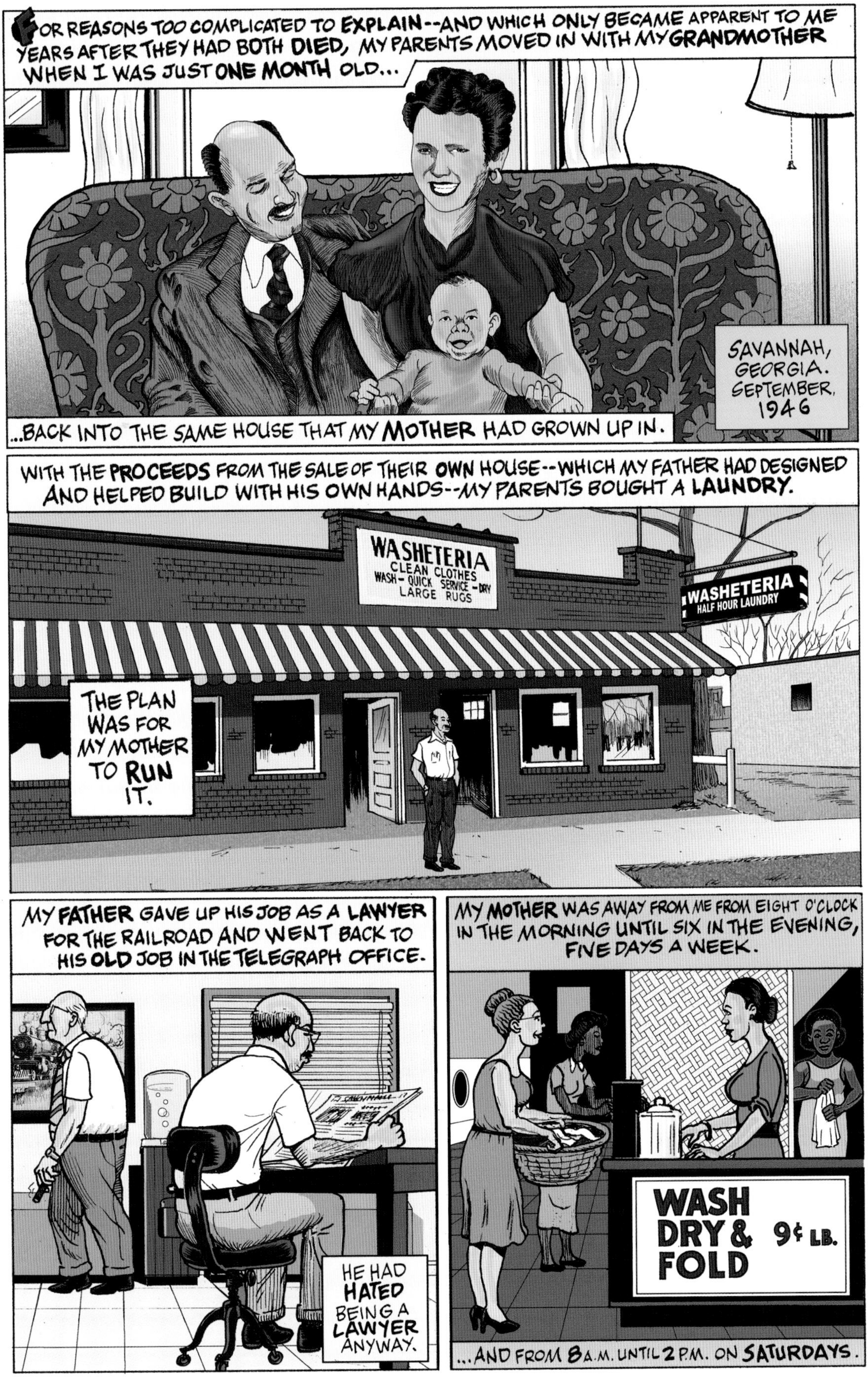
FOR REASONS TOO COMPLICATED TO EXPLAIN--AND WHICH ONLY BECAME APPARENT TO ME YEARS AFTER THEY HAD BOTH DIED, MY PARENTS MOVED IN WITH MY GRANDMOTHER WHEN I WAS JUST ONE MONTH OLD...
SAVANNAH, GEORGIA. SEPTEMBER, 1946
...BACK INTO THE SAME HOUSE THAT MY MOTHER HAD GROWN UP IN.
WITH THE PROCEEDS FROM THE SALE OF THEIR OWN HOUSE--WHICH MY FATHER HAD DESIGNED AND HELPED BUILD WITH HIS OWN HANDS--MY PARENTS BOUGHT A LAUNDRY.
WASHETERIA
CLEAN CLOTHES
WASH - QUICK SERVICE - DRY
LARGE RUGS
WASHETERIA
HALF HOUR LAUNDRY
THE PLAN WAS FOR MY MOTHER TO RUN IT.
MY FATHER GAVE UP HIS JOB AS A LAWYER FOR THE RAILROAD AND WENT BACK TO HIS OLD JOB IN THE TELEGRAPH OFFICE.
HE HAD HATED BEING A LAWYER ANYWAY.
MY MOTHER WAS AWAY FROM ME FROM EIGHT O'CLOCK IN THE MORNING UNTIL SIX IN THE EVENING, FIVE DAYS A WEEK.
WASH
DRY &
FOLD
9¢ LB.
...AND FROM 8 A.M. UNTIL 2 P.M. ON SATURDAYS.

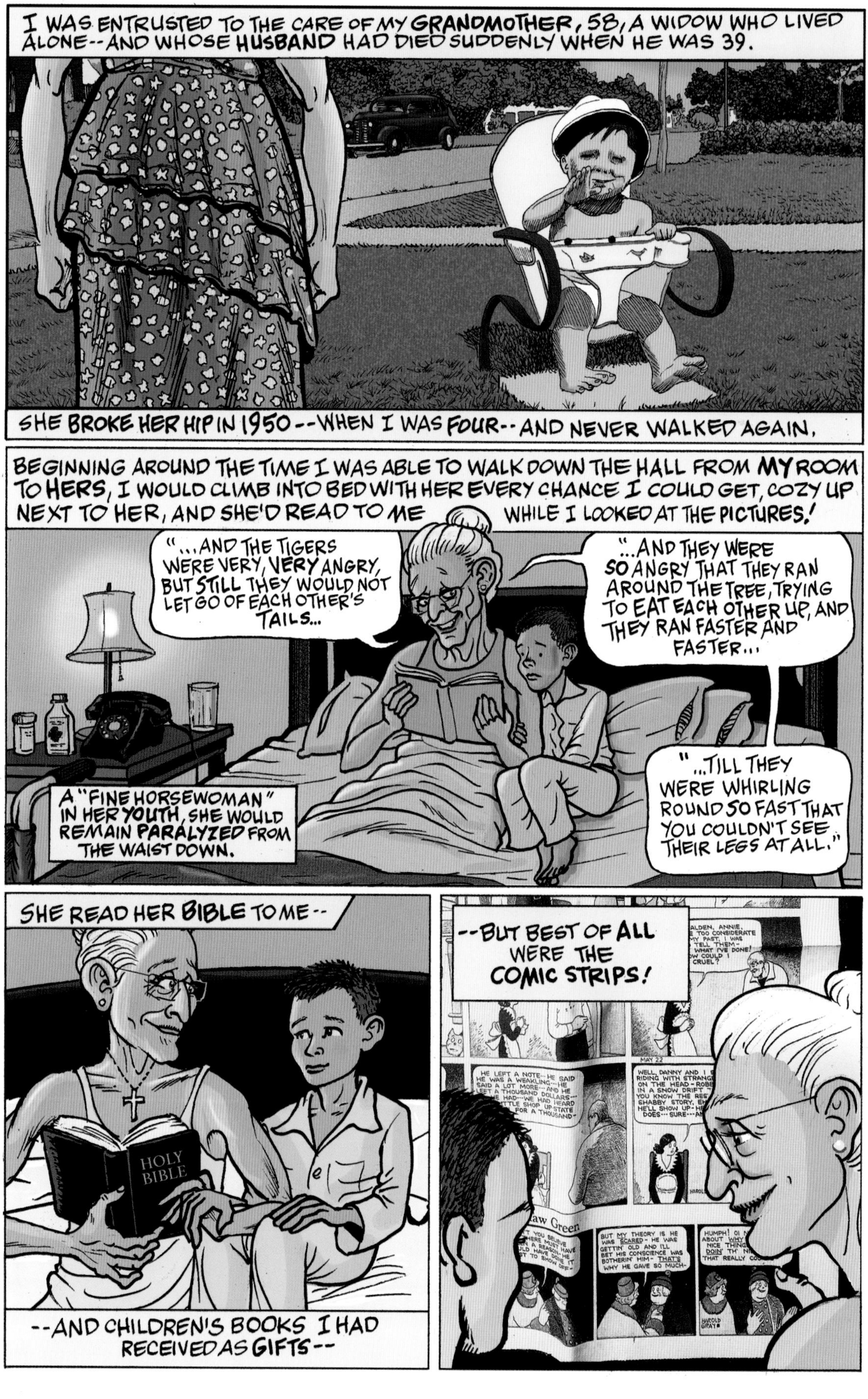
I WAS ENTRUSTED TO THE CARE OF MY GRANDMOTHER, 58, A WIDOW WHO LIVED ALONE--AND WHOSE HUSBAND HAD DIED SUDDENLY WHEN HE WAS 39.
SHE BROKE HER HIP IN 1950--WHEN I WAS FOUR--AND NEVER WALKED AGAIN.
BEGINNING AROUND THE TIME I WAS ABLE TO WALK DOWN THE HALL FROM MY ROOM TO HERS, I WOULD CLIMB INTO BED WITH HER EVERY CHANCE I COULD GET, COZY UP NEXT TO HER, AND SHE'D READ TO ME WHILE I LOOKED AT THE PICTURES!
"...AND THE TIGERS WERE VERY, VERY ANGRY, BUT STILL THEY WOULD NOT LET GO OF EACH OTHER'S TAILS...
"...AND THEY WERE SO ANGRY THAT THEY RAN AROUND THE TREE, TRYING TO EAT EACH OTHER UP, AND THEY RAN FASTER AND FASTER...
A "FINE HORSEWOMAN" IN HER YOUTH, SHE WOULD REMAIN PARALYZED FROM THE WAIST DOWN.
"...TILL THEY WERE WHIRLING ROUND SO FAST THAT YOU COULDN'T SEE THEIR LEGS AT ALL."
SHE READ HER BIBLE TO ME--
HOLY BIBLE
--AND CHILDREN'S BOOKS I HAD RECEIVED AS GIFTS--
--BUT BEST OF ALL WERE THE COMIC STRIPS!

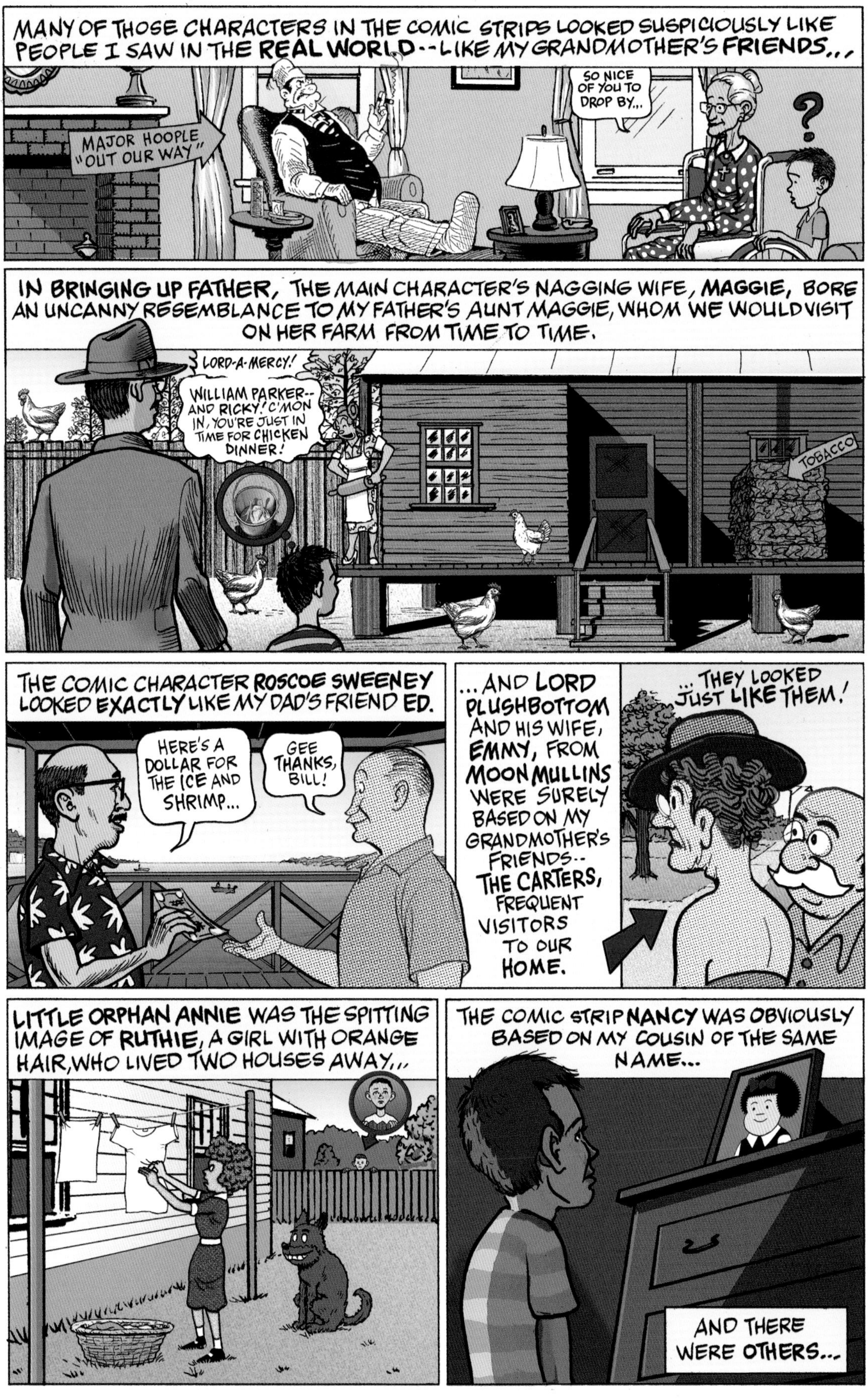
MANY OF THOSE CHARACTERS IN THE COMIC STRIPS LOOKED SUSPICIOUSLY LIKE PEOPLE I SAW IN THE REAL WORLD--LIKE MY GRANDMOTHER'S FRIENDS...
MAJOR HOOPLE "OUT OUR WAY"
SO NICE OF YOU TO DROP BY...
?
IN BRINGING UP FATHER, THE MAIN CHARACTER'S NAGGING WIFE, MAGGIE, BORE AN UNCANNY RESEMBLANCE TO MY FATHER'S AUNT MAGGIE, WHOM WE WOULD VISIT ON HER FARM FROM TIME TO TIME.
LORD-A-MERCY!
WILLIAM PARKER-- AND RICKY! C'MON IN, YOU'RE JUST IN TIME FOR CHICKEN DINNER!
TOBACCO
THE COMIC CHARACTER ROSCOE SWEENEY LOOKED EXACTLY LIKE MY DAD'S FRIEND ED.
HERE'S A DOLLAR FOR THE ICE AND SHRIMP...
GEE THANKS, BILL!
...AND LORD PLUSHBOTTOM AND HIS WIFE, EMMY, FROM MOON MULLINS WERE SURELY BASED ON MY GRANDMOTHER'S FRIENDS-- THE CARTERS, FREQUENT VISITORS TO OUR HOME.
...THEY LOOKED JUST LIKE THEM!
LITTLE ORPHAN ANNIE WAS THE SPITTING IMAGE OF RUTHIE, A GIRL WITH ORANGE HAIR, WHO LIVED TWO HOUSES AWAY...
THE COMIC STRIP NANCY WAS OBVIOUSLY BASED ON MY COUSIN OF THE SAME NAME...
AND THERE WERE OTHERS...

BUT THE ONE THAT REALLY STRUCK ME WAS CALLED HENRY --A STRIP ABOUT A LITTLE BOY WITH A BALD HEAD AND BIG EARS...
OKAY, GRANDMA...LET'S SEE... IT LOOKS LIKE THE BOY RINGS THE DOORBELL...AND HENRY FILLS UP A BUCKET WITH WATER...
Henry
I WONDER WHAT THEY MAKE IN DAT FACTORY
VERY GOOD!
THERE WAS NO QUESTION IT WAS BASED ON THE BOY NEXT DOOR, WHOSE NAME WAS --YOU GUESSED IT-- HENRY.
HE LOOKED EXACTLY LIKE HIM!
WHEN I GROW UP, I THINK I'D LIKE TO SWING THROUGH THE JUNGLE ON VINES LIKE TARZAN...
ATOMIZERS
FROM ONE LOFTY BRANCH TO ANOTHER, RICKY SWEPT WITH INCREDIBLE SPEED, THE LEOPARD SCENT GROWING EVER STRONGER.
I KNEW IT WAS JUST A MATTER OF TIME UNTIL SOMEONE DID A COMIC STRIP ABOUT ME...

SOMETIMES YOU HAVE TO TAKE MATTERS INTO YOUR OWN HANDS.

IT WAS LATE FEBRUARY, AND THE SKY, A COLD GRAY, MATCHED MY MOOD...

THE BARRACKS WERE HEATED BY BURNING BIG LUMPS OF BLACK ANTHRACITE COAL, AND THE BURNED CINDERS AND ASH DRIFTED DOWN LIKE UGLY BLACK GERMS AND LANDED ON EACH SHAVED HEAD, AND ROW UPON ROW OF DRAB WOODEN BUILDINGS.
INDUCTION STATION FORT JACKSON, SOUTH CAROLINA. FEBRUARY, 1966
AS I PLODDED ALONG, AMID ALL THE JOYLESS INDUCTEES, I KEPT REMINDING MYSELF THAT I WAS JUST IN THE ARMY, AND NOT IN SOME PRISON OR CONCENTRATION CAMP.
PARKER
U.S. ARMY
GOMES
JONES
TITUS
EADES
I STARED AT THE SHAVED HEAD OF THE POOR BASTARD IN FRONT OF ME AND CAME TO A STARTLING REALIZATION.
I'D BEEN IN THE ARMY FOR NEARLY A WEEK AND I STILL HADN'T TAKEN A DUMP.
THE WHOLE THING WAS BEGINNING TO SEEM LIKE SOME KIND OF BAD DREAM FROM WHICH I COULD NOT WAKE UP.
PARKER
U.S. ARMY
HOW DID I EVER GET MYSELF INTO THIS PREDICAMENT?

1

CALLED UP

MOST LIKELY, I WAS DAYDREAMING ABSENTMINDEDLY IN HOMEROOM THE MORNING MY TEACHER MADE THE ANNOUNCEMENT.
TODAY'S DATE: SEPTEMBER 2, 1963
...REPRESENTATIVES OF VARIOUS COLLEGES AND UNIVERSITIES...
...WILL MEET WITH PROSPECTIVE APPLICANTS THIS AFTERNOON IN THE AUDITORIUM AT 2 P.M....
...THE REST OF YOU WILL ATTEND CLASS AS USUAL...
ME
INTEGRATION IN GEORGIA BEGAN MY SENIOR YEAR.
EVEN IF I WASN'T DAYDREAMING, I PROBABLY DIDN'T THINK THE ANNOUNCEMENT PERTAINED TO ME.
NO ONE HAD EVER DISCUSSED COLLEGE WITH ME--NOT MY TEACHERS--NOT OTHER STUDENTS--
SAVANNAH EVE
--NOT EVEN MY PARENTS!
MY MOTHER, A BRIGHT YOUNG WOMAN WHO GRADUATED FROM HIGH SCHOOL WHEN SHE WAS 16--
--DROPPED OUT OF COLLEGE AFTER ONLY ONE YEAR.
IT WAS THE HEIGHT OF THE DEPRESSION. SHE HAD BEEN OFFERED A GOOD JOB WITH THE RAILROAD...
...IN THE SAME OFFICE HER FATHER HAD WORKED IN BEFORE HE DIED SEVEN YEARS EARLIER.
SHE SAID SHE USED TO SEE HER FATHER'S HANDWRITING ON THE OFFICE PAPERWORK.
HE LEFT MY GRANDMOTHER TO RAISE FOUR CHILDREN, THE OLDEST OF WHOM WAS ONLY 19.
GOODSON
MY MOTHER, THE YOUNGEST CHILD AND HIS FAVORITE (OR SO SHE TOLD ME) WAS ONLY 10.

MY FATHER'S EDUCATION WAS CUT SHORT AT 16 WHEN HE WAS SUMMONED BACK TO GEORGIA FROM ASBURY COLLEGE IN KENTUCKY--
--TO ATTEND THE FUNERAL OF HIS 21-YEAR-OLD SISTER WHO HAD DIED UNEXPECTEDLY.
SHE SUCCUMBED TO VIRAL MENINGITIS, THE SAME ILLNESS THAT HAD TAKEN THE LIFE OF HER ONE-YEAR-OLD SON A MONTH EARLIER.
WHO IS THIS, GRANDMA?
SHE WAS YOUR AUNT.
MY GRANDMOTHER TOLD ME, "SHE DIED OF A BROKEN HEART."
RATHER THAN RETURN TO SCHOOL, MY FATHER TOOK A JOB SWEEPING UP AT A LITTLE COUNTRY RAILROAD STATION IN AN EFFORT TO HELP SUPPORT HIS WIDOWED MOTHER.
WESTERN UNION
W P PARKER JR
NICHOLLS, GEORGIA
STATION HELPER POSITION AVAILABLE IMMEDIATELY
SALARY $1.50 PER WEEK
INQUIRE STATION MANAGER
P.D. BRITTINGHAM
ALMA, GEORGIA
HIS MOTHER HAD LOST HER HUSBAND WHEN MY FATHER, ALSO THE YOUNGEST OF FOUR CHILDREN, WAS ONLY 13.
HE WOUND UP WORKING FOR THE RAILROAD FOR THE NEXT 52 YEARS...
CHOLLS
STATION HELPER
TAP TAP
TELEGRAPH OPERATOR
LAWYER
MANAGER TELEGRAPH OFFICE

IN HIGH SCHOOL, I SHOWED A MARKED TALENT IN WRITING AND ART--
YOU WANTED TO SEE ME, MR. BELFORD?
YES... YOU'RE THE MOST ARTICULATE STUDENT IN MY CLASS...
I HAD TO LOOK UP THE WORD "ARTICULATE."
I ONLY MANAGED TO GRADUATE BY REPEATING ALGEBRA 1 & 2 IN SUMMER SCHOOL.
I WAS JUST A FEW MONTHS SHY OF MY 18TH BIRTHDAY.
I ONLY APPLIED TO TWO COLLEGES--
JABBO, THIS IS BILL PARKER.
--DARTMOUTH--
--AND PRATT INSTITUTE IN BROOKLYN--
--AND WAS SUMMARILY REJECTED BY BOTH.
U.S. MAIL
HMPH! I KNEW IT...
I HAD EVEN BOUGHT BLAZER BUTTONS!
ALTHOUGH I HAD NO WAY OF KNOWING IT AT THE TIME--
--I WOULD RECEIVE MY MASTER'S DEGREE FROM PRATT ABOUT 10 YEARS LATER.

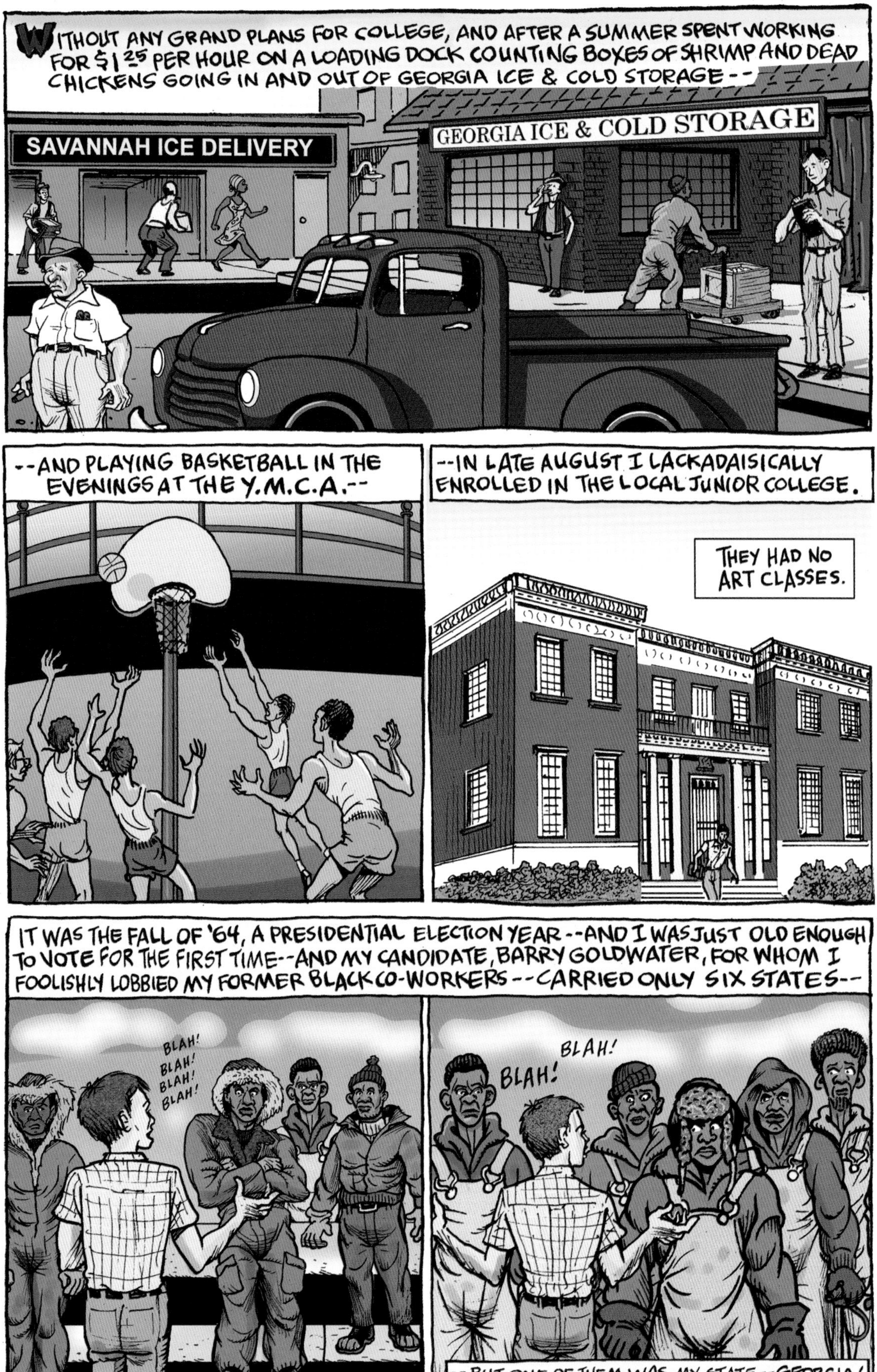
WITHOUT ANY GRAND PLANS FOR COLLEGE, AND AFTER A SUMMER SPENT WORKING FOR $1.25 PER HOUR ON A LOADING DOCK COUNTING BOXES OF SHRIMP AND DEAD CHICKENS GOING IN AND OUT OF GEORGIA ICE & COLD STORAGE--
SAVANNAH ICE DELIVERY
GEORGIA ICE & COLD STORAGE
--AND PLAYING BASKETBALL IN THE EVENINGS AT THE Y.M.C.A.--
--IN LATE AUGUST I LACKADAISICALLY ENROLLED IN THE LOCAL JUNIOR COLLEGE.
THEY HAD NO ART CLASSES.
IT WAS THE FALL OF '64, A PRESIDENTIAL ELECTION YEAR--AND I WAS JUST OLD ENOUGH TO VOTE FOR THE FIRST TIME--AND MY CANDIDATE, BARRY GOLDWATER, FOR WHOM I FOOLISHLY LOBBIED MY FORMER BLACK CO-WORKERS--CARRIED ONLY SIX STATES--
BLAH! BLAH! BLAH! BLAH!
BLAH!
BLAH!
--BUT ONE OF THEM WAS MY STATE--GEORGIA!

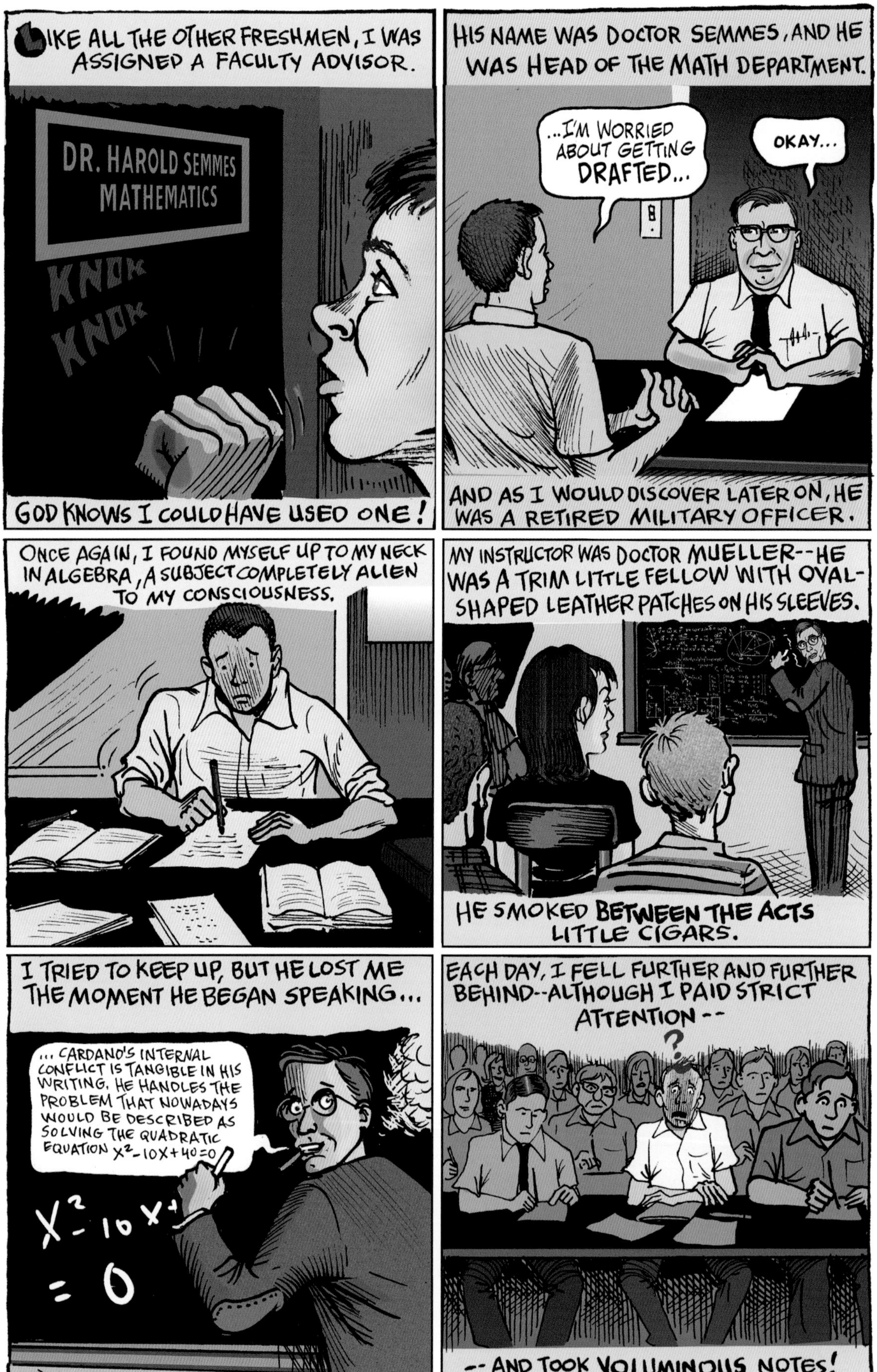
LIKE ALL THE OTHER FRESHMEN, I WAS ASSIGNED A FACULTY ADVISOR.
DR. HAROLD SEMMES MATHEMATICS
KNOK KNOK
GOD KNOWS I COULD HAVE USED ONE!
HIS NAME WAS DOCTOR SEMMES, AND HE WAS HEAD OF THE MATH DEPARTMENT.
...I'M WORRIED ABOUT GETTING DRAFTED...
OKAY...
AND AS I WOULD DISCOVER LATER ON, HE WAS A RETIRED MILITARY OFFICER.
ONCE AGAIN, I FOUND MYSELF UP TO MY NECK IN ALGEBRA, A SUBJECT COMPLETELY ALIEN TO MY CONSCIOUSNESS.
MY INSTRUCTOR WAS DOCTOR MUELLER--HE WAS A TRIM LITTLE FELLOW WITH OVAL-SHAPED LEATHER PATCHES ON HIS SLEEVES.
HE SMOKED BETWEEN THE ACTS LITTLE CIGARS.
I TRIED TO KEEP UP, BUT HE LOST ME THE MOMENT HE BEGAN SPEAKING...
... CARDANO'S INTERNAL CONFLICT IS TANGIBLE IN HIS WRITING. HE HANDLES THE PROBLEM THAT NOWADAYS WOULD BE DESCRIBED AS SOLVING THE QUADRATIC EQUATION X²-10X+40=0
EACH DAY, I FELL FURTHER AND FURTHER BEHIND--ALTHOUGH I PAID STRICT ATTENTION--
?
--AND TOOK VOLUMINOUS NOTES!

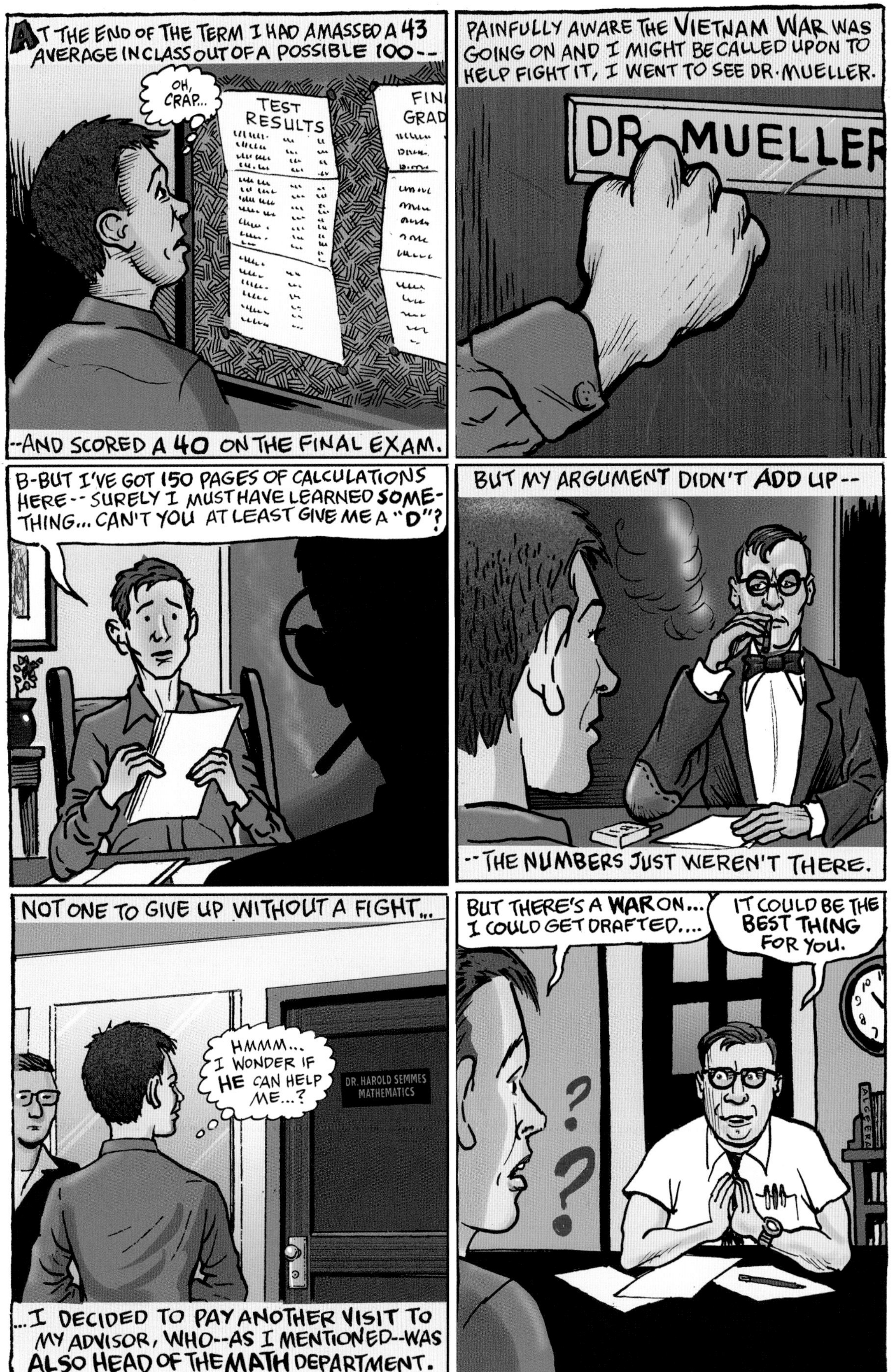
AT THE END OF THE TERM I HAD AMASSED A 43 AVERAGE IN CLASS OUT OF A POSSIBLE 100--
OH, CRAP...
TEST RESULTS
--AND SCORED A 40 ON THE FINAL EXAM.
PAINFULLY AWARE THE VIETNAM WAR WAS GOING ON AND I MIGHT BE CALLED UPON TO HELP FIGHT IT, I WENT TO SEE DR. MUELLER.
DR. MUELLER
B-BUT I'VE GOT 150 PAGES OF CALCULATIONS HERE-- SURELY I MUST HAVE LEARNED SOME-THING... CAN'T YOU AT LEAST GIVE ME A "D"?
BUT MY ARGUMENT DIDN'T ADD UP--
--THE NUMBERS JUST WEREN'T THERE.
NOT ONE TO GIVE UP WITHOUT A FIGHT...
HMMM... I WONDER IF HE CAN HELP ME...?
DR. HAROLD SEMMES MATHEMATICS
...I DECIDED TO PAY ANOTHER VISIT TO MY ADVISOR, WHO--AS I MENTIONED--WAS ALSO HEAD OF THE MATH DEPARTMENT.
BUT THERE'S A WAR ON... I COULD GET DRAFTED....
IT COULD BE THE BEST THING FOR YOU.
ALGEBRA

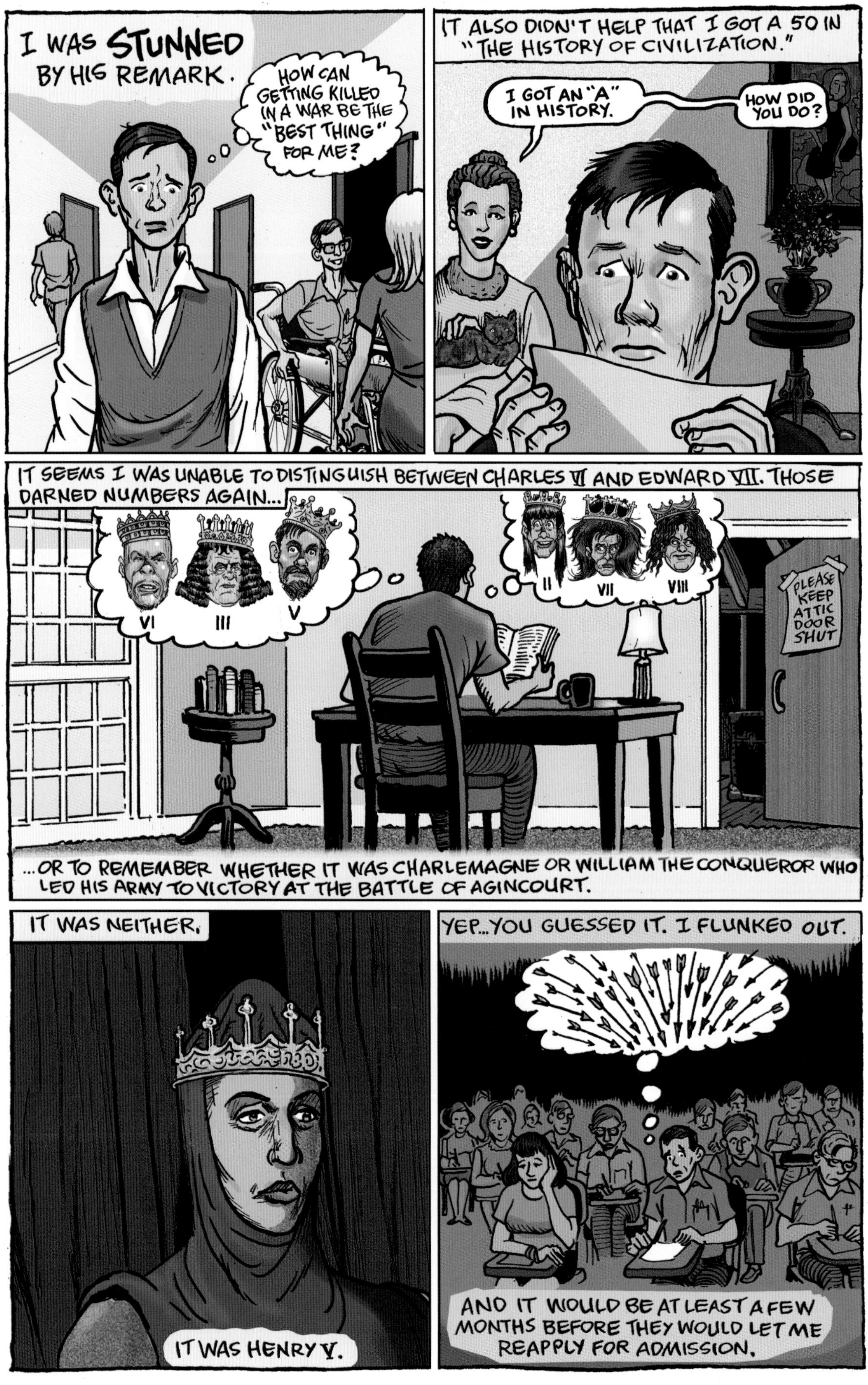
I WAS STUNNED BY HIS REMARK.
HOW CAN GETTING KILLED IN A WAR BE THE "BEST THING" FOR ME?
IT ALSO DIDN'T HELP THAT I GOT A 50 IN "THE HISTORY OF CIVILIZATION."
I GOT AN "A" IN HISTORY.
HOW DID YOU DO?
IT SEEMS I WAS UNABLE TO DISTINGUISH BETWEEN CHARLES VI AND EDWARD VII. THOSE DARNED NUMBERS AGAIN...
VI
III
V
II
VII
VIII
PLEASE KEEP ATTIC DOOR SHUT
...OR TO REMEMBER WHETHER IT WAS CHARLEMAGNE OR WILLIAM THE CONQUEROR WHO LED HIS ARMY TO VICTORY AT THE BATTLE OF AGINCOURT.
IT WAS NEITHER.
IT WAS HENRY V.
YEP...YOU GUESSED IT. I FLUNKED OUT.
AND IT WOULD BE AT LEAST A FEW MONTHS BEFORE THEY WOULD LET ME REAPPLY FOR ADMISSION.

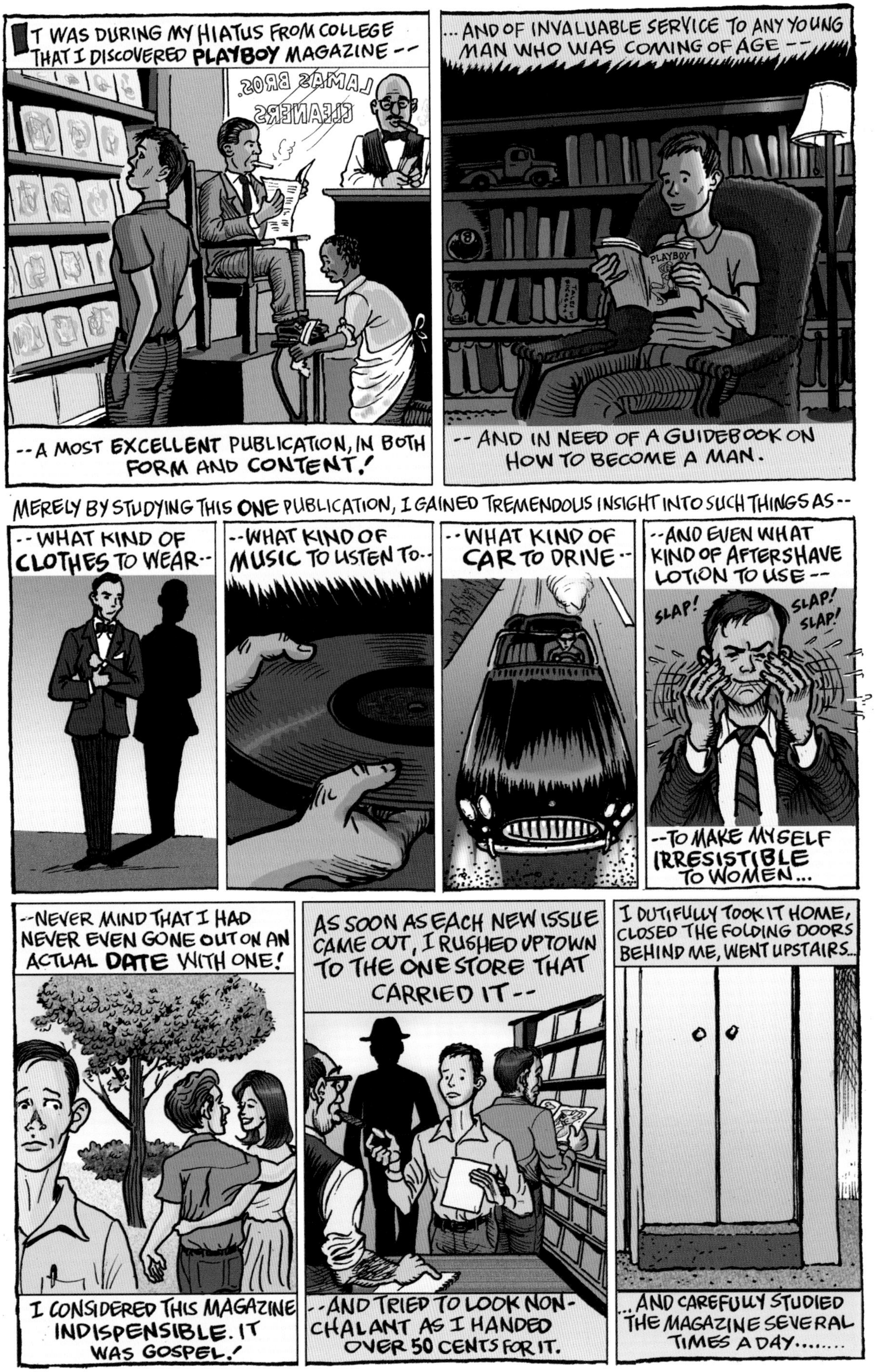
IT WAS DURING MY HIATUS FROM COLLEGE THAT I DISCOVERED PLAYBOY MAGAZINE --
LAMAS BROS. CLEANERS
--A MOST EXCELLENT PUBLICATION, IN BOTH FORM AND CONTENT!
...AND OF INVALUABLE SERVICE TO ANY YOUNG MAN WHO WAS COMING OF AGE --
PLAYBOY
-- AND IN NEED OF A GUIDEBOOK ON HOW TO BECOME A MAN.
MERELY BY STUDYING THIS ONE PUBLICATION, I GAINED TREMENDOUS INSIGHT INTO SUCH THINGS AS --
-- WHAT KIND OF CLOTHES TO WEAR --
-- WHAT KIND OF MUSIC TO LISTEN TO --
-- WHAT KIND OF CAR TO DRIVE --
-- AND EVEN WHAT KIND OF AFTERSHAVE LOTION TO USE --
SLAP!
SLAP! SLAP!
-- TO MAKE MYSELF IRRESISTIBLE TO WOMEN...
-- NEVER MIND THAT I HAD NEVER EVEN GONE OUT ON AN ACTUAL DATE WITH ONE!
I CONSIDERED THIS MAGAZINE INDISPENSIBLE. IT WAS GOSPEL!
AS SOON AS EACH NEW ISSUE CAME OUT, I RUSHED UPTOWN TO THE ONE STORE THAT CARRIED IT --
-- AND TRIED TO LOOK NON-CHALANT AS I HANDED OVER 50 CENTS FOR IT.
I DUTIFULLY TOOK IT HOME, CLOSED THE FOLDING DOORS BEHIND ME, WENT UPSTAIRS...
...AND CAREFULLY STUDIED THE MAGAZINE SEVERAL TIMES A DAY.......

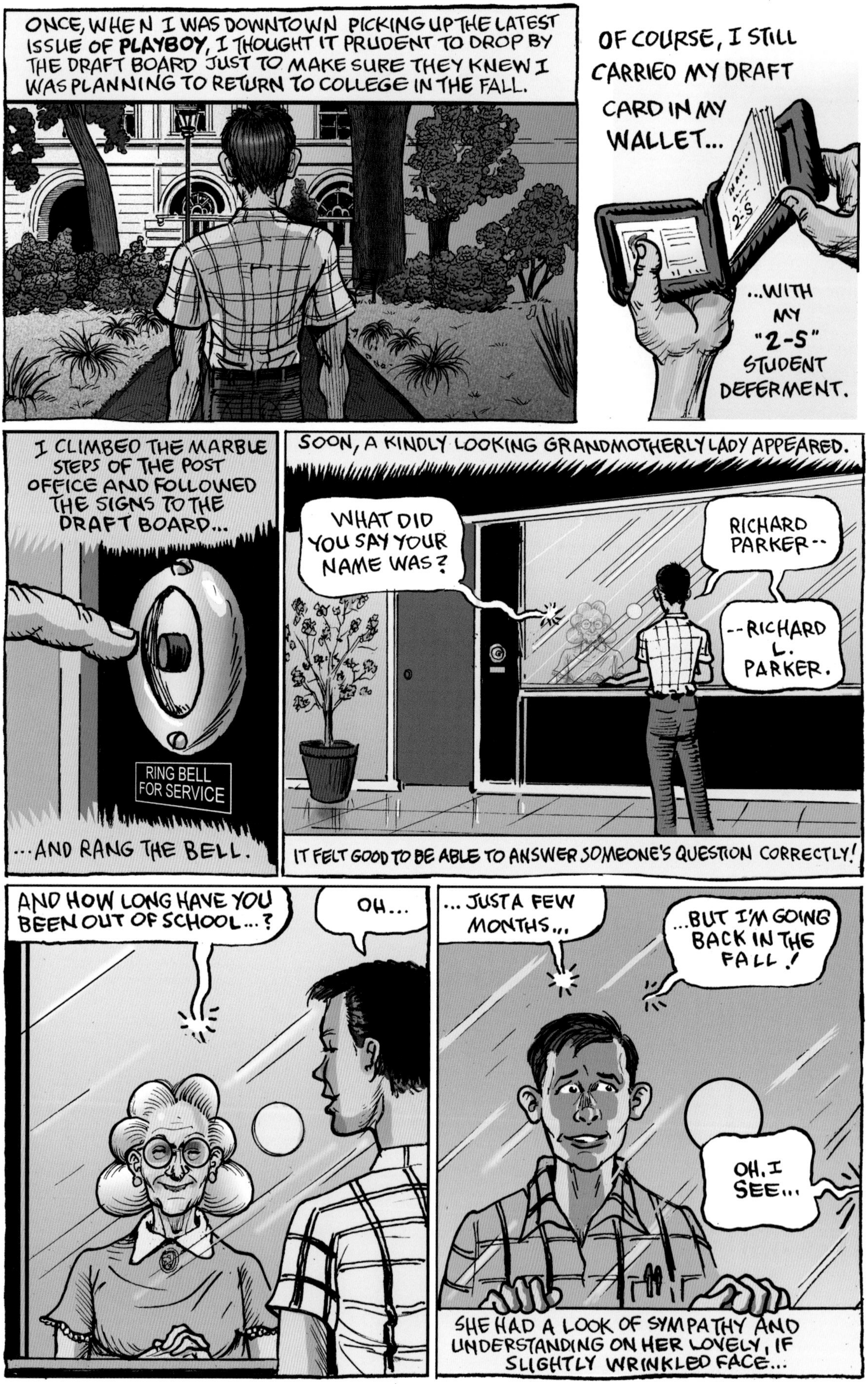
ONCE, WHEN I WAS DOWNTOWN PICKING UP THE LATEST ISSUE OF PLAYBOY, I THOUGHT IT PRUDENT TO DROP BY THE DRAFT BOARD JUST TO MAKE SURE THEY KNEW I WAS PLANNING TO RETURN TO COLLEGE IN THE FALL.
OF COURSE, I STILL CARRIED MY DRAFT CARD IN MY WALLET...
2-S
...WITH MY "2-S" STUDENT DEFERMENT.
I CLIMBED THE MARBLE STEPS OF THE POST OFFICE AND FOLLOWED THE SIGNS TO THE DRAFT BOARD...
RING BELL FOR SERVICE
...AND RANG THE BELL.
SOON, A KINDLY LOOKING GRANDMOTHERLY LADY APPEARED.
WHAT DID YOU SAY YOUR NAME WAS?
RICHARD PARKER--
--RICHARD L. PARKER.
IT FELT GOOD TO BE ABLE TO ANSWER SOMEONE'S QUESTION CORRECTLY!
AND HOW LONG HAVE YOU BEEN OUT OF SCHOOL...?
OH...
...JUST A FEW MONTHS...
...BUT I'M GOING BACK IN THE FALL!
OH, I SEE...
SHE HAD A LOOK OF SYMPATHY AND UNDERSTANDING ON HER LOVELY, IF SLIGHTLY WRINKLED FACE...

SECURE IN THE KNOWLEDGE THAT I HAD EXPLAINED MY SITUATION QUITE CLEARLY...
...AND RELIEVED TO HAVE CIRCUMVENTED ANY POSSIBLE MISUNDERSTANDING REGARDING MY ELIGIBILITY STATUS...
...I STEPPED AWAY FROM THE WINDOW...
...DID AN ABOUT-FACE... AND MARCHED AWAY FEELING QUITE SATISFIED...
...I PUSHED OPEN THE BIG PLATE GLASS DOORS WITH BOTH HANDS --
-- AND STEPPED OUT ONTO THE WHITE MARBLE PORTICO OF THE UNITED STATES POST OFFICE INTO THE CRISP AUTUMN AIR...

YES-SIR-REE!
IT'S A GORGEOUS DAY TO BE ALIVE.
THE SUN WAS FILTERING SOFTLY THROUGH THE LEAVES OF THE OAK TREES IN TELFAIR SQUARE...
OLD MEN IN GRAY SUITS SAT ON PARK BENCHES READING THEIR NEWSPAPERS...
...A MOTHER AND CHILD FED THE PIGEONS...
YESSIR! I HAD TO ADMIT...
...LIFE WAS GOOD!
ALL WAS RIGHT WITH THE WORLD!
EXACTLY ONE WEEK LATER...
...I GOT DRAFTED.

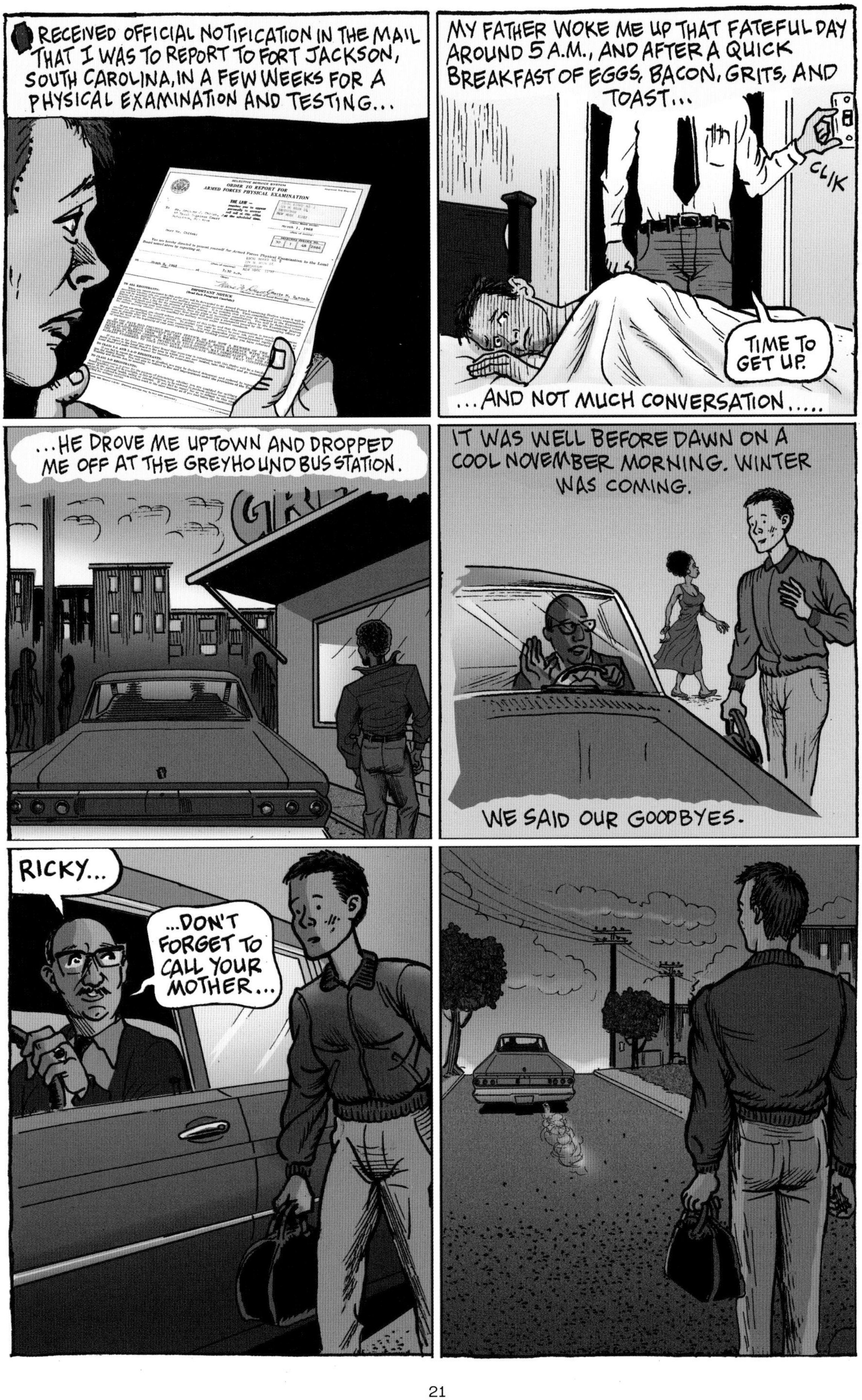
I RECEIVED OFFICIAL NOTIFICATION IN THE MAIL THAT I WAS TO REPORT TO FORT JACKSON, SOUTH CAROLINA, IN A FEW WEEKS FOR A PHYSICAL EXAMINATION AND TESTING...
MY FATHER WOKE ME UP THAT FATEFUL DAY AROUND 5 A.M., AND AFTER A QUICK BREAKFAST OF EGGS, BACON, GRITS, AND TOAST...
CLIK
TIME TO GET UP.
...AND NOT MUCH CONVERSATION.....
...HE DROVE ME UPTOWN AND DROPPED ME OFF AT THE GREYHOUND BUS STATION.
IT WAS WELL BEFORE DAWN ON A COOL NOVEMBER MORNING. WINTER WAS COMING.
WE SAID OUR GOODBYES.
RICKY...
...DON'T FORGET TO CALL YOUR MOTHER...

INSIDE THE BUS STATION, SEVERAL PEOPLE WERE CURLED UP IN THEIR SEATS TRYING TO SLEEP. THE STALE SMELL OF TOBACCO HUNG IN THE AIR--AND NO ONE SEEMED HAPPY OR IN VERY MUCH OF A HURRY TO GO ANYWHERE.
GREYHOUND
I LOOKED AROUND--I DIDN'T SEE ANYONE WHO LOOKED EVEN REMOTELY LIKE ME...
...THEN I NOTICED A LINE FORMING OUTSIDE NEXT TO ONE OF THE BUSES.
THEY WERE ALL YOUNG GUYS LIKE ME. I GOT IN THE BACK OF THE LINE.
NO ONE SAID MUCH--OR EVEN LOOKED UP.
WE WERE ALL LOST IN OUR OWN PRIVATE THOUGHTS.
MOST OF THE GUYS ON THE BUS SEEMED TO BE FROM THE "OTHER SIDE OF THE TRACKS." A ROUGHER CROWD THAN I WAS USED TO ASSOCIATING WITH....
THE BUS PULLED OUT AND BEGAN THE TWO-HOUR JOURNEY TO FORT JACKSON.

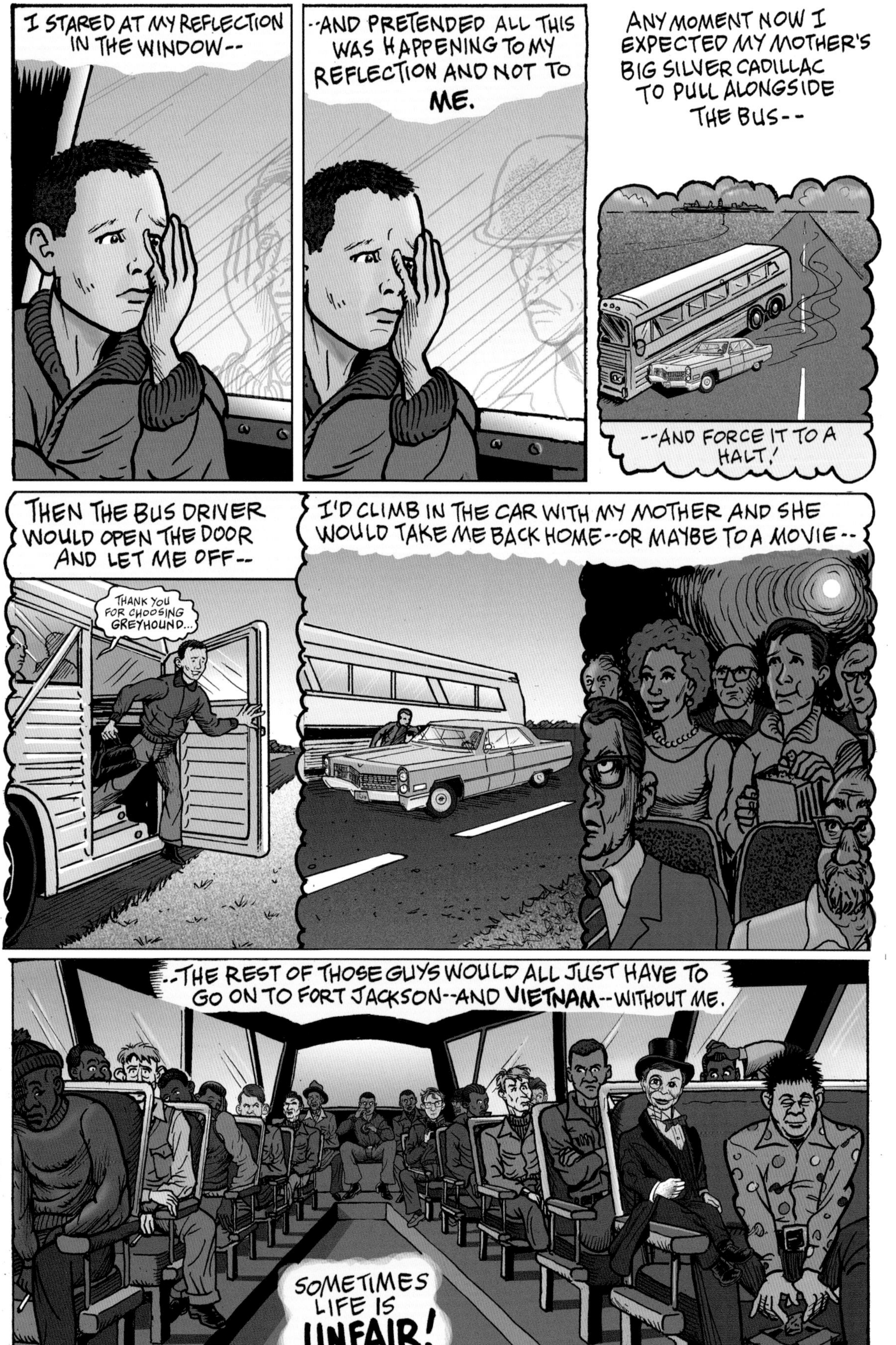
I STARED AT MY REFLECTION IN THE WINDOW--
--AND PRETENDED ALL THIS WAS HAPPENING TO MY REFLECTION AND NOT TO ME.
ANY MOMENT NOW I EXPECTED MY MOTHER'S BIG SILVER CADILLAC TO PULL ALONGSIDE THE BUS--
--AND FORCE IT TO A HALT!
THEN THE BUS DRIVER WOULD OPEN THE DOOR AND LET ME OFF--
THANK YOU FOR CHOOSING GREYHOUND...
I'D CLIMB IN THE CAR WITH MY MOTHER AND SHE WOULD TAKE ME BACK HOME--OR MAYBE TO A MOVIE--
--THE REST OF THOSE GUYS WOULD ALL JUST HAVE TO GO ON TO FORT JACKSON--AND VIETNAM--WITHOUT ME.
SOMETIMES LIFE IS UNFAIR!
FOR John

AS WE CROSSED INTO SOUTH CAROLINA, I CAUGHT A FLEETING GLIMPSE OF A LITTLE FIREWORKS STAND--
FIREWORKS
CHERRY BOMBS M80's
--I HAD GONE TO IT ONCE ON THE BACK OF JERRY'S MOTOR SCOOTER.
JERRY, A FRIEND'S OLDER BROTHER, HAD ALMOST STRANGLED ME TO DEATH IN HIS ATTIC ONLY SIX OR SEVEN YEARS EARLIER...
HA-HA-HA! LOOK--!!
HE PEED IN HIS PANTS!!
WE PASSED THE LARGE EXPANSE OF SALT MARSH THAT BORDERED THE RIVER--
--I THOUGHT BACK TO A TIME WHEN I HAD TRAVELED THIS SAME ROAD WITH MY PARENTS--
--WE WERE ON OUR WAY TO SPEND THE DAY AT THE BEACH AT HILTON HEAD.
RICKY-- WOULD YOU LIKE A PIMENTO CHEESE SANDWICH?
YUCK!
NO THANK YOU.
MY MUSINGS WERE RUDELY INTERRUPTED BY A GUY IN A SEAT ACROSS THE AISLE FROM ME.
LET ME TELL YOU HOW TO GET AUTOMATICALLY REJECTED.
HIS FACE WAS COVERED WITH WHAT COULD ONLY BE DESCRIBED AS PUSTULATING BOILS.
ALTHOUGH I WAS FAR FROM THE "PATRIOTIC TYPE", IT WOULD NEVER HAVE OCCURRED TO ME TO DO WHAT HE HAD DONE....
I USED A HYPODERMIC NEEDLE DIPPED IN MY OWN SHIT.

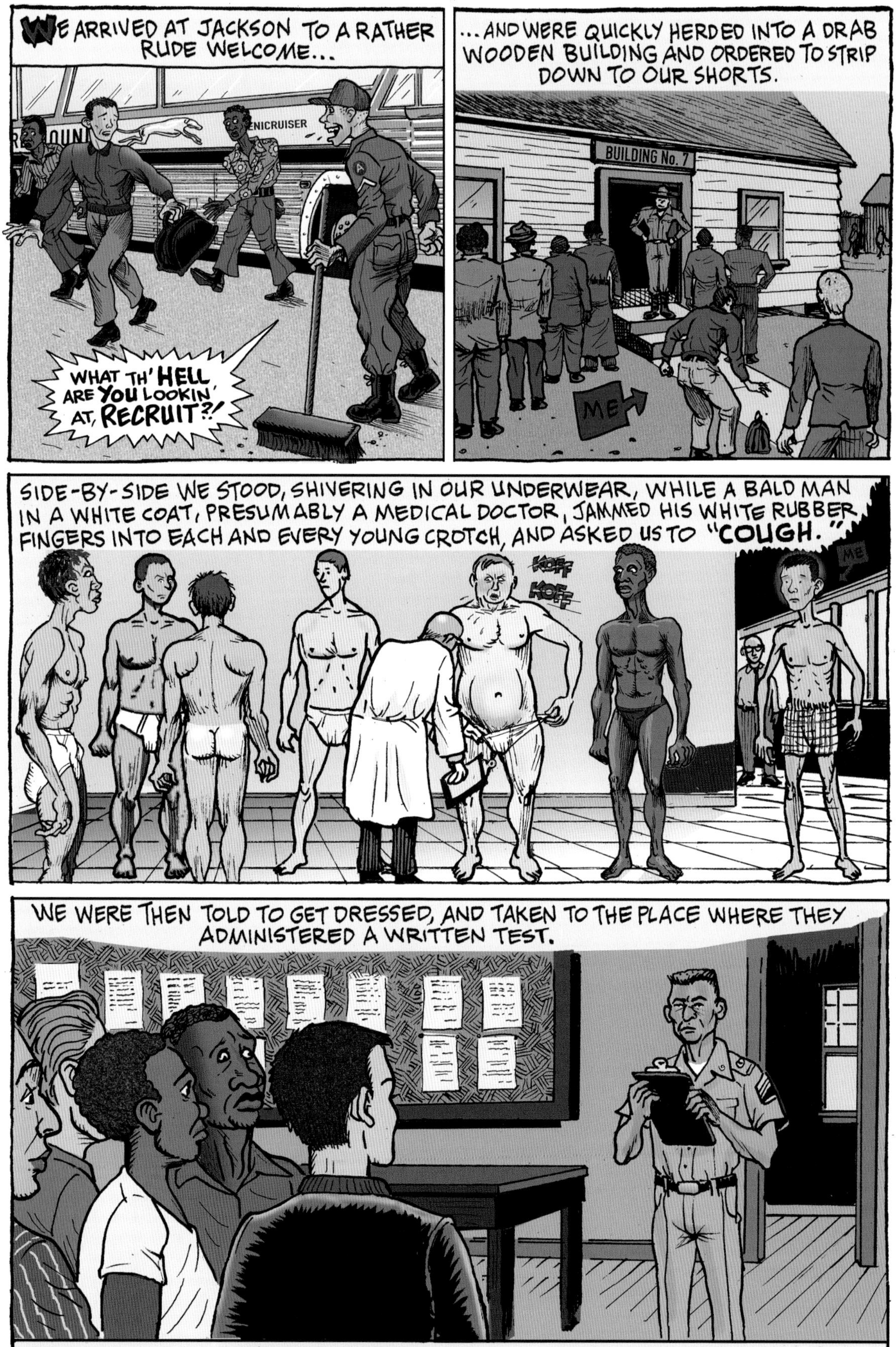
WE ARRIVED AT JACKSON TO A RATHER RUDE WELCOME...
ENICRUISER
WHAT TH' HELL ARE YOU LOOKIN' AT, RECRUIT?!
...AND WERE QUICKLY HERDED INTO A DRAB WOODEN BUILDING AND ORDERED TO STRIP DOWN TO OUR SHORTS.
BUILDING No. 7
ME
SIDE-BY-SIDE WE STOOD, SHIVERING IN OUR UNDERWEAR, WHILE A BALD MAN IN A WHITE COAT, PRESUMABLY A MEDICAL DOCTOR, JAMMED HIS WHITE RUBBER FINGERS INTO EACH AND EVERY YOUNG CROTCH, AND ASKED US TO "COUGH."
KOFF
KOFF
ME
WE WERE THEN TOLD TO GET DRESSED, AND TAKEN TO THE PLACE WHERE THEY ADMINISTERED A WRITTEN TEST.
BEFORE WE BEGAN, AN ARMY SERGEANT STOOD IN THE FRONT OF THE ROOM AND ASKED WHAT I THOUGHT WAS A RATHER STRANGE QUESTION.

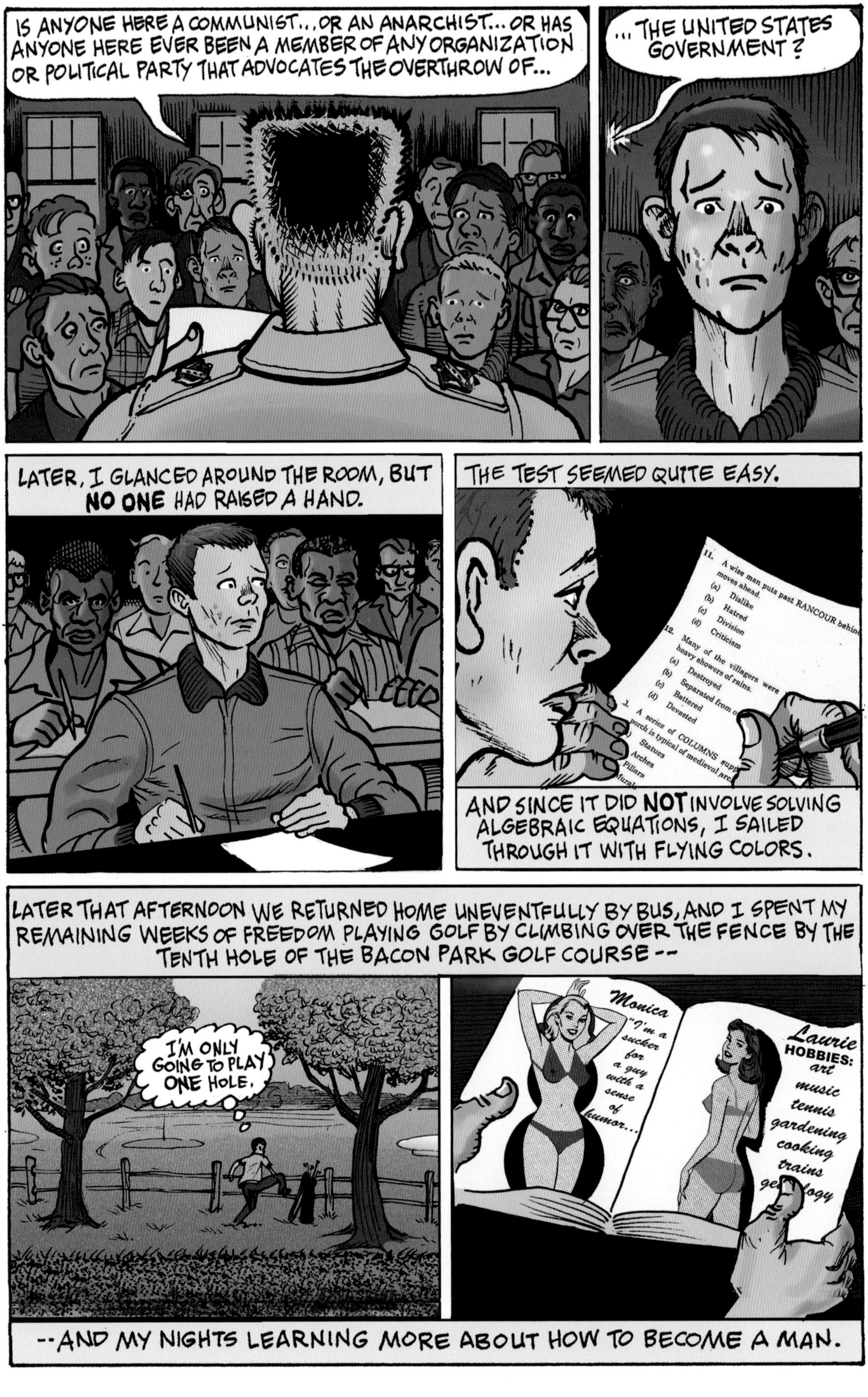
IS ANYONE HERE A COMMUNIST...OR AN ANARCHIST...OR HAS ANYONE HERE EVER BEEN A MEMBER OF ANY ORGANIZATION OR POLITICAL PARTY THAT ADVOCATES THE OVERTHROW OF...
...THE UNITED STATES GOVERNMENT?
LATER, I GLANCED AROUND THE ROOM, BUT **NO ONE** HAD RAISED A HAND.
THE TEST SEEMED QUITE EASY.
11. A wise man puts past RANCOUR behind
moves ahead.
(a) Dislike
(b) Hatred
(c) Division
(d) Criticism
12. Many of the villagers were
heavy showers of rains.
(a) Destroyed
(b) Separated from
(c) Battered
(d) Devasted
AND SINCE IT DID **NOT** INVOLVE SOLVING ALGEBRAIC EQUATIONS, I SAILED THROUGH IT WITH FLYING COLORS.
LATER THAT AFTERNOON WE RETURNED HOME UNEVENTFULLY BY BUS, AND I SPENT MY REMAINING WEEKS OF FREEDOM PLAYING GOLF BY CLIMBING OVER THE FENCE BY THE TENTH HOLE OF THE BACON PARK GOLF COURSE--
I'M ONLY GOING TO PLAY **ONE** HOLE.
Monica
"I'm a sucker for a guy with a sense of humor..."
Laurie
HOBBIES:
art
music
tennis
gardening
cooking
trains
--AND MY NIGHTS LEARNING MORE ABOUT HOW TO BECOME A MAN.

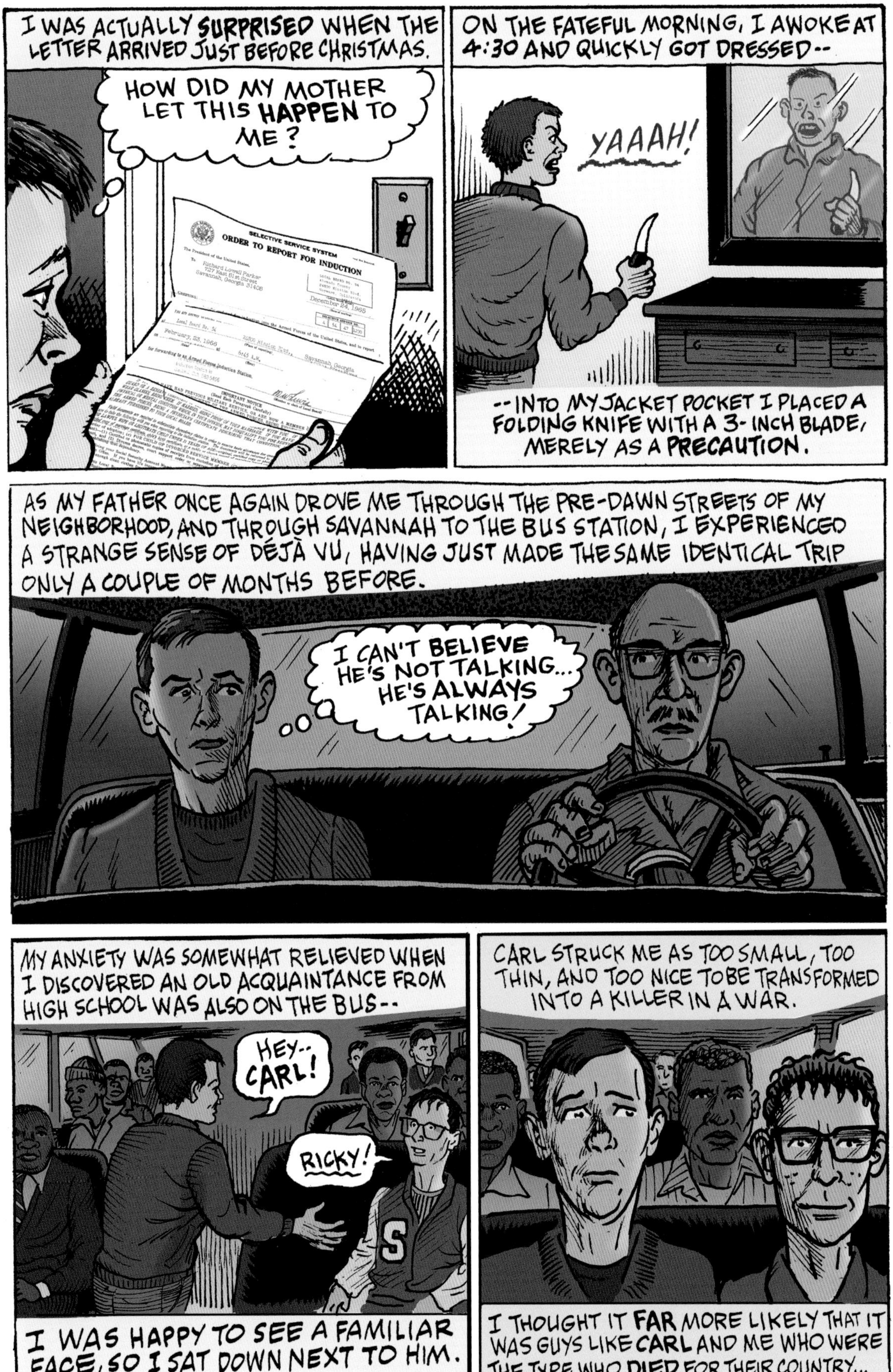

I WAS ACTUALLY SURPRISED WHEN THE LETTER ARRIVED JUST BEFORE CHRISTMAS.
HOW DID MY MOTHER LET THIS HAPPEN TO ME?
SELECTIVE SERVICE SYSTEM
ORDER TO REPORT FOR INDUCTION
ON THE FATEFUL MORNING, I AWOKE AT 4:30 AND QUICKLY GOT DRESSED--
YAAAH!
--INTO MY JACKET POCKET I PLACED A FOLDING KNIFE WITH A 3-INCH BLADE, MERELY AS A PRECAUTION.
AS MY FATHER ONCE AGAIN DROVE ME THROUGH THE PRE-DAWN STREETS OF MY NEIGHBORHOOD, AND THROUGH SAVANNAH TO THE BUS STATION, I EXPERIENCED A STRANGE SENSE OF DÉJÀ VU, HAVING JUST MADE THE SAME IDENTICAL TRIP ONLY A COUPLE OF MONTHS BEFORE.
I CAN'T BELIEVE HE'S NOT TALKING... HE'S ALWAYS TALKING!
MY ANXIETY WAS SOMEWHAT RELIEVED WHEN I DISCOVERED AN OLD ACQUAINTANCE FROM HIGH SCHOOL WAS ALSO ON THE BUS--
HEY.. CARL!
RICKY!
I WAS HAPPY TO SEE A FAMILIAR FACE, SO I SAT DOWN NEXT TO HIM.
CARL STRUCK ME AS TOO SMALL, TOO THIN, AND TOO NICE TO BE TRANSFORMED INTO A KILLER IN A WAR.
I THOUGHT IT FAR MORE LIKELY THAT IT WAS GUYS LIKE CARL AND ME WHO WERE THE TYPE WHO DIED FOR THEIR COUNTRY...

ONCE OFF THE BUS, THE THIRTY OF US WERE LED INTO A WINDOWLESS WOODEN BUILDING.
BUILDING No.2
LOST IN OUR THOUGHTS, WE CIRCLED AROUND A WAIST-HIGH TABLE THAT TOOK UP MOST OF THE ROOM. ONCE WE WERE ALL INSIDE...
?
?
?
?
?
...THEY LOCKED US IN AND WE TURNED TO FACE THE TABLE.
OKAY! NOW PLACE ALL GUNS, KNIVES AND OTHER WEAPONS ON THE TABLE IN FRONT OF YOU.
DICK
GUNS?!! WHAT DO THEY THINK WE ARE--? A BUNCH OF COMMON CRIMINALS?
THEN I REMEMBERED THAT I MYSELF HAD STUCK A KNIFE INSIDE MY JACKET POCKET.
WHILE I PONDERED THIS, THERE WAS A SUDDEN SHUFFLING OF FEET, A REACHING INTO POCKETS, ACCOMPANIED BY THE SOUNDS OF HEAVY METAL OBJECTS BEING PLACED UPON A WOODEN TABLE.
KLUMP
KOMP
CLOMP
DONK
I REACHED INTO MY POCKET...
...SWALLOWED HARD...
...AND SURRENDERED MY KNIFE.
KLOMP
YOUR PERSONAL PROPERTY WILL FOLLOW YOU WHEREVER YOU ARE STATIONED IN THIS MAN'S ARMY.
NEEDLESS TO SAY, I NEVER SAW THAT KNIFE AGAIN.

THUS, IN SHORT ORDER, HAVING NOW BEEN STRIPPED OF OUR SIDEARMS, WE WERE HERDED, LIKE COMMON CRIMINALS, INTO A NEARBY BUILDING TO BE SWORN INTO THE MILITARY....
C'MON! C'MON! MOVE IT!
ONCE INSIDE, WE WERE FORMED INTO A LONG LINE...
EACH OF US WAS HANDED A SHEET OF PAPER...
(CHECK ONE) I WOULD LIKE TO BE IN THE:
ARMY
MARINE CORPS
DOESN'T MATTER
I THOUGHT TO MYSELF, "I'M NO JOHN WAYNE."
ARMY
MARINE
SOON, A MARINE CORPS SERGEANT COLLECTED OUR FORMS...
H-HERE YOU ARE, SIR...
NOT "SIR," SERGEANT, YOUNG HERO!

IF YOU CHECKED "ARMY"...
...YOU GOT ARMY.
IF YOU CHECKED "MARINE CORPS"...
...YOU GOT MARINE CORPS.
IF YOU CHECKED "DOESN'T MATTER"...
...YOU GOT MARINE CORPS!
APPARENTLY, THERE WERE STILL NOT ENOUGH NEW RECRUITS FOR THE MARINE CORPS.
IT WAS 1966--THE "HIPPIE" ERA--AND A FEW OF THE GUYS HAD LONG HAIR.
FORTUNATELY, FOR ME, I WASN'T ONE OF THEM. AND ON THE ADVICE OF A FAMILY FRIEND, I HAD JUST GOTTEN A HAIRCUT THE DAY BEFORE.

THE MARINE SERGEANT STOPPED NEXT TO ME!
PERKINS
I STARED STRAIGHT AHEAD, AVOIDING EYE CONTACT, TRYING MY BEST TO BECOME INVISIBLE...
...BUT I COULD FEEL HIS EYES BURNING TWO HOLES IN THE SIDE OF MY PIMPLY FACE.
YOU'RE GONNA BE A MARINE!
I MOMENTARILY PANICKED...
...I FELT THE BLOOD RUSH OUT OF MY HEAD.
I THOUGHT ABOUT HOW "UN-MARINELIKE" I WOULD LOOK LYING THERE ON THE FLOOR...
...BEING STARED AT BY A CROWD OF COMPLETE STRANGERS.

THEN, TO MY EVERLASTING RELIEF, I REALIZED THE SERGEANT WAS ADDRESSING THE GUY BEHIND ME....
YOU! HIPPIE--!
YER GONNA BE A MARINE!
BUT I DON' WANNA BE A MUH-REEN.
I SAID, YER GONNA BE A MARINE...
BUT I DON' WANNA BE A MUH-REEN.
YER GONNA BE A MARINE!
B-BUT I DON' WANNA BE A MUH-REEN.
YER GONNA BE A MARINE!
BUT I DON' WANNA BE A MUH-REEN!
AND THE SERGEANT TOOK HIM AWAY TO BECOME A "MUH-REEN." HOPEFULLY HE LIVED HAPPILY EVER AFTER.

SOON, A GROUP OF STRANGERS STOOD UP AND RAISED THEIR RIGHT HANDS...
BEN
...AND AFTER SWEARING TO "DEFEND THE CONSTITUTION OF THE UNITED STATES FROM ALL ENEMIES, FOREIGN AND DOMESTIC, AND OBEY THE LAWFUL ORDERS OF THE PRESIDENT AND THOSE OFFICERS APPOINTED ABOVE US"-- WE STEPPED FORWARD AND INTO THE ARMY OF THE UNITED STATES OF AMERICA!
INDEED, THERE WOULD BE MUCH FORWARD-STEPPING AND MARCHING IN THE YEARS TO COME...
THE FIRST PLACE WE WERE MARCHED WAS TO GET A "HAIRCUT."
BZZZZZZZ
AND THEN WE WENT TO DRAW OUR UNIFORMS AND RELATED EQUIPMENT.
UHM...
...THIS ONE'S TOO SMALL.
DO YOU HAVE A LARGER ONE?
DUMMY.
FOSS
U.S. ARMY
TRY LOOSENING THE HEADBAND.

EARLY ON, AS WE WERE GETTING SQUARED AWAY AT THE INDUCTION STATION, IT SUDDENLY BECAME APPARENT THAT I WAS TO SHARE A BUNK WITH THIS GUY WHO LOOKED AT ME LIKE HE WANTED TO KILL ME...
OH--! Y-YOU SCARED ME.
I'M TAKIN' TH' BOTTOM BUNK.
I WASN'T ABOUT TO ARGUE WITH HIM.
AFTER WE HAD MADE UP OUR BUNKS, I SHEEPISHLY ASKED HIM A QUESTION.
WHERE ARE YOU FROM?
NEW YORK.
I TOLD HIM I WAS AN ARTIST--SECRETLY HOPING THAT SOMEHOW THAT INFORMATION MIGHT PREVENT HIM FROM DOING ME BODILY HARM.
I'M AN ARTIST...
AFTER ALL, I HAD ONLY BEEN IN THE ARMY FOR LESS THAN ONE DAY-- SO IT WAS FAR TOO SOON FOR ME TO BEGIN SHEDDING BLOOD FOR MY COUNTRY!
HE REACHED AROUND AND PULLED A WALLET FROM HIS BACK POCKET.
HE ASKED ME IF I COULD DRAW A PICTURE OF HIS GIRLFRIEND.
TINKER
THANKFULLY I WAS VERY ADEPT AT COPYING PHOTOGRAPHS.
I WORRIED THAT IF IT DIDN'T LOOK ENOUGH LIKE HER HE MIGHT KICK MY ASS!

I HAD NEVER DRAWN A BLACK PERSON BEFORE.
With Love, Darlene
FROM SOMEWHERE, I SCROUNGED UP A PIECE OF PAPER AND A PENCIL.
AS I STUDIED HER FACE, I WONDERED IF SHE WOULD STILL BE WAITING FOR HIM TWO YEARS LATER WHEN HE GOT OUT.
I WONDERED HOW DEVASTATED SHE WOULD BE IF HE GOT KILLED IN VIETNAM.
IN ABOUT AN HOUR, I FELT GOOD ENOUGH ABOUT THE DRAWING TO SHOW IT TO HIM.
NOW THA'S TH' SHIT...
TO SAY I WAS CONFUSED WOULD BE PUTTING IT MILDLY.
THE NEXT DAY, I HAD 17 MORE REQUESTS!

ALTHOUGH IT WAS COLD AS HELL OUTSIDE THAT FIRST WEEK, WE HAD TO SLEEP WITH THE WINDOWS OPEN BECAUSE WE'D BEEN TOLD THERE WAS AN OUTBREAK OF SPINAL MENINGITIS.
FREEZING MY ASS OFF.
THAT NIGHT, AFTER LIGHTS OUT AND EVERYONE WAS IN HIS BUNK, I THOUGHT, "NOW WOULD BE A GOOD TIME FOR ME TO USE THE BATHROOM."
ZZZZ
UNFORTUNATELY, THERE WAS ALREADY A GUY ON ONE OF THE TOILETS, SO THERE WAS NO WAY I WAS GOING TO BE ABLE TO DO ANYTHING WITH HIM THERE...
GOD DANG IT!
...SO I WALKED OVER TO THE SINK, SPLASHED SOME WATER ON MY FACE, AND WENT BACK OUT!

FOR A LONG TIME I LAY SHIVERING ON MY BUNK, UNABLE TO FALL ASLEEP.
A FEW HOURS LATER, I WAS JOLTED AWAKE AT 5 A.M. BY A LOUDSPEAKER NEXT TO MY BUNK.
GET YOUR HEAD OUTTA YO ASS!
ALMOST IMMEDIATELY, AN ENLISTED MAN CAME IN, SWITCHED ON THE LIGHTS, AND GOT EVERYONE UP.
OKAY GET UP!
LET'S GO!
KLANG
KLANG
KLANG

AS WE STOOD OUTSIDE, RESPLENDENT IN OUR NEW UNIFORMS, EAGER TO BEGIN DEFENDING THE CONSTITUTION, A REGULAR-ARMY SERGEANT ADDRESSED US.
HAS ANYONE HERE EVER BEEN IN THE ARMY BEFORE?
I THOUGHT IT WAS A RATHER STRANGE QUESTION...
WHY WOULD ANYONE COME BACK?
DAVIS
SUDDENLY, AN OLDER-LOOKING FELLOW SPOKE UP.
YEAH...
...I HAVE!
TURNS OUT HE WAS 37.
"POP" WYATT WAS PUT IN CHARGE OF OUR SMALL MOB, AND IMMEDIATELY STEPPED FORWARD AND BEGAN ISSUING ORDERS...
TENCH----
--HUT!

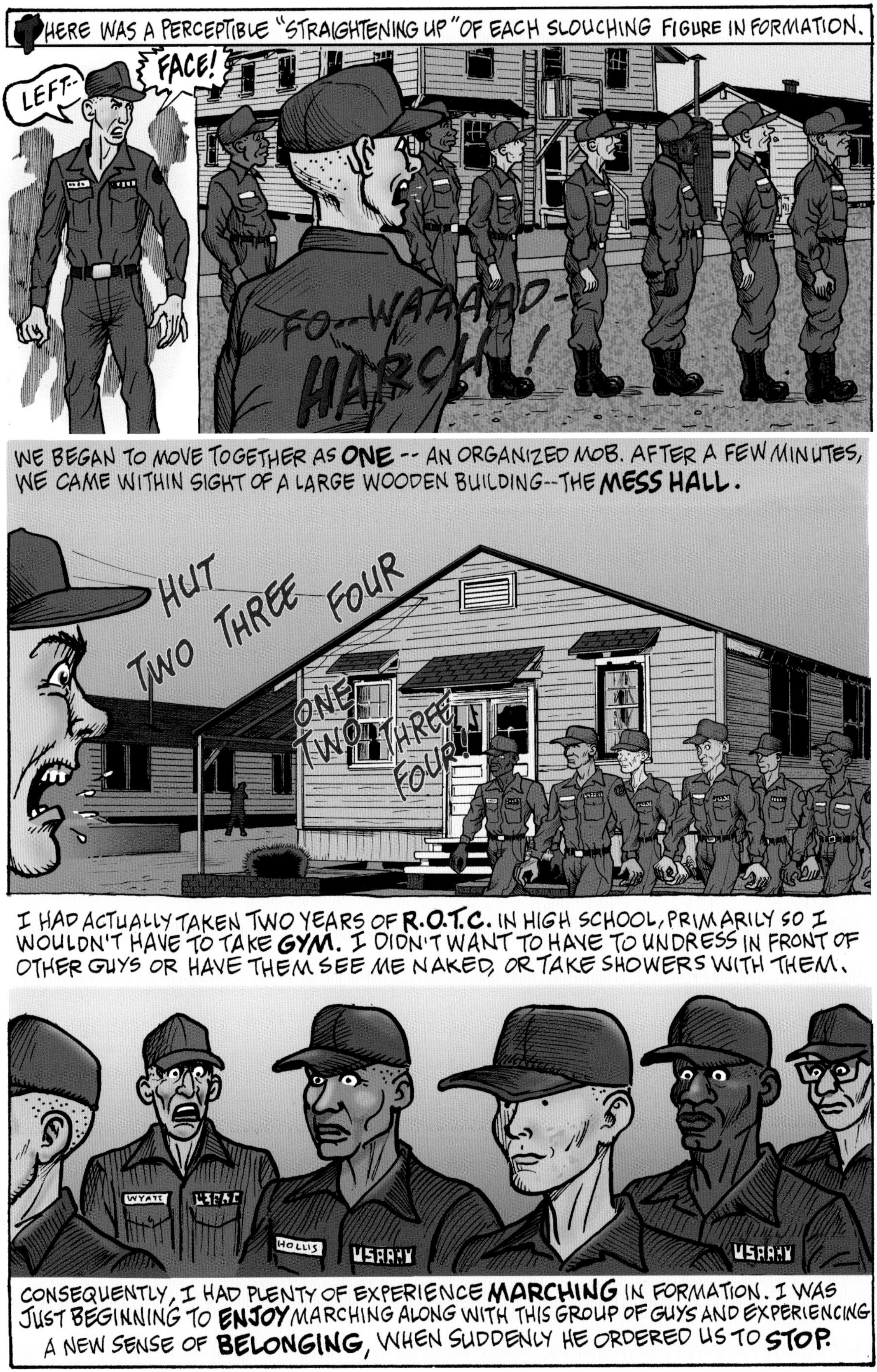
THERE WAS A PERCEPTIBLE "STRAIGHTENING UP" OF EACH SLOUCHING FIGURE IN FORMATION.
LEFT--
FACE!
FO--WAAAAD--
HARCH!
WE BEGAN TO MOVE TOGETHER AS ONE -- AN ORGANIZED MOB. AFTER A FEW MINUTES, WE CAME WITHIN SIGHT OF A LARGE WOODEN BUILDING--THE MESS HALL.
HUT TWO THREE FOUR
ONE TWO THREE FOUR!
I HAD ACTUALLY TAKEN TWO YEARS OF R.O.T.C. IN HIGH SCHOOL, PRIMARILY SO I WOULDN'T HAVE TO TAKE GYM. I DIDN'T WANT TO HAVE TO UNDRESS IN FRONT OF OTHER GUYS OR HAVE THEM SEE ME NAKED, OR TAKE SHOWERS WITH THEM.
WYATT
HOLLIS
USARMY
USARMY
CONSEQUENTLY, I HAD PLENTY OF EXPERIENCE MARCHING IN FORMATION. I WAS JUST BEGINNING TO ENJOY MARCHING ALONG WITH THIS GROUP OF GUYS AND EXPERIENCING A NEW SENSE OF BELONGING, WHEN SUDDENLY HE ORDERED US TO STOP.

MUTHAFUKKAS... HALT!
MESS HALL
"MOTHER FUCKERS"?
I HAD NEVER HEARD THAT WORD BEFORE. IT LITERALLY STOPPED ME IN MY TRACKS!
A SICKENING FEELING DEEP IN THE PIT OF MY STOMACH SUDDENLY OVERWHELMED ME...
OH... MY... GOD...
WHAT KIND OF ANIMALS AM I STUCK IN HERE WITH--?
US ARMY
IN A LITTLE OVER A WEEK, I WAS BACK HOME ON LEAVE BEFORE BASIC. MY MOTHER'S CAT, BLUE, WAS UP ON THE KITCHEN COUNTER CHECKING OUT THE FRESHLY BAKED TURKEY MY MOM HAD JUST TAKEN OUT OF THE OVEN. I TURNED TO MY MOTHER AND CASUALLY INQUIRED...
WHAT IS THAT FUCKING CAT DOING UP THERE ON THE COUNTER?

THE FOLLOWING DAY, A SUNDAY, A FAMILY FRIEND DROVE ME BACK UP TO FORT JACKSON IN COLUMBIA, SOUTH CAROLINA, A DISTANCE OF ABOUT 160 MILES.
MY MOTHER AND FATHER WENT ALONG FOR THE RIDE.
ED HAD BEEN IN WORLD WAR TWO AND HAD SOME ADVICE FOR ME AS I GOT OUT OF HIS CAR.
OH, RICKY...
GEORGIA
ICEMAN
PEACH STATE
...NEVER VOLUNTEER FOR ANYTHING...
I BENT DOWN AND LEANED IN TO GIVE MY MOTHER A GOODBYE KISS.
SHE OFFERED ME HER CHEEK.
I STOOD THERE UNTIL THEIR CAR HAD COMPLETELY DISAPPEARED FROM VIEW.
THE VERY NEXT DAY AT FORT STEWART, GEORGIA, I WAS SLATED TO BEGIN BASIC TRAINING.

2
BOOT CAMP

SPIFFY IN OUR DRESS GREENS, WE HOPPED THE DOG TO STEWART.
GREYHOUND
I WAS CHEERED BY THE PROSPECT OF BEING STATIONED ONLY 39 MILES FROM MY HOMETOWN.
AS THE BUS ROLLED PAST SAVANNAH, MY SPIRITS BEGAN TO LIFT AS I CAUGHT FLEETING GLIMPSES OF FAMILIAR SIGHTS ALONG HIGHWAY 17--
ZZZZZ
WE PASSED THE SPOT WHERE I HAD ONCE SEEN A DEAD ALLIGATOR THAT HAD BEEN RUN OVER BY A TRUCK...
...AND THAT BEND IN THE ROAD WHERE MY DAD LOST CONTROL OF HIS CAR AND RAN INTO A DITCH WHEN HE FIRST CAME TO SAVANNAH IN 1927...
US 53 417 848
THE PLANTATION INN...
...ART'S CAFÉ.
ART'S CAFE
EATS
...THE DIXIE JUNGLE--THAT JOINT I RODE MY BIKE TO WHEN I WAS JUST 13, TO BUY FIREWORKS.
DIXIE JUNGLE 1 MI.
SEE MAUDE SINGING JACKASS
FIREWORKS
IT WAS 17 MILES EACH WAY.
...CHARLIE'S RENDEZVOUS LOUNGE...
...EVEN THE LITTLE ONE-PUMP GAS STATION WHERE MY DAD ALWAYS BOUGHT GAS...
COMET
GAS
THEY WERE ALL STILL RIGHT THERE, JUST AS THEY ALWAYS HAD BEEN MY ENTIRE LIFE, IN THOSE HALCYON DAYS OF YORE, BEFORE MY ASS BELONGED TO UNCLE SAM!!

WE ARRIVED AT FORT STEWART JUST BEFORE NOON.
THEN, ONE BY ONE, WE STUMBLED OUT INTO THE CRISP, COOL MARCH AIR -- TO THE ROUSING SOUND OF TRUMPETS, TROMBONES, TUBAS, DRUMS, AND PICCOLOS.
HINESVILLE
1966
IT WAS LOVELY.
BUT MY ENJOYMENT WAS SOMEWHAT DIMINISHED WHEN I OVERHEARD SOMEONE SAY THAT THE REASON THEY WERE PLAYING WAS BECAUSE THEY WERE EXPECTING MUHAMMAD ALI TO BE ON OUR BUS. BUT AFTER THE "WELCOME" WE HAD RECEIVED AT THE INDUCTION STATION AT FORT JACKSON, I FELT LIKE I'D DIED AND GONE TO HEAVEN!
HINESVILLE
1966
SCENICRUISER
THE FIRST THING WE DID WAS DRAW SHEETS AND BLANKETS.
THEN SOMEONE EXPLAINED HOW THEIR LAUNDRY SYSTEM WORKED.
... AND THEN WE WERE MARCHED TO OUR BILLETS.
COMPARED TO THE OLD WOODEN BARRACKS AT FORT JACKSON, OUR NEW HOME WAS MORE LIKE A COLLEGE DORMITORY.

BACK AT THE INDUCTION STATION, WE HAD TAKEN A SERIES OF WRITTEN TESTS THAT WERE DESIGNED TO HELP SOMEBODY SOMEWHERE DECIDE WHAT TO DO WITH US ONCE WE HAD FINISHED BASIC.
I WAS 19 YEARS OLD, 6 FEET TALL, AND WEIGHED 143 POUNDS.
WILL I BE DEAD A YEAR FROM NOW?
MY FATHER USED TO CALL ME A "PICKY EATER."
NOW THE U.S. WAS INVOLVED IN A WAR IN SOUTHEAST ASIA, AND IF I WAS GOING TO HAVE TO GO AND HELP FIGHT IT, I FIGURED I'D BETTER EAT WHATEVER FOOD THE ARMY PUT IN FRONT OF ME--
"SHIT ON A SHINGLE"
CHIPPED BEEF ON TOAST
--WHETHER I LIKED IT OR NOT.
BUT WHAT REALLY STRENGTHENED MY RESOLVE WAS ONE OF THE VERY FIRST THINGS THAT THEY TOLD US--
...THE VIETNAMESE ARE HIGHLY SKILLED IN HAND-TO-HAND COMBAT...
...AND FROM A VERY EARLY AGE--
GRAVES
HAVING BEEN PICKED ON BY BULLIES MY ENTIRE LIFE, I KNEW I WOULD HAVE NO CHANCE AGAINST AN ENEMY LIKE THAT.
SO I WAS DETERMINED TO BECOME AS BIG AND STRONG AS I POSSIBLY COULD. MAYBE THAT WOULD MAKE ME A LITTLE HARDER TO KILL.
17...18...19...20!
...AN' ONE MORE FOR YOUR GRANNY!
I WAS NOT READY TO DIE--BECAUSE THE WAY I LOOKED AT IT-- I HAD NOT YET BEGUN TO LIVE!

OUR PLATOON LEADER WAS SGT. ALLEN, A FINE SPECIMEN OF A SOLDIER, WHO TOLD US WE WERE FIGHTING FOR "MOTHERHOOD AND APPLE PIE!"
YO LEFF...
YO LEFF...
ME
I LIKE APPLE PIE!
YO LEFF
RIGHT
LEFF...
HE REMINDED ME OF PAUL NEWMAN, AND HE WELCOMED US BY ANNOUNCING THAT WE WERE NOW IN "THIS MAN'S ARMY" -- HIS ARMY.
REMEMBER! YOUR ASS IS GRASS--
--AND I'M TH' LAWNMOWER!
ALLEN
US ARMY
FOR THE NEXT EIGHT WEEKS OF BASIC, WHENEVER HE ASKED US...
DO I MAKE MYSELF PERFECTLY CLEAR?
EVEN WHEN WE HAD NO IDEA WHAT HE SAID OR MEANT-- WHICH WAS MOST OF THE TIME-- WE ALWAYS ANSWERED HIM WITH A HEARTY--
YES, SERGEANT!
DEEMER
DeCESARE
MESERVE
TO WHICH HE WOULD INVARIABLY REPLY IN AN ELEVATED SINGSONG VOICE--
I CAN'T HEAR YOU...
...TO WHICH, IN UNISON, WE WOULD THEN ALL REPLY...
YES, SERGEANT!
TO WHICH HE WOULD ALWAYS REPLY IN A LOUD, COMMANDING VOICE...
I STILL CAN'T HEAR YOU!
WHAT HE REALLY LOOKED LIKE
TO WHICH WE WOULD THEN ALL REPLY IN ONE LOUD SYNCHRONIZED VOICE--
YES, SERGEANT!!!
--TO WHICH HE WOULD ALWAYS REPLY...
MY GRANNY CAN YELL LOUDER THAN THAT--AN' SHE AIN'T GOT BUT ONE BALL!

BACK IN THE BARRACKS -- AND ALL THE REST OF THE TIME, WE WERE OVERSEEN BY SGT. MOXLEY -- A SHIFTY-EYED LITTLE GUY WITH A NAPOLEON COMPLEX.
FLIP FLOPS
ME
3
HURRY UP! LIGHTS OUT IN TWO MINUTES!
CHROME HELMET
CUSTOM FIT UNIFORM
HE GOT US UP AT 0500, AND WE DID AN HOUR OF P.T. EACH MORNING BEFORE BREAKFAST -- EXCEPT ON SUNDAY. (CHAPEL WAS OPTIONAL.)
ME
IN SPITE OF ALL THE PHYSICAL DEMANDS, I WAS BEGINNING TO THINK THAT I JUST MIGHT ACTUALLY LIKE BEING IN SGT. ALLEN'S ARMY...
I HAD ALWAYS WANTED TO HAVE FRIENDS -- AND HERE WERE A BUNCH OF GUYS MY OWN AGE -- AND A FEW A COUPLE OF YEARS OLDER --
GLUG! GLUG!
ME
TRIER
FIRST TIME DRINKING BEER
-- WHO, WHETHER THEY LIKED IT OR NOT -- WERE NOW STUCK WITH ME.

BUT I STILL FELT LIKE A LOSER FOR FLUNKING OUT OF COLLEGE.
LISTEN UP!
ANY OF YOU JOKERS EVER BEEN IN THE ARMY BEFORE?
?
MAYBE THERE WAS STILL SOME WAY I COULD REDEEM MYSELF...
NO, BUT I TOOK R.O.T.C. IN HIGH SCHOOL.
...YOU'RE SQUAD LEADER.
AS A SQUAD LEADER IN BASIC, I DON'T REMEMBER DOING MUCH LEADING...
I WAS IN BETTER PHYSICAL SHAPE THAN MANY OF MY FELLOW RECRUITS, AND HAD NO TROUBLE DOING ALL OF THE MARCHING, DOUBLE-TIMING, PUSH-UPS, SIT-UPS, SQUAT THRUSTS, AND SIDE-STRADDLE HOPS WE HAD DO TO EVERY SINGLE DAY.
45... 46... 47... 48...
49...
ONE DAY MY NAME WAS CALLED, ALONG WITH SOME OTHERS ON A LIST. IT SEEMED WE HAD SCORED WELL ENOUGH ON THOSE STANDARDIZED ARMY TESTS TO QUALIFY FOR ADMISSION TO OFFICER CANDIDATE SCHOOL (O.C.S.). MOST DRAFTEES PREFERRED TO JUST DO THEIR TWO YEARS, THEN GET OUT.
...OSBORN...... PARKER... SIMON...
I, ON THE OTHER HAND, SAW THIS AS A CHANCE TO REDEEM MYSELF. IT ALSO OCCURRED TO ME THAT MY CHANCES OF SURVIVAL MIGHT BE ENHANCED WERE I TO BECOME AN OFFICER. BUT NOTHING COULD HAVE BEEN FURTHER FROM THE TRUTH!

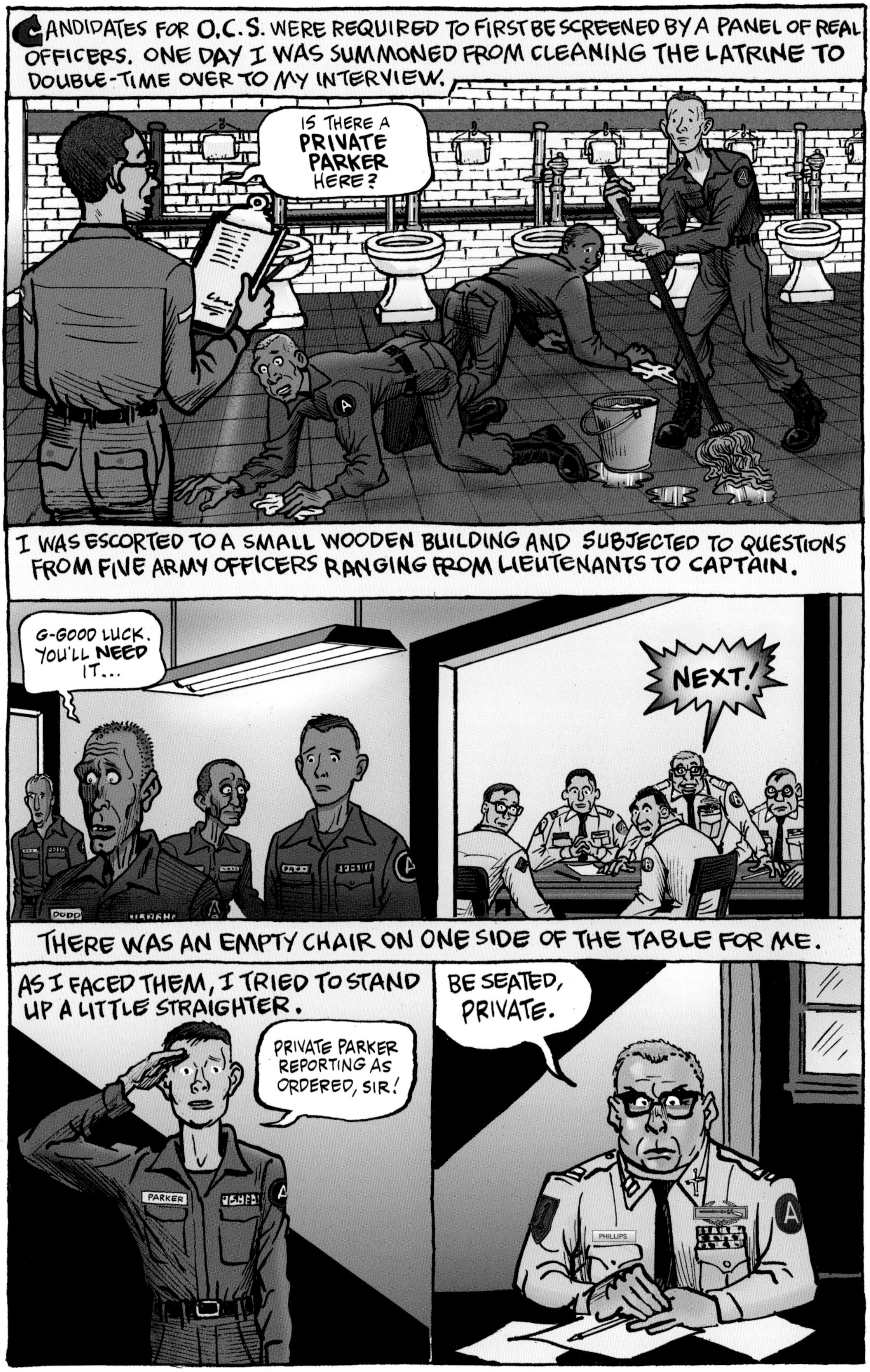
CANDIDATES FOR O.C.S. WERE REQUIRED TO FIRST BE SCREENED BY A PANEL OF REAL OFFICERS. ONE DAY I WAS SUMMONED FROM CLEANING THE LATRINE TO DOUBLE-TIME OVER TO MY INTERVIEW.
IS THERE A PRIVATE PARKER HERE?
I WAS ESCORTED TO A SMALL WOODEN BUILDING AND SUBJECTED TO QUESTIONS FROM FIVE ARMY OFFICERS RANGING FROM LIEUTENANTS TO CAPTAIN.
G-GOOD LUCK. YOU'LL NEED IT...
NEXT!
DODD
THERE WAS AN EMPTY CHAIR ON ONE SIDE OF THE TABLE FOR ME.
AS I FACED THEM, I TRIED TO STAND UP A LITTLE STRAIGHTER.
PRIVATE PARKER REPORTING AS ORDERED, SIR!
PARKER
BE SEATED, PRIVATE.
PHILLIPS

STARTING WITH THE OFFICER ON MY LEFT AND PROCEEDING IN AN ORDERLY FASHION, I WAS ASKED A SERIES OF QUESTIONS, THE DETAILS OF WHICH NOW ESCAPE ME.
PHILLIPS
HASPIEL
FORTIER
BALDINI
SNAP!
MY RECOLLECTION IS THAT I WAS ABLE TO ANSWER EVERY ONE OF THEM SATISFACTORILY. THERE WERE NO FOLLOW-UP QUESTIONS AND NO ONE ASKED ME ABOUT MATH.
JUST BEFORE RELEASING ME, THE CAPTAIN SUDDENLY THOUGHT OF ONE MORE QUESTION.
PRIVATE PARKER...
...IF YOU WERE TO STAY IN THE ARMY...
PHILLIPS
...HOW HIGH UP THE CHAIN OF COMMAND DO YOU THINK YOU WOULD RISE?
I LOOKED HIM STRAIGHT IN THE EYE. WITHOUT A MOMENT'S HESITATION, I TOLD HIM...
SIR-- FIVE STAR GENERAL.
FOR A BRIEF SECOND, HE LOOKED TAKEN ABACK--ALMOST AS IF IN AWE OF ME.
THERE WAS AN AWKWARD SILENCE. THEN HE RELEASED ME.
THAT WILL BE ALL, PRIVATE PARKER.
YES, SIR!
PHILLIPS
I STOOD UP, SALUTED, DID AN ABOUT-FACE, AND MARCHED SMARTLY OUT OF THE ROOM AND BACK TO MY BARRACKS--
PARKER
U.S. ARMY
--WHEREUPON I IMMEDIATELY RE-ENGAGED IN CLEANING THE LATRINE!

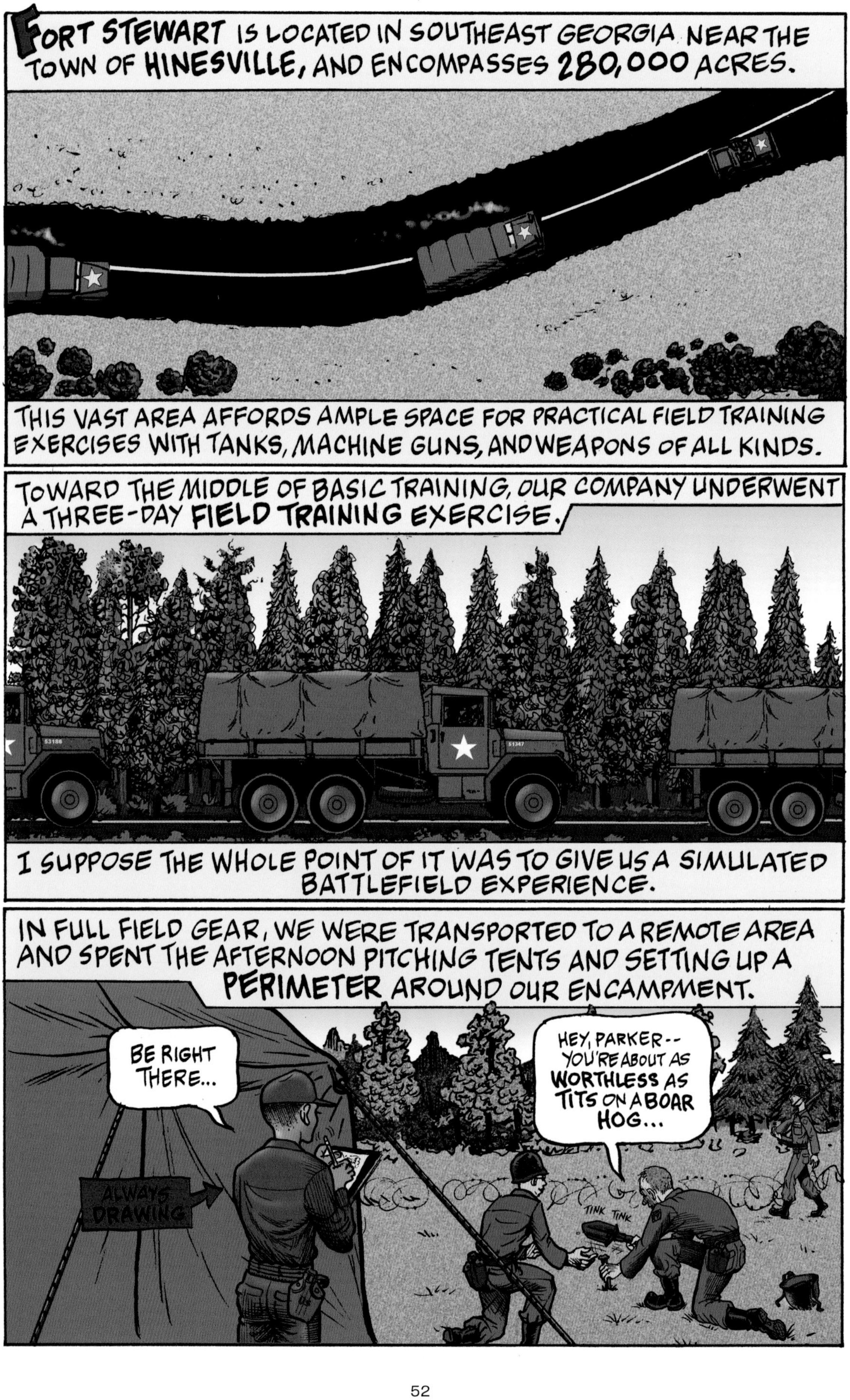
FORT STEWART IS LOCATED IN SOUTHEAST GEORGIA NEAR THE TOWN OF HINESVILLE, AND ENCOMPASSES 280,000 ACRES.
THIS VAST AREA AFFORDS AMPLE SPACE FOR PRACTICAL FIELD TRAINING EXERCISES WITH TANKS, MACHINE GUNS, AND WEAPONS OF ALL KINDS.
TOWARD THE MIDDLE OF BASIC TRAINING, OUR COMPANY UNDERWENT A THREE-DAY FIELD TRAINING EXERCISE.
I SUPPOSE THE WHOLE POINT OF IT WAS TO GIVE US A SIMULATED BATTLEFIELD EXPERIENCE.
IN FULL FIELD GEAR, WE WERE TRANSPORTED TO A REMOTE AREA AND SPENT THE AFTERNOON PITCHING TENTS AND SETTING UP A PERIMETER AROUND OUR ENCAMPMENT.
BE RIGHT THERE...
ALWAYS DRAWING
HEY, PARKER-- YOU'RE ABOUT AS WORTHLESS AS TITS ON A BOAR HOG...
TINK TINK

WE USED OUR ENTRENCHING TOOLS TO DIG IN-- AND TWO MEN WERE ASSIGNED TO EACH FOXHOLE.
SHUK
HEY--!
SOON.
WE TOOK TURNS STANDING WATCH--IT WAS TWO HOURS ON AND TWO HOURS OFF...
WHAT TIME IS IT?
YOU'VE GOT ANOTHER HOUR AN'A HALF TO GO...
PARKER
THERE WAS A VAST OPEN AREA DIRECTLY IN FRONT OF US WITH SOME SCATTERED VEGETATION AND A TREE LINE OFF IN THE DISTANCE.
IT'S GETTIN' DARK... DO YOU WANT TO GO TO SLEEP FIRST?
TOO EARLY TO SLEEP--LET'S BOTH KEEP WATCH.
PARKER
OUR MISSION WAS TO GUARD THE PERIMETER AND TO KEEP A WATCHFUL EYE OUT FOR "AGGRESSOR FORCES" IN THE AREA.
LATER.
HEY, PARKER...
...DON'T SHOOT TILL YOU SEE TH' WHITES OF THEIR ASSES!
HA HA
VERY FUNNY.
IT WAS A MOONLESS, CLOUDLESS NIGHT, WITH ONLY THE STARS TO ILLUMINATE THE LANDSCAPE.

WE HAD BEEN TAUGHT IN TRAINING THAT WHEN SCANNING THE AREA FOR THE ENEMY IN DARKNESS, THAT YOU COULD ACTUALLY DETECT MOVEMENT BETTER BY USING YOUR "PERIPHERAL VISION."
AT NIGHT, IT'S BETTER TO LOOK AT SOMETHING OUT OF THE CORNER OF YOUR EYE, RATHER THAN DIRECTLY AT IT.
I WAS SHARING A FOXHOLE WITH PRIVATE JERRY EVATT, ANOTHER GUY IN MY COMPANY WHOM I KNEW ONLY VAGUELY.
GUESS WHAT...
...I ASKED SERGEANT MADDY WHY WE'RE FIGHTIN' IN VIETNAM...
HE SAID "SO WE WON'T HAVE TO FIGHT 'EM IN CALIFORNIA."
OH...
I THOUGHT IT WAS FOR APPLE PIE.
EARLIER, WE HAD BEEN ISSUED BLANK AMMUNITION FOR OUR M-14s AND HAD THEM LOCKED AND LOADED.
AT MIDNIGHT, IT WAS MY TURN TO STAND GUARD--WHILE PRIVATE EVATT TRIED TO GET SOME SLEEP.

AS I STARED OUT INTO THE VASTNESS, ALL WAS QUIET AND STILL-- WITHOUT EVEN THE SLIGHTEST HINT OF WIND.
AT PRECISELY 0137 HOURS, AT A DISTANCE OF PERHAPS 100 METERS, AND FOR JUST AN INSTANT, I THOUGHT I SAW A BUSH MOVE.
I KEPT MY EYES FIXED ON THE BUSH FOR A WHILE, BUT DETECTED NO FURTHER MOVEMENT.
I CONTINUED TO SCAN THE HORIZON...

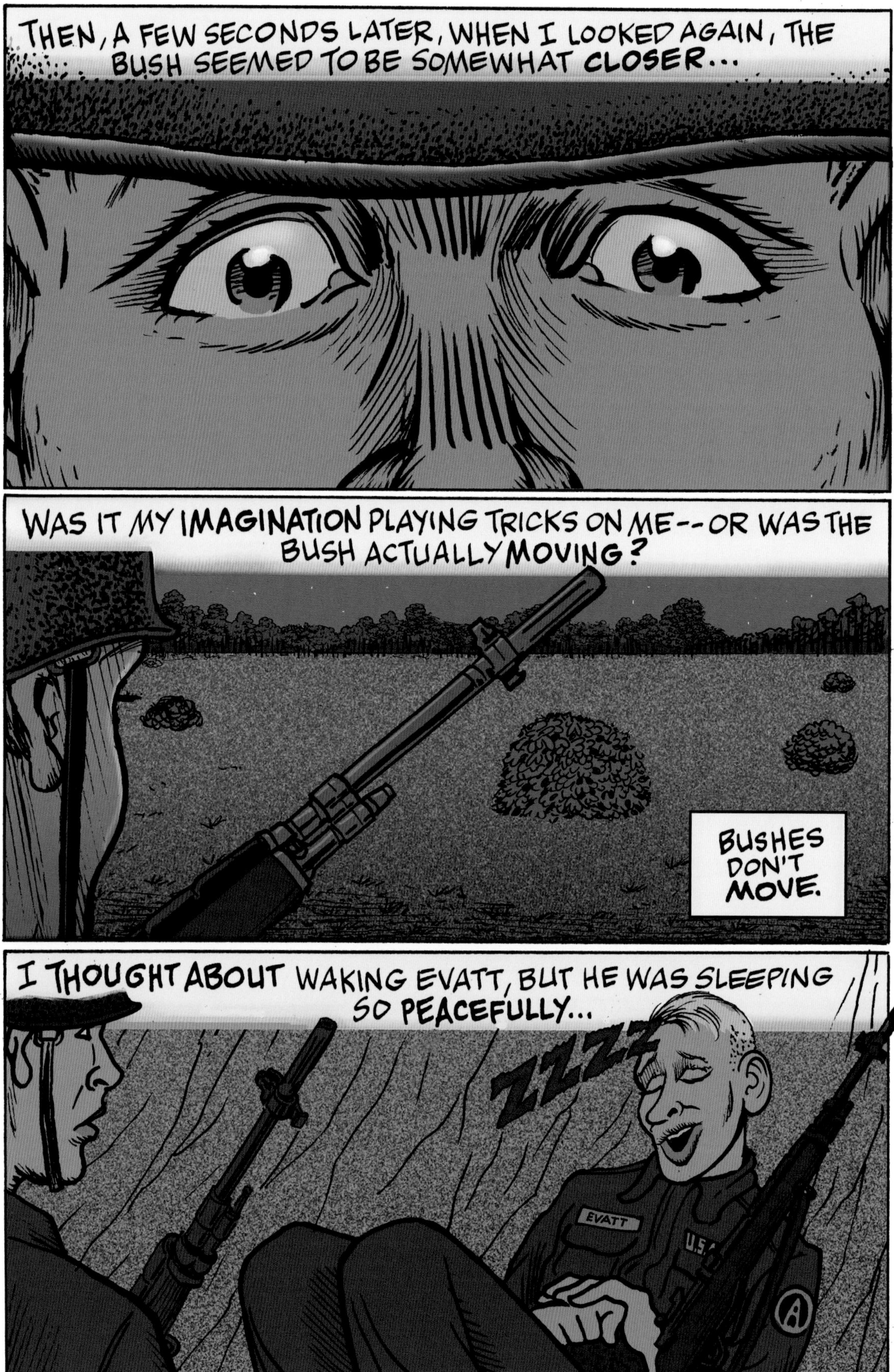
THEN, A FEW SECONDS LATER, WHEN I LOOKED AGAIN, THE BUSH SEEMED TO BE SOMEWHAT CLOSER...
WAS IT MY IMAGINATION PLAYING TRICKS ON ME--OR WAS THE BUSH ACTUALLY MOVING?
BUSHES DON'T MOVE.
I THOUGHT ABOUT WAKING EVATT, BUT HE WAS SLEEPING SO PEACEFULLY...
ZZZZ
EVATT
U.S.

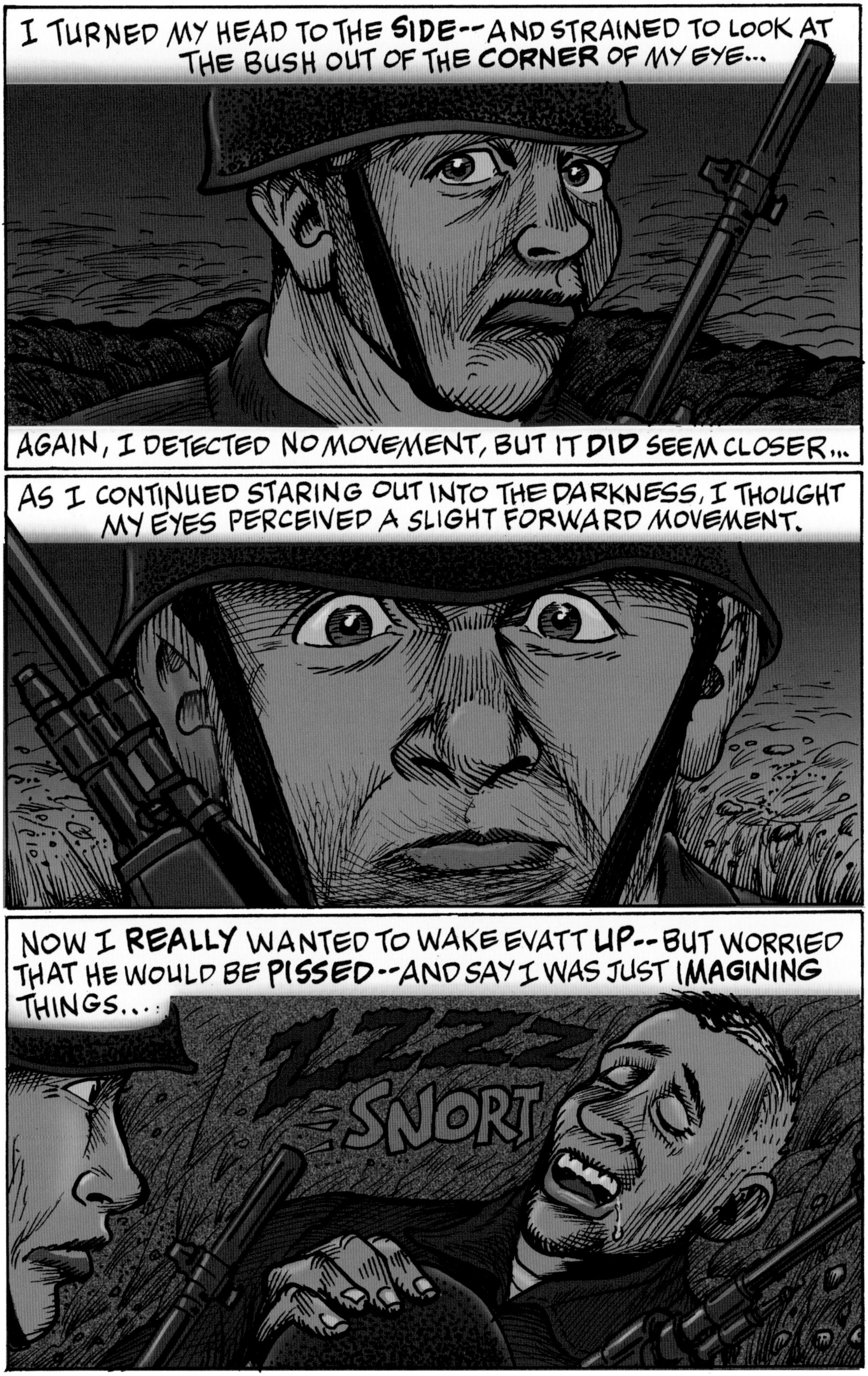
I TURNED MY HEAD TO THE SIDE--AND STRAINED TO LOOK AT THE BUSH OUT OF THE CORNER OF MY EYE...
AGAIN, I DETECTED NO MOVEMENT, BUT IT DID SEEM CLOSER...
AS I CONTINUED STARING OUT INTO THE DARKNESS, I THOUGHT MY EYES PERCEIVED A SLIGHT FORWARD MOVEMENT.
NOW I REALLY WANTED TO WAKE EVATT UP--BUT WORRIED THAT HE WOULD BE PISSED--AND SAY I WAS JUST IMAGINING THINGS...
ZZZZ
SNORT

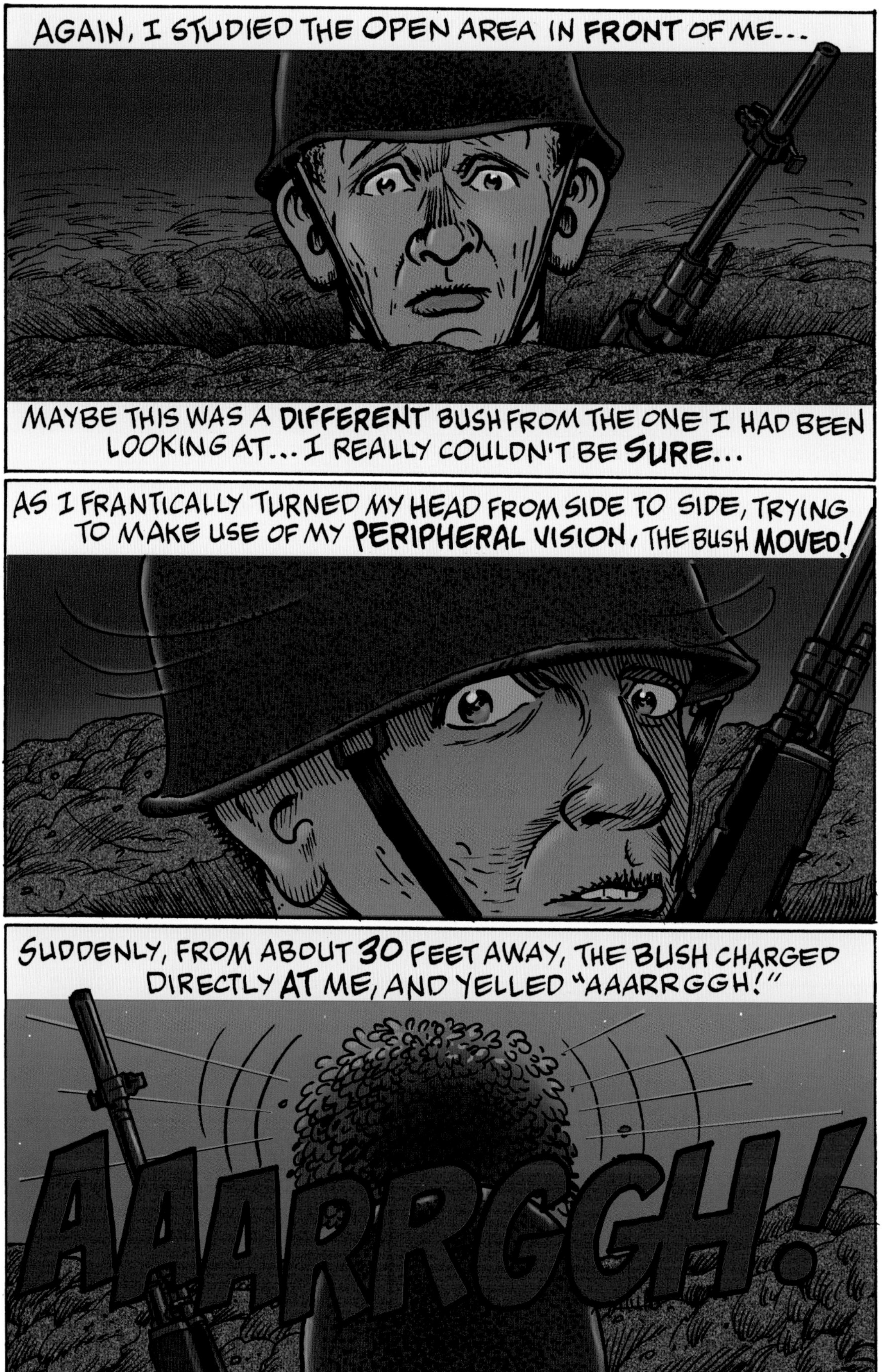
AGAIN, I STUDIED THE OPEN AREA IN FRONT OF ME...
MAYBE THIS WAS A DIFFERENT BUSH FROM THE ONE I HAD BEEN LOOKING AT... I REALLY COULDN'T BE SURE...
AS I FRANTICALLY TURNED MY HEAD FROM SIDE TO SIDE, TRYING TO MAKE USE OF MY PERIPHERAL VISION, THE BUSH MOVED!
SUDDENLY, FROM ABOUT 30 FEET AWAY, THE BUSH CHARGED DIRECTLY AT ME, AND YELLED "AAARRGGH!"
AAARRGGH!

AAARRGGH!

AND AS THAT BUSH HURLED ITSELF INTO MY FOXHOLE, I INSTINCTIVELY RAISED MY M-14, AND SQUEEZED OFF SEVERAL ROUNDS IN RAPID SUCCESSION...
BLAM
BLAM
BLAM
ALLEN
EVATT

THEN THE BUSH **SCREAMED** AT ME...
WHAT TH' FUCK ?!
ALLEN
...THEN THAT BUSH SUDDENLY TURNED INTO SERGEANT ALLEN!
YOU'RE NOT SUPPOSED TO SHOOT ME IN THE FACE!
WHAT COULD I SAY?
I-I'M REALLY **SORRY**, SERGEANT ALLEN...
YOU JUST DID WHAT WE WERE TRAINED TO DO...
ALLEN
U.S. ARMY
U.S. ARMY

MY BASE SALARY AS A PRIVATE E-1 WAS $96.90 PER MONTH, ALWAYS PAID IN CASH, PLUS COMPLIMENTARY ROOM AND BOARD, CLOTHING, AND MEDICAL.
-- AND BURIAL INSURANCE!
UPON INDUCTION, WE HAD BEEN INFORMED THAT EVERY SOLDIER IS ENTITLED TO A FREE MILITARY FUNERAL WITH FULL MILITARY HONORS...
ANY QUESTIONS...?
YOU CAN'T IMAGINE WHAT A RELIEF THAT WAS TO HEAR!
ONE FINE SPRING DAY, AFTER WE HAD EARNED OUR FIRST PAYCHECK, WE WERE MARCHED TO THE P.X. -- THE POST EXCHANGE -- OR ARMY STORE.
WHILE SOME GUYS STOCKED UP ON CIGARETTES FOR 19 CENTS A PACK...
... I MYSELF, NOT BEING A SMOKER, LOOKED AROUND FOR SOMETHING A BIT MORE SUBSTANTIAL TO SPEND MY PAY ON.
I CAME TO A GLASS CASE -- AND INSIDE I SAW A WATCH, BUT NOT JUST ANY WATCH.
THIS ONE WAS DARK GRAY WITH AN OLIVE DRAB BAND AND A LUMINOUS DIAL.
I WANTED THAT WATCH VERY MUCH BECAUSE I KNEW I COULD USE IT MONTHS LATER, WHEN, IF ON PATROL IN THE JUNGLES OF VIETNAM --
-- I GOT SHOT AND MORTALLY WOUNDED, I WOULD BE ABLE TO GLANCE DOWN AT MY USELESS ARM --
-- AND ASCERTAIN THE PRECISE TIME AT WHICH THE UNFORTUNATE INCIDENT OCCURRED.

THE ONE IN THE CASE WAS A DISPLAY MODEL, SO I PLACED MY ORDER, PAID $33.00--THE EQUIVALENT OF TWO WEEKS' SALARY..
HOW MUCH IS THIS ONE?
THIRTY-THREE DOLLARS.
I'LL TAKE IT.
IT'S A DISPLAY MODEL, HONEY.
THE LADY BEHIND THE COUNTER ASSURED ME THAT MY WATCH WOULD BE MAILED "IN DUE TIME"--
...IT TAKES A WHILE.
I HAD NOTHING BUT TIME.
TWO WEEKS LATER, TOWARD THE END OF BASIC, WE WERE ON ANOTHER FIELD EXERCISE, MILES FROM THE POST, IN THE MIDDLE OF NOWHERE...
SUDDENLY, I WAS UNEXPECTEDY CALLED OUT OF TRAINING BY ONE OF THE SERGEANTS...
PRIVATE PARKER!
YOU HAVE A VERY IMPORTANT TELEGRAM WAITING FOR YOU BACK AT HEADQUARTERS.
PARKER

A JEEP AND DRIVER HAD BEEN DISPATCHED TO TAKE ME BACK TO FORT STEWART.
GETTING A TELEGRAM IN THOSE DAYS WAS A BIG DEAL, AND USUALLY ONLY HAPPENED WHEN SOME AWFUL EVENT HAD TAKEN PLACE.
I HAVE TO ADMIT I WAS WORRIED.
I WAS AN ONLY CHILD AND ALL FOUR OF MY GRAND-PARENTS HAD LONG SINCE PASSED AWAY.
THE ONLY POSSIBLE EXPLANATION WAS THAT SOMETHING TERRIBLE HAD HAPPENED TO MY PARENTS.
PERHAPS OUR HOUSE HAD BURNED DOWN--
--OR MAYBE THEY HAD BEEN KILLED IN A CAR ACCIDENT...
EEE-GAD!!
...THEY DID SEEM TO GO A LOT OF PLACES BY CAR.

THAT SEEMED THE MOST LIKELY EXPLANATION.
IT DIDN'T HELP THAT THE DRIVER DIDN'T SAY A WORD TO ME DURING THE ENTIRE HOUR IT TOOK TO GET BACK.
HE PROBABLY KNEW I WAS IN MOURNING.
AND DIDN'T WANT TO INTRUDE ON MY SOLITUDE.
I LOVED MY PARENTS.
I THOUGHT ABOUT ALL THE GOOD TIMES WE'D SHARED--
--AT THE BEACH...
...AT THE MOVIES...
...GOING OUT TO DINNER.
THE TOWN HOUSE
SAVANNAH, GEORGIA
1951
THE DRIVER WOULD HAVE NO DOUBT BEEN CONCERNED HAD HE LOOKED OVER AT ME. BUT HE JUST DROVE ON AND TOOK LONG DRAGS ON HIS CIGARETTE. IF HE HAD ANY THOUGHTS ABOUT ME--
--HE KEPT THEM TO HIMSELF.

EACH SMOKY EXHALATION SEEMED TO REINFORCE THE HOPELESSNESS OF MY SITUATION.
HE HAS PROBABLY DONE THIS MANY TIMES BEFORE.
HE KNOWS SOMETHING AWFUL HAS HAPPENED.
THOUSANDS OF TALL PINE TREES STOOD SILENTLY AND RESPECTFULLY ALONG EITHER SIDE OF THE ROAD AS WE PASSED.
THEY KNEW WHAT WAS IN THAT TELEGRAM.
FINALLY WE ARRIVED BACK AT HEADQUARTERS.
HEADQUARTERS
THE C.Q. (CHARGE OF QUARTERS) HANDED ME THE TELEGRAM.
PRIVATE PARKER ?
PRIVATE RICHARD L. PARKER ?
WITH A HEAVY HEART I TORE IT OPEN...
MY WATCH HAD ARRIVED AT THE P.X.

AFTER...
...56 STRAIGHT DAYS OF RISING BEFORE DAWN...
MESS HALL
...ENDLESS PHYSICAL TRAINING...
...EXERCISE ONE NUMBER ONE IS THE SIDE-STRADDLE HOP...
...LONG HOT MARCHES DOWN DRIED-OUT RIVER BEDS...
...IN FULL FIELD GEAR...
...PULLING MY ASS UP AND OVER WALLS...
...FIRING HUNDREDS OF ROUNDS OF AMMUNITION FROM EVERY CONCEIVABLE KIND OF WEAPON...
BLAM
JUST LIKE IN A WAR COMIC I HAD READ AS A CHILD, MY SHOT WITH THE M-6 ROCKET LAUNCHER--OR "BAZOOKA"--WENT DOWN THE HATCH AND EXPLODED INSIDE THE TANK!
DOING HUNDREDS OF PUSH-UPS A DAY...
47... 47... 47...
...YELLING, AND BEING YELLED AT BY EVERYBODY ALL THE TIME--
I SAID...
PARKER
US ARMY
DROP AN' GIMME 50!
...FINALLY...
...THERE WAS STILL ONE LAST OBSTACLE TO OVERCOME...

THE NIGHTCRAWLER!
I JOINED A COLUMN AT ONE END OF THE COURSE, AND WHEN MY TURN CAME I DROPPED TO MY KNEES, AND LAY ON MY BELLY, MY M-14 CRADLED ATOP MY ELBOWS. I WAS TOLD ALL I HAD TO DO WAS FOLLOW THE MAN IN FRONT OF ME...
...THAT SEEMED SIMPLE ENOUGH...
--EXCEPT WE WOULD BE CRAWLING UNDERNEATH A BARBED-WIRE CANOPY SUSPENDED JUST 30 INCHES OFF THE GROUND---
I'VE GOTTA TAKE A PISS...
...I'M GONNA STAND UP!
ARE YOU CRAZY?!!
--WHILE A MACHINE-GUN FIRED LIVE AMMUNITION--TRACERS--OVER OUR HEADS!
RATATATATATATATAT!
FUCK THIS!
GET DOWN AND STAY DOWN!
DON'T WORRY.
I'M ALREADY LOWER THAN WHALESHIT!

I HAD BEEN AMONG THE LAST TO GO.
RATATATATATATATATATATATAT!
AT FIRST, ALL WENT WELL...
SLOSH
SLOSH
SLOSH
SLOSH
...AT FIRST.
IT WAS LIGHT ENOUGH FROM THE TRACERS TO ALMOST MAKE OUT THE TWO GUYS ON EITHER SIDE OF ME.
...ALMOST.
SO, I FOLLOWED THE GRUNTING NOISES COMING FROM THE GUY AHEAD OF ME.
RATATATATATATATATATATATAT!
UNGH
UNGH
UNNGH!
AND ONCE OR TWICE, MY RIFLE ACCIDENTALLY TOUCHED HIS BOOTS.
OOPS... SORRY...
WHUT TH' FUCK?

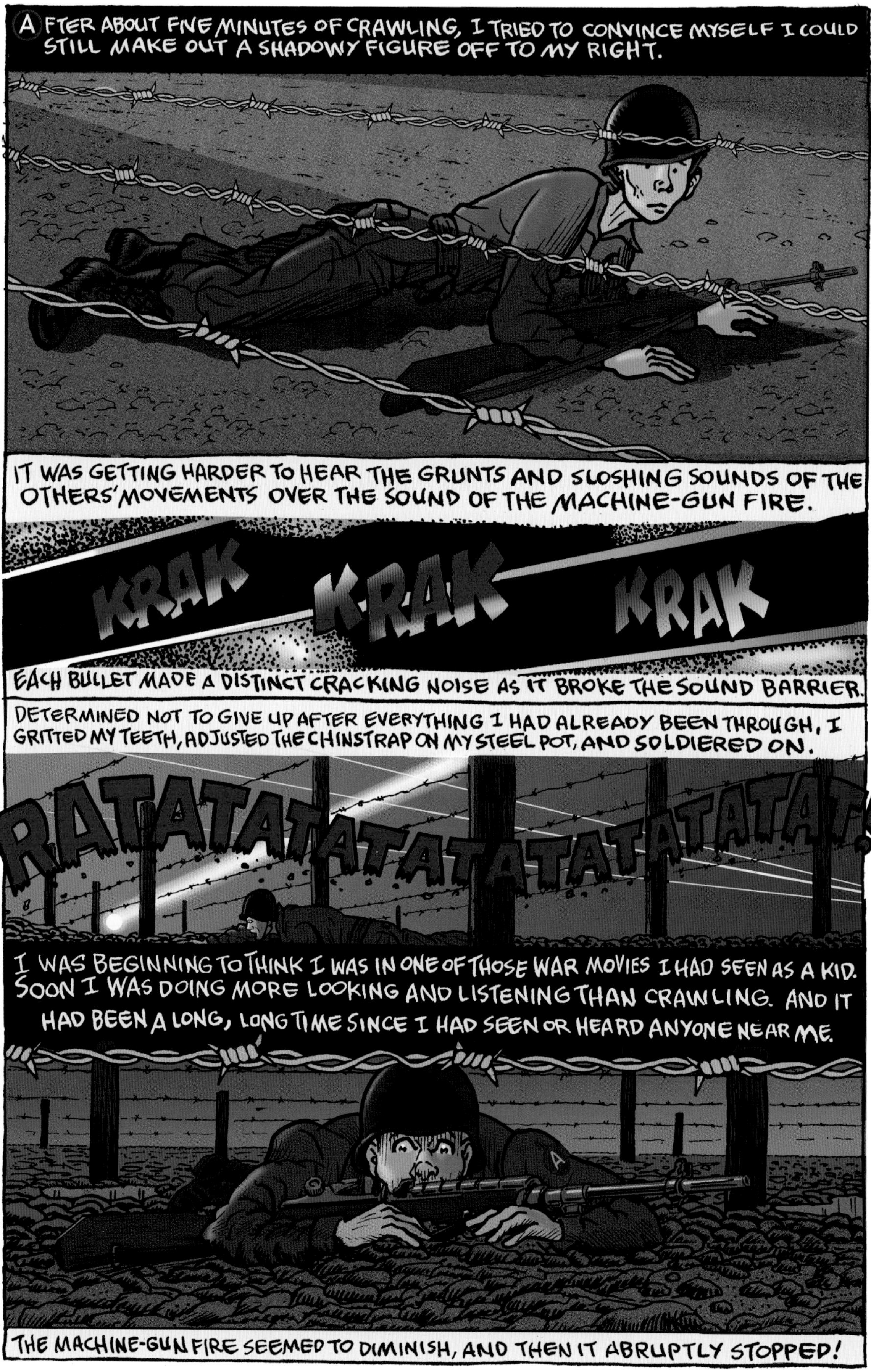
AFTER ABOUT FIVE MINUTES OF CRAWLING, I TRIED TO CONVINCE MYSELF I COULD STILL MAKE OUT A SHADOWY FIGURE OFF TO MY RIGHT.
IT WAS GETTING HARDER TO HEAR THE GRUNTS AND SLOSHING SOUNDS OF THE OTHERS' MOVEMENTS OVER THE SOUND OF THE MACHINE-GUN FIRE.
KRAK
KRAK
KRAK
EACH BULLET MADE A DISTINCT CRACKING NOISE AS IT BROKE THE SOUND BARRIER.
DETERMINED NOT TO GIVE UP AFTER EVERYTHING I HAD ALREADY BEEN THROUGH, I GRITTED MY TEETH, ADJUSTED THE CHINSTRAP ON MY STEEL POT, AND SOLDIERED ON.
RATATATATATATATATATAT!
I WAS BEGINNING TO THINK I WAS IN ONE OF THOSE WAR MOVIES I HAD SEEN AS A KID. SOON I WAS DOING MORE LOOKING AND LISTENING THAN CRAWLING. AND IT HAD BEEN A LONG, LONG TIME SINCE I HAD SEEN OR HEARD ANYONE NEAR ME.
THE MACHINE-GUN FIRE SEEMED TO DIMINISH, AND THEN IT ABRUPTLY STOPPED!

SEARCHLIGHTS BEGAN COMBING BACK AND FORTH ACROSS THE AREA. I ADVANCED A FEW MORE METERS THROUGH THE MUD, TRYING TO AVOID BEING SEEN.
SUDDENLY A VOICE ON A LOUDSPEAKER ASKED:
IS ANYONE STILL OUT THERE?
I WONDERED IF THEY WERE TALKING ABOUT ME.
I DIDN'T MEAN TO BE RUDE, BUT I REALLY DIDN'T FEEL LIKE SHOUTING, "YES! THERE IS! I'M STILL OUT HERE! PLEASE DON'T SHOOT!"
SO I MADE A CONCERTED EFFORT TO QUICKLY CRAWL THE LAST TWENTY METERS OR SO...
...AND JOINED THE OTHERS.
MERCIFULLY, IT WAS SO DARK THAT NO ONE COULD SEE THE LOOK OF HUMILIATION ON MY FACE.

After BASIC, I stayed at Fort Stewart and began A.I.T.* in ARMOR, while I awaited orders for Officer Candidate School. I had gotten my DRIVER'S LICENSE only one year before by learning how to drive my mother's 1959 CADILLAC--so I felt perfectly at home at the controls of an M48A1 PATTON TANK!

*Advanced Individual Training

A TANK doesn't have a STEERING WHEEL...instead, it is operated by means of two big LEVERS. These levers control the TRACKS. Pulling back on the LEFT lever locks the left tread--and the tank turns to the LEFT.
Pulling back on the RIGHT lever turns the tank to the RIGHT.
There are two large PEDALS--which you operate with your feet. One is the GAS--and the other is the BRAKE.
It takes BOTH HANDS and BOTH FEET to drive a TANK.

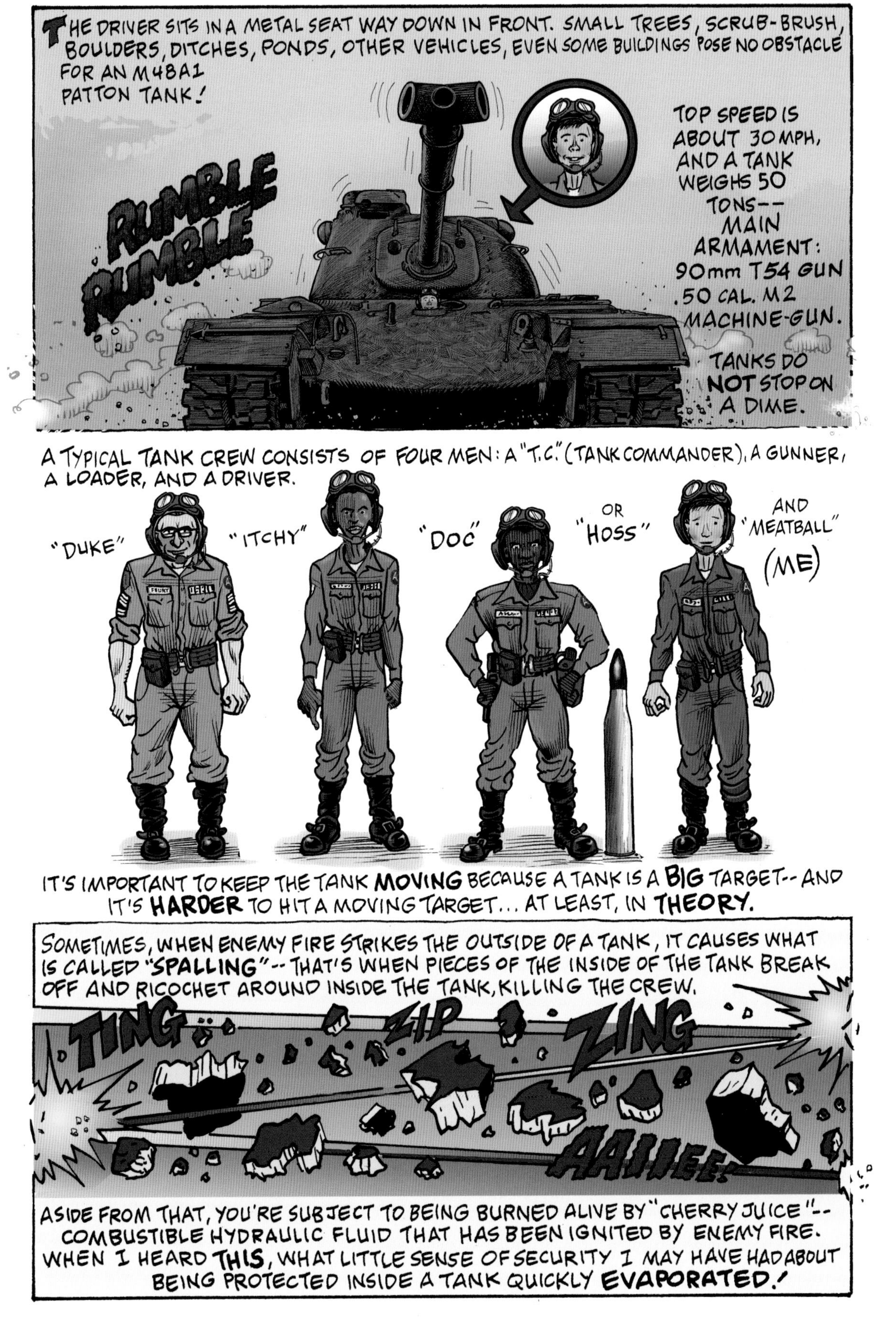
THE DRIVER SITS IN A METAL SEAT WAY DOWN IN FRONT. SMALL TREES, SCRUB-BRUSH, BOULDERS, DITCHES, PONDS, OTHER VEHICLES, EVEN SOME BUILDINGS POSE NO OBSTACLE FOR AN M48A1 PATTON TANK!
RUMBLE RUMBLE
TOP SPEED IS ABOUT 30 MPH, AND A TANK WEIGHS 50 TONS-- MAIN ARMAMENT: 90mm T54 GUN .50 CAL. M2 MACHINE-GUN.
TANKS DO NOT STOP ON A DIME.
A TYPICAL TANK CREW CONSISTS OF FOUR MEN: A "T.C." (TANK COMMANDER), A GUNNER, A LOADER, AND A DRIVER.
"DUKE"
"ITCHY"
"DOC"
OR "HOSS"
AND "MEATBALL"
(ME)
IT'S IMPORTANT TO KEEP THE TANK MOVING BECAUSE A TANK IS A BIG TARGET-- AND IT'S HARDER TO HIT A MOVING TARGET... AT LEAST, IN THEORY.
SOMETIMES, WHEN ENEMY FIRE STRIKES THE OUTSIDE OF A TANK, IT CAUSES WHAT IS CALLED "SPALLING"-- THAT'S WHEN PIECES OF THE INSIDE OF THE TANK BREAK OFF AND RICOCHET AROUND INSIDE THE TANK, KILLING THE CREW.
TING
ZIP
ZING
AAIIEE!
ASIDE FROM THAT, YOU'RE SUBJECT TO BEING BURNED ALIVE BY "CHERRY JUICE"-- COMBUSTIBLE HYDRAULIC FLUID THAT HAS BEEN IGNITED BY ENEMY FIRE. WHEN I HEARD THIS, WHAT LITTLE SENSE OF SECURITY I MAY HAVE HAD ABOUT BEING PROTECTED INSIDE A TANK QUICKLY EVAPORATED!

WHEN THE HATCH IS CLOSED, THE DRIVER "SEES" THROUGH A PERISCOPE, AND "HEARS" THROUGH A HEADSET BUILT INTO HIS HELMET. THE T.C., WHO HAS A BETTER VIEW OF WHERE THE TANK IS HEADED (PRESUMABLY), ISSUES ORDERS AND DIRECTIONS.
SLOW DOWN! YOU'RE GOIN' TO KILL US!
SPEED UP! NOW YER GOIN' TOO SLOW!
HAVING THE T.C. YELLING AT YOU OVER THE RUMBLE OF THE TRACKS AS YOU HURTLE THROUGH SPACE IN A 50-TON TANK, AT NIGHT, WHILE PEERING AT THE WORLD THROUGH A PERISCOPE, IS THE ULTIMATE BACKSEAT DRIVER EXPERIENCE... I KNOW-- BECAUSE IT HAPPENED TO ME!
WE WERE ON NIGHT MANEUVERS...
MY ONLY INSTRUCTIONS WERE TO FOLLOW THE TANK IN FRONT OF ME.
SEEMED SIMPLE ENOUGH.
BUT I HAVE NEVER BEEN ESPECIALLY GOOD AT FOLLOWING SIMPLE INSTRUCTIONS.
I WAS TO KEEP MY EYE ON THE DUAL RED TAILLIGHTS OF THE TANK DIRECTLY IN FRONT OF ME. AS LONG AS I COULD SEE TWO DISTINCT LIGHTS, I WAS THE CORRECT DISTANCE BEHIND HIM. BUT THAT WAS EASIER SAID THAN DONE.
KRONK-A-GRONNK!

IF, ON THE OTHER HAND, I FELL TOO FAR BEHIND WHEN FOLLOWING, THEN THE TWO LIGHTS WOULD APPEAR AS ONE--AND I'D HAVE TO SPEED UP!
KLONK-A-KLONK-A-KLONK
IT'S VERY TRICKY, BECAUSE THERE ARE OTHER TANKS FOLLOWING YOU, AND YOU HAVE TO STAY TOGETHER--ESPECIALLY AT NIGHT.
RUMBLE
RUMBLE
IT GETS DARK OUT THERE. AND BESIDES--
--TANKS DON'T HAVE REARVIEW MIRRORS!

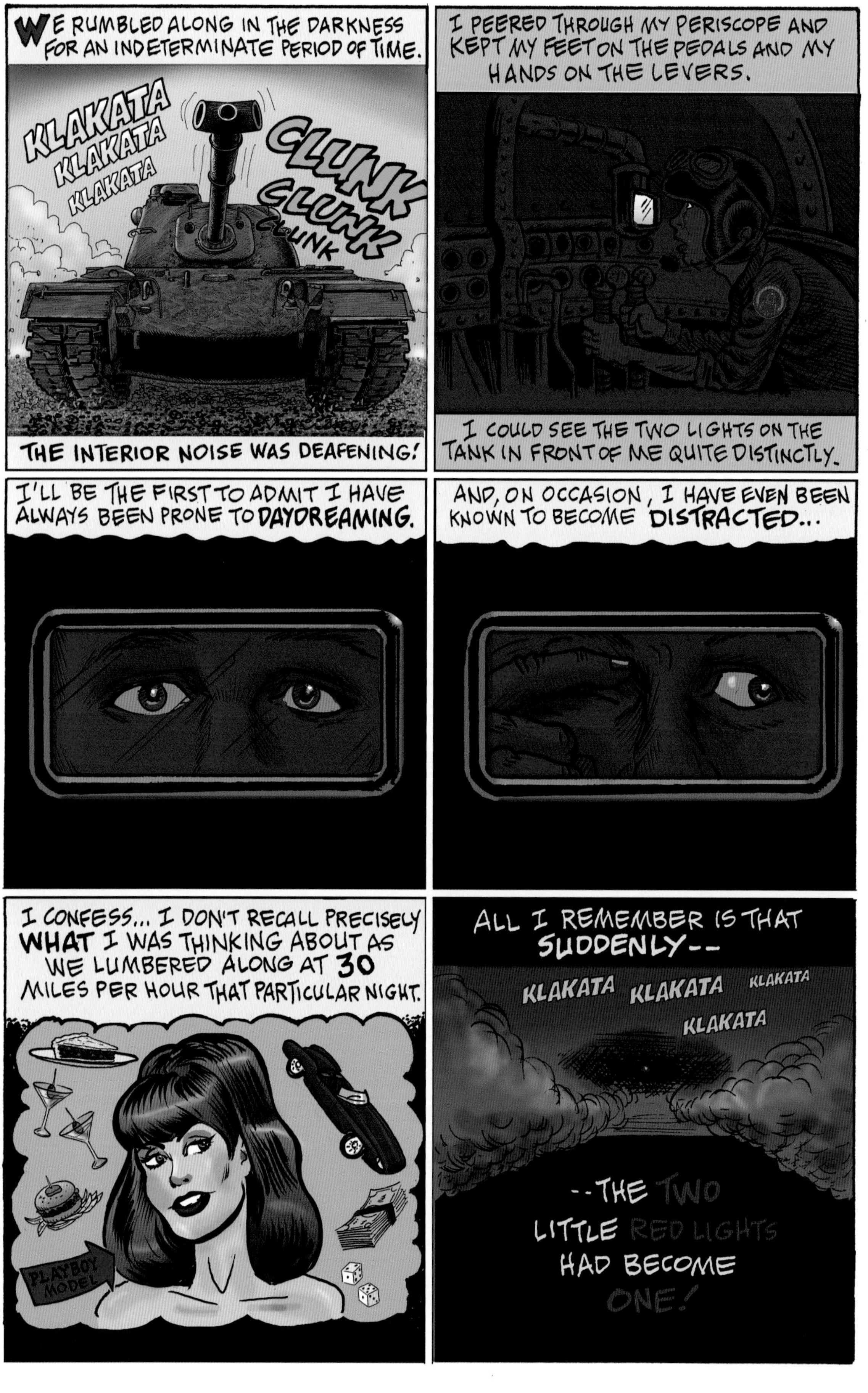
WE RUMBLED ALONG IN THE DARKNESS FOR AN INDETERMINATE PERIOD OF TIME.
KLAKATA KLAKATA KLAKATA
CLUNK CLUNK CLUNK
THE INTERIOR NOISE WAS DEAFENING!
I PEERED THROUGH MY PERISCOPE AND KEPT MY FEET ON THE PEDALS AND MY HANDS ON THE LEVERS.
I COULD SEE THE TWO LIGHTS ON THE TANK IN FRONT OF ME QUITE DISTINCTLY.
I'LL BE THE FIRST TO ADMIT I HAVE ALWAYS BEEN PRONE TO DAYDREAMING.
AND, ON OCCASION, I HAVE EVEN BEEN KNOWN TO BECOME DISTRACTED...
I CONFESS... I DON'T RECALL PRECISELY WHAT I WAS THINKING ABOUT AS WE LUMBERED ALONG AT 30 MILES PER HOUR THAT PARTICULAR NIGHT.
PLAYBOY MODEL
ALL I REMEMBER IS THAT SUDDENLY--
KLAKATA KLAKATA KLAKATA KLAKATA
--THE TWO LITTLE RED LIGHTS HAD BECOME ONE!

SUDDENLY, THE T.C. WAS SCREAMING ORDERS AT SOMEONE OVER MY HEADSET. IT WAS IMPOSSIBLE TO UNDERSTAND HIM WITH THE ROAR OF THE TRACKS AND THE RADIO STATIC! POOR BASTARD.
ER-WAAH-DIZZ GUT-AH-RHEA!
ERRRR-WAH DIZZ GUTT!
?
GOD! I THINK HE'S TALKIN' TO ME!
SHIT...
ERRWAH--DIZZ-GUT-AH-RHEA!
SAY AGAIN..?
OVER.
I WASN'T SURE HOW TO RESPOND, SO I EASED UP ON THE GAS PEDAL THINKING THAT WITH LESS ENGINE NOISE I MIGHT BE ABLE TO UNDERSTAND HIM BETTER.
ERR-RARRH! DIZZ-GUT!
SAY AGAIN?
OVER.
ERRWAGH! DIZGUTT--!
UHH...SORRY... I C-CAN'T UNDERSTAND...
OVER.
GRONK-GARUNK-KA-KLACKKA
WHILE I WAS TRYING TO FIGURE OUT WHAT TO DO NEXT, I GRADUALLY BECAME ACUTELY AWARE OF SOMEONE APPROACHING FROM BEHIND. THE T.C. GRABBED ME BY THE RIGHT SHOULDER AND RIPPED MY HELMET OFF AND THEN WHISPERED SOMETHING IN MY EAR.....
EXCUSE ME, PRIVATE PARKER... I HATE TO BOTHER YOU, BUT IT OCCURRED TO ME THAT WE ARE JUST A TAD TOO FAR BEHIND THE LEAD TANK... WOULD YOU MIND TERRIBLY IF I SUGGESTED THAT YOU SPEED UP A TINY BIT?
WELL, THAT'S NOT EXACTLY WHAT HE SAID, BUT YOU GET THE IDEA!

BECAUSE I WAS DESTINED FOR O.C.S., I WAS PULLED OUT OF ARMOR A.I.T. AFTER JUST ONE MONTH AND SENT BACK TO FORT JACKSON TO BEGIN INFANTRY A.I.T.
I GUESS THEY THOUGHT INFANTRY TRAINING WOULD SOMEHOW PREPARE ME BETTER IF I EVER HAD TO LEAD MEN INTO COMBAT.
FOLLOW ME!
ZING
HOW I IMAGINED THE FUTURE ME AFTER O.C.S.
ZING
ZING
NO WAY I'M GOIN' OUT THERE...
YOU FIRST...
IS HE NUTS?
GET DOWN, YOU FOOL!
VIP
VIP
VIP

BUT THE BEST PART ABOUT THE TRANSFER WAS THAT AS A "TANKER," I GOT TO BLOUSE MY BOOTS (TUCK PANTS INTO BOOTS) WHEN TRAVELING IN MY CLASS "A" UNIFORM...
ME
SCENICRUISER
...WHEREAS OTHER SOLDIERS HAD TO WEAR "LOW QUARTERS" WITH THEIR DRESS UNIFORMS.

THE INFANTRY IS KNOWN AS THE "QUEEN OF BATTLE," AND IT'S THE INFANTRY THAT IS ON THE FRONT LINES IN WAR. THE "GRUNTS" ARE LITERALLY THE "BOOTS ON THE GROUND" OUR GOVERNMENT OFFICIALS SO OFTEN SPEAK OF.
EEE-YAAH KILL
ALONG WITH THE U.S. MARINES, THEY'RE USUALLY THE FIRST TO GO INTO ANY HOSTILE ENVIRONMENT--AND THE LAST TO LEAVE. AS A RESULT, THEY SUFFER THE GREATEST NUMBER OF CASUALTIES.
BY 1969, A LARGE PART OF THE ARMY'S INFANTRY CONSISTED OF DRAFTEES--AND OVER HALF OF ALL THE U.S. ARMY'S CASUALTIES IN VIETNAM WERE INFANTRY.
TROMP TROMP
TROMP
CONSEQUENTLY, OUR TRAINING WAS PRETTY RIGOROUS. IF YOU WANTED TO FIGHT--YOU EITHER JOINED THE MARINES--OR YOU BECAME AN INFANTRYMAN!

WE "DOUBLE-TIMED" IT WHEREVER WE WENT-- AND OUR DRILL SERGEANT EVEN TAUGHT US SOME NEW SONGS.
I DUNNO BUT I'VE BEEN TOLD--
...I DUNNO BUT I'VE BEEN TOLD...
ESKIMO PIE IS MIGHTY COLD--
ESKIMO PIE IS MIGHTY COLD...

UNDER THE CAREFUL INSTRUCTION OF SOME SEASONED COMBAT VETERANS, WE WERE QUICKLY TRANSFORMED INTO TRAINED KILLERS BY BECOMING FAMILIAR WITH SUCH VALUABLE SKILLS AS....
...HOW TO SNEAK UP ON THE ENEMY AND SLIT HIS THROAT BEFORE HE COULD EVEN UTTER A SOUND...
...OR HOW TO "GUT" HIM WITH A KNIFE!
NOT TO MENTION LEARNING HOW TO FIELD-STRIP, CLEAN, AND FIRE EVERY SINGLE WEAPON IN THE INFANTRY'S VAST ARSENAL OF "SMALL ARMS."

ALTHOUGH I ABSOLUTELY DREADED EVEN THE THOUGHT OF HAVING TO "GUT" SOMEONE, ALL THAT FIRING OF ALL THOSE WEAPONS WAS ESPECIALLY SATISFYING TO ME...
BLAM
...BECAUSE MY PARENTS WOULDN'T EVEN LET ME HAVE A BB GUN! BY THE TIME I WAS IN HIGH SCHOOL, I HAD FINALLY SAVED UP ENOUGH MONEY TO GO OUT AND BUY ONE, BUT IT WASN'T HALF AS EXCITING AS ANY OF THIS!

BUT BEFORE WE ACTUALLY GOT OUR HANDS ON ANY OF THOSE WEAPONS, THEY SAT US DOWN IN FRONT OF THE FIRING RANGE, WHERE WE WERE INSTRUCTED ON THE FINER POINTS OF EACH INDIVIDUAL WEAPON.
THE M60 IS A GAS-OPERATED, AIR-COOLED, BELT-FED, AUTOMATIC MACHINE GUN THAT FIRES FROM THE OPEN-BOLT POSITION AND IS CHAMBERED FOR THE 7.62mm NATO CARTRIDGE.....
AMMUNITION IS USUALLY FED INTO THE WEAPON FROM A 100-ROUND BANDOLIER CONTAINING A DISINTEGRATING, METALLIC SPLIT-LINK BELT... BLAH... BLAH... BLAH...
BICKMORE
A SERIES OF WHITE CUT-OUT TARGETS, EACH ABOUT 36 INCHES HIGH-- ROUGHLY THE SHAPE OF A HUMAN BEING AND MARKED WITH A BIG BLACK BULLSEYE ON ITS CHEST--HAD BEEN SET UP IN THE FIELD IN FRONT OF US.
"THE PIG"
ON AN ORDER FROM THE INSTRUCTOR, A TWO-MAN GUN CREW TROTTED OUT FROM ONE SIDE. THEY CARRIED A WEAPON THAT HAD A SMALL TRIPOD ATTACHED TO ITS BARREL, AND AWAITED HIS ORDERS TO FIRE.

THE FIRST TARGET LAY FLAT ON THE GROUND AT A MERE 100 METERS.
ON A SIGNAL FROM OUR INSTRUCTOR, THE TARGET POPPED UP.
IT REMINDED ME OF A GRAVESTONE IN AN OLD CEMETERY.
POP!
NO SOONER HAD IT POPPED UP THAN IT WAS FALLING BACK OVER AGAIN WITH A LARGE HOLE IN ITS CENTER OF MASS.
A SINGLE ROUND WAS ENOUGH TO DROP IT AFTER ONLY A SECOND OR TWO AT MOST.
THEN THE SERGEANT CALLED FOR THE TARGET AT 200 METERS...
KA-POP!
... AND SUDDENLY THERE IT WAS.
USARMY
AS QUICKLY AS THE TARGET POPPED UP, THE M-60 JUST AS QUICKLY MADE A SINGLE POPPING SOUND, AND IN ABOUT A SECOND AND A HALF, THIS TARGET, TOO, FELL SILENTLY BACKWARD, THE VICTIM OF A SINGLE ROUND FROM "THE PIG."
THEN THINGS GOT REALLY INTERESTING.
500 METERS...
NOW ALL EYES STRAINED TO FIND THE TARGET ON THE DISTANT HORIZON...
POP!
...AND DOWN IT WENT.!
PARKER

1,000 METERS...
I LOOKED TO THE FRONT AND SQUINTED-- BUT ALL I COULD SEE WERE SOME GENTLY ROLLING HILLS DOTTED WITH SCRUB BRUSH --AND FURTHER OFF, SOME TREES. AT LEAST, I THINK THEY WERE TREES. THEY COULD HAVE BEEN CLOUDS...
THEN, AS I VAINLY SCANNED THE HORIZON FOR THE DISTANT TARGET, OUT OF THE CORNER OF MY EYE I THOUGHT I SAW SOMETHING MOVE... A TINY WHITE OBJECT APPEARED THAT HADN'T BEEN THERE A SECOND BEFORE...
OUT IN FRONT OF US, THE GUNNER SHIFTED HIS BODY SLIGHTLY AND SQUEEZED OUT A "BURST OF FIVE"...
RATATATATATATATAT!
AFTER A DELAY OF ABOUT THREE SECONDS, THE TINY TARGET ROLLED OVER BACKWARD, JUST AS SILENTLY AS IT HAD ARCHED UP. I WAS IMPRESSED. EVERYONE WAS...
...EXCEPT FOR MAYBE OUR INSTRUCTOR, WHO HAD SEEN THE PIG IN ACTION MANY TIMES BEFORE...
BICKMORE
...AND NO DOUBT, EVEN KILLED WITH IT.

THE SERGEANT DISMISSED THE TWO-MAN MACHINE GUN CREW, AND THEY JUMPED UP AND TROTTED OFF SMARTLY WITH THE M60.
I FELT LIKE APPLAUDING.
BUT IT JUST DIDN'T SEEM RIGHT SOMEHOW.
LATER THAT DAY, WE WERE PRACTICING THE ASSEMBLY AND THE DISASSEMBLY OF THE M-60 WHEN AN ARMY CLERK ENTERED.
HEY, JONES... PASS ME THAT BORE CLEANER...
ANYONE HERE KNOW. ANYTHING ABOUT MATH..?
I WONDERED IF FLUNKING OUT OF COLLEGE MY FIRST YEAR WITH A 43 AVERAGE IN MATH COUNTED FOR ANYTHING.
I TOOK MATH IN COLLEGE!
THE CLERK WROTE DOWN MY NAME AND SERVICE NUMBER. LATER, I LEARNED THE ARMY COULD ONLY SEND TWO CANDIDATES TO THE ARTILLERY OFFICER CANDIDATE SCHOOL. ARTILLERY, THE "KING OF BATTLE", USES TRIGONOMETRY TO "PUT HIS BALLS" WHERE THE QUEEN OF BATTLE"--THE INFANTRY--WANTS THEM. ALL THE REST OF THE GUYS IN MY UNIT WENT TO INFANTRY O.C.S. AT FORT BENNING, AND BECAME PLATOON LEADERS IN 'NAM.
400 Pennsylvania Ave
Quantico, Virginia
Allocations for Officer Candidate School
June 20, 1966
To: Headquarters Training Battalion
Fort Jackson, South Carolina
RE: ALLOCATIONS FOR OFFICER CANDIDATE SCHOOL
Infantry (67)
Fort Benning, Georgia
AND SO, MY OLD NEMESIS, MATH--WHICH GOT ME DRAFTED IN THE FIRST PLACE--WOULD PROVE TO BE MY SALVATION... AND KEEP MY SORRY ASS FROM GETTING SENT TO VIETNAM! FOR NOW, AT LEAST!

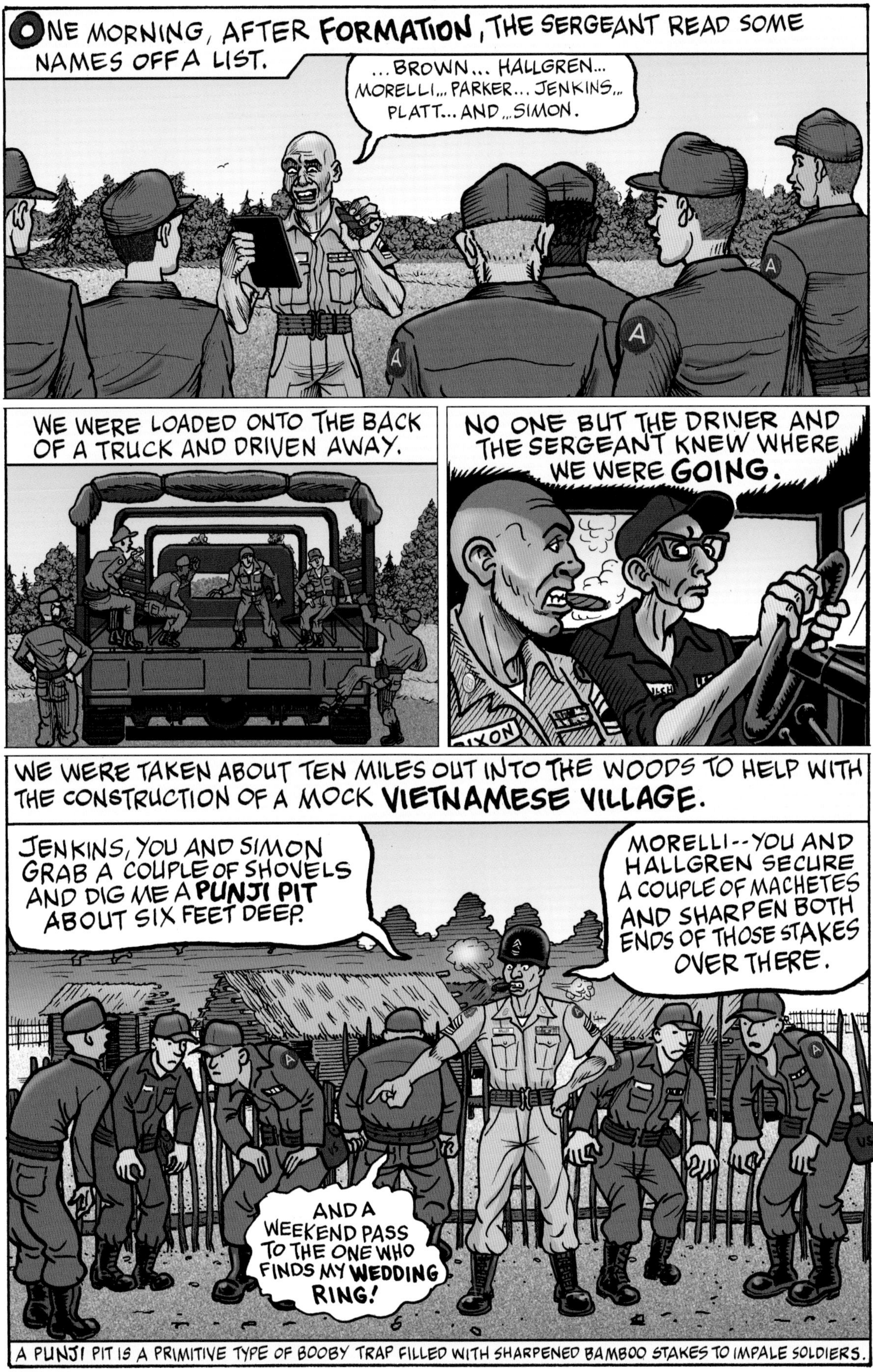
ONE MORNING, AFTER FORMATION, THE SERGEANT READ SOME NAMES OFF A LIST.
...BROWN... HALLGREN... MORELLI... PARKER... JENKINS... PLATT... AND... SIMON.
WE WERE LOADED ONTO THE BACK OF A TRUCK AND DRIVEN AWAY.
NO ONE BUT THE DRIVER AND THE SERGEANT KNEW WHERE WE WERE GOING.
DIXON
WE WERE TAKEN ABOUT TEN MILES OUT INTO THE WOODS TO HELP WITH THE CONSTRUCTION OF A MOCK VIETNAMESE VILLAGE.
JENKINS, YOU AND SIMON GRAB A COUPLE OF SHOVELS AND DIG ME A PUNJI PIT ABOUT SIX FEET DEEP.
MORELLI--YOU AND HALLGREN SECURE A COUPLE OF MACHETES AND SHARPEN BOTH ENDS OF THOSE STAKES OVER THERE.
AND A WEEKEND PASS TO THE ONE WHO FINDS MY WEDDING RING!
A PUNJI PIT IS A PRIMITIVE TYPE OF BOOBY TRAP FILLED WITH SHARPENED BAMBOO STAKES TO IMPALE SOLDIERS.

THERE WERE ONLY A COUPLE OF US LEFT. ME AND PERKINS...
PARKER
PERKINS
EITHER OF YOU TWO JOKERS KNOW HOW TO DRIVE A PICKUP?
THINKING THAT WOULDN'T BE SUCH A HARD JOB, I SPOKE UP.
I DO!
PARKER
OKAY...TAKE THAT WHEELBARROW AND PICK UP ALL THAT SHIT OVER THERE!
IT WAS THEN I REMEMBERED THE ONE PIECE OF ADVICE A FAMILY FRIEND HAD GIVEN ME....
NEVER VOLUNTEER FOR ANYTHING...

AFTER EIGHT WEEKS OF **A.I.T.** (ADVANCED INFANTRY TRAINING), I TOOK A WEEK'S LEAVE IN SAVANNAH TO VISIT MY PARENTS. THEN THEY DROVE ME BACK TO FORT JACKSON TO AWAIT ORDERS FOR **O.C.S.**

SO LONG!
CALL US! ...DON'T FORGET!
19 GEORGIA 66
LS 612
PEACH STATE
CHATHAM

BY NOW IT WAS AUGUST... THE DAYS WERE LONG AND HOT--AND THE AREA WE WERE IN WAS KNOWN AFFECTIONATELY AS "**TANK HILL**." TO HONE MY LEADERSHIP SKILLS, THEY GAVE ME THREE STRIPES--MADE ME AN "ACTING JACK"--AND PUT ME IN CHARGE OF THE "**HOLDOVER PLATOON**."

ME
YOUR LEFT... YOUR LEFT... YOUR LEFT, RIGHT, LEFT...

THE HOLDOVER PLATOON WAS COMPRISED OF A MOTLEY ASSORTMENT OF **INDIVIDUALS** DEEMED **UNFIT** FOR MILITARY SERVICE FOR ONE REASON OR ANOTHER. THEY WERE AWAITING ORDERS TO BE MUSTERED **OUT** OF THE SERVICE AND RELEASED BACK INTO AN UNSUSPECTING CIVILIAN POPULATION.

I WAS IN CHARGE OF ALL TWELVE OF THEM!
"CYCLOPS"
Dayton, Ohio
Domestic Violence
"SPIDER"
Las Vegas
Stealing
"BIG MAC"
Rincon, Georgia
Weight Control
"ANIMAL"
Miami, Florida
A.W.O.L.
"STINKY"
Cleveland, Ohio
Personal Hygiene Issues
"JOEL th' HOSE"
Madison, Wisconsin
Indecent Exposure
"SMILEY"
Stark, Florida
Anger Management Issues
"CLAM"
Canton, Ohio
Bedwetting
"WEIRDO"
Manassas, Georgia
Inability to Adapt to Military Life
"SLEEPY"
Bronx, New York
Sleepwalking
"SPEEDY"
Barstow, California
Drug Abuse
"GRAMPS"
Presque Isle, Maine
Under Strength

AND WE ALL BUNKED TOGETHER IN ONE BARRACKS.

MY IMMEDIATE SUPERIOR WAS STAFF SERGEANT KING, WHO APPEARED BRIEFLY EACH MORNING TO INSPECT THE BARRACKS.
FOLLOW ME!
PARKER
I ACCOMPANIED HIM ON HIS ROUNDS.

WHILE HE DID THE INSPECTION, MY "MEN" WERE IN THE MESS HALL...MAKING A MESS.
ZZZ
TYLER

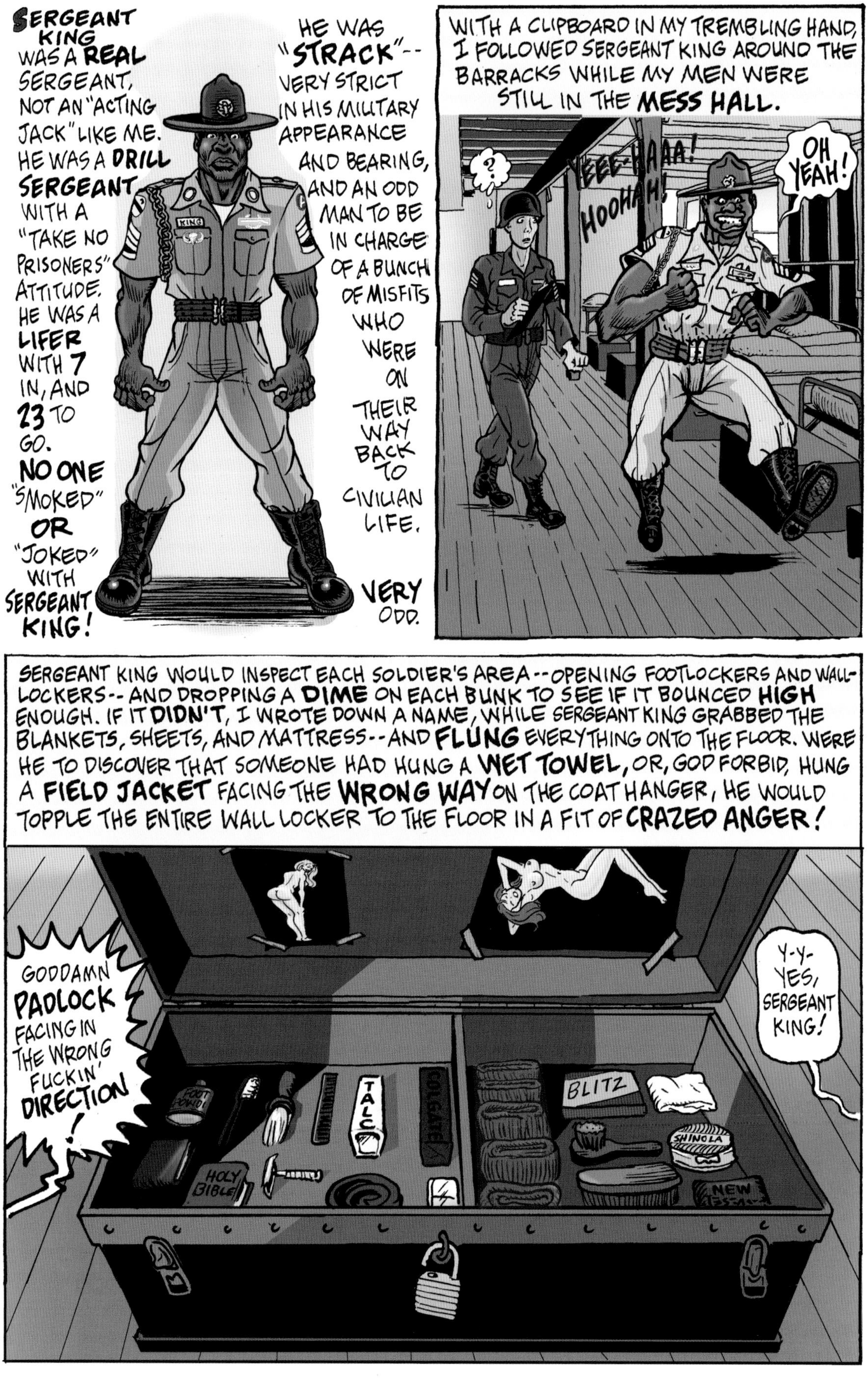
SERGEANT KING WAS A REAL SERGEANT, NOT AN "ACTING JACK" LIKE ME. HE WAS A DRILL SERGEANT WITH A "TAKE NO PRISONERS" ATTITUDE. HE WAS A LIFER WITH 7 IN, AND 23 TO GO. NO ONE "SMOKED" OR "JOKED" WITH SERGEANT KING!
KING
HE WAS "STRACK"-- VERY STRICT IN HIS MILITARY APPEARANCE AND BEARING, AND AN ODD MAN TO BE IN CHARGE OF A BUNCH OF MISFITS WHO WERE ON THEIR WAY BACK TO CIVILIAN LIFE.
VERY ODD.
WITH A CLIPBOARD IN MY TREMBLING HAND, I FOLLOWED SERGEANT KING AROUND THE BARRACKS WHILE MY MEN WERE STILL IN THE MESS HALL.
?
YEEE-HAAA!
HOOHAH!
OH YEAH!
SERGEANT KING WOULD INSPECT EACH SOLDIER'S AREA--OPENING FOOTLOCKERS AND WALL-LOCKERS--AND DROPPING A DIME ON EACH BUNK TO SEE IF IT BOUNCED HIGH ENOUGH. IF IT DIDN'T, I WROTE DOWN A NAME, WHILE SERGEANT KING GRABBED THE BLANKETS, SHEETS, AND MATTRESS--AND FLUNG EVERYTHING ONTO THE FLOOR. WERE HE TO DISCOVER THAT SOMEONE HAD HUNG A WET TOWEL, OR, GOD FORBID, HUNG A FIELD JACKET FACING THE WRONG WAY ON THE COAT HANGER, HE WOULD TOPPLE THE ENTIRE WALL LOCKER TO THE FLOOR IN A FIT OF CRAZED ANGER!
GODDAMN PADLOCK FACING IN THE WRONG FUCKIN' DIRECTION!
Y-Y-YES, SERGEANT KING!
FOOT POWDER
TALC
COLGATE
HOLY BIBLE
BLITZ
SHINOLA
NEW

PADLOCK IMPROPERLY SECURED... GOT IT.
SOCKS IMPROPERLY ROLLED!
GOT IT.
FUCK!
I DO NOT LIKE WHAT I'M LOOKIN' AT...
THAT BETTER NOT BE WHAT I THINK IT IS...!
IT IS...! THAT IS A GODDAMN HAIR!
GROSS!
FLING

WHEN "INSPECTION" WAS OVER, IT LITERALLY LOOKED AS IF A TORNADO HAD HIT THE BARRACKS.
NOW MARCH THEIR SORRY ASSES BACK HERE AND CLEAN UP THIS DISASTER AREA...
YES, SERGEANT.
THE HOLDOVER PLATOON DIDN'T HAVE ANY "OFFICIAL" DUTIES SINCE EACH OF THEM WOULD BE OUT OF THE ARMY IN A MONTH. BUT INANE TASKS AND SERGEANT KING'S TRASHING OF THEIR QUARTERS EVERY DAY KEPT THEM BUSY AND DEMORALIZED.
CIGARETTE PATROL
I FOUND ONE, SERGEANT PARKER!
CIVILIAN LIFE MUST HAVE SEEMED LIKE A BLESSING AFTER WHAT THEY HAD EXPERIENCED DURING THEIR LAST FEW WEEKS IN THE ARMY. I KNOW IT TOOK A TOLL ON ME!
MANY OF THESE "MISFITS" HAD A SLIPPERY GRIP ON SANITY IN THE FIRST PLACE. SO I TOOK IT UPON MYSELF TO ENCOURAGE THEM, CHEER THEM UP IF I COULD, AND TRY TO MOTIVATE THEM TO GET THE PLACE BACK IN ORDER...
OKAY, WHO'S WITH ME ON THIS?
...EVEN THOUGH SERGEANT KING WOULD COME BACK THE NEXT DAY AND DO IT ALL OVER AGAIN!

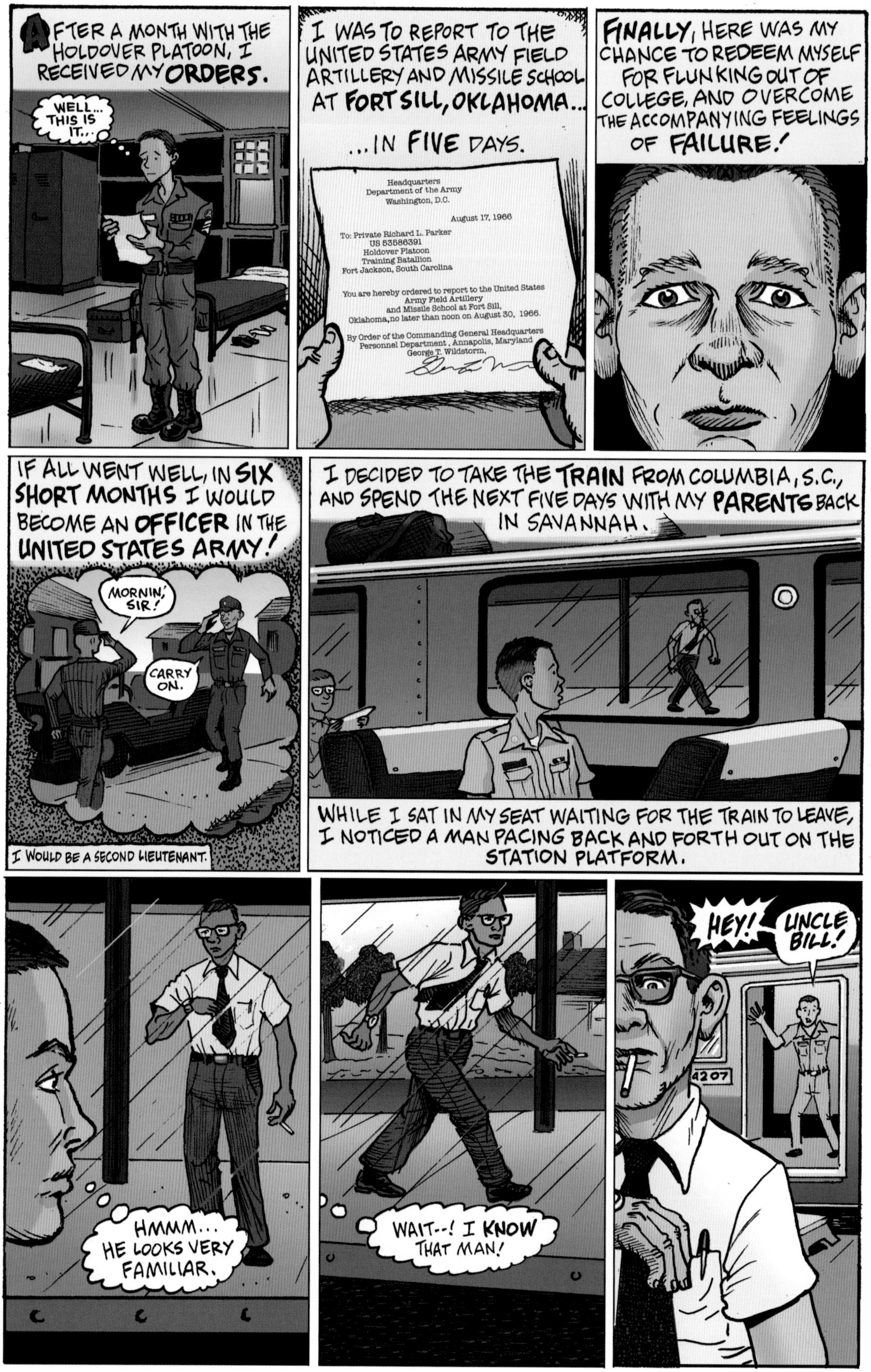
AFTER A MONTH WITH THE HOLDOVER PLATOON, I RECEIVED MY ORDERS.
WELL... THIS IS IT...
I WAS TO REPORT TO THE UNITED STATES ARMY FIELD ARTILLERY AND MISSILE SCHOOL AT FORT SILL, OKLAHOMA...
...IN FIVE DAYS.
Headquarters
Department of the Army
Washington, D.C.
August 17, 1966
To: Private Richard L. Parker
US 53586391
Holdover Platoon
Training Batallion
Fort Jackson, South Carolina
You are hereby ordered to report to the United States Army Field Artillery and Missile School at Fort Sill, Oklahoma, no later than noon on August 30, 1966.
By Order of the Commanding General Headquarters
Personnel Department, Annapolis, Maryland
George T. Wildstorm,
FINALLY, HERE WAS MY CHANCE TO REDEEM MYSELF FOR FLUNKING OUT OF COLLEGE, AND OVERCOME THE ACCOMPANYING FEELINGS OF FAILURE!
IF ALL WENT WELL, IN SIX SHORT MONTHS I WOULD BECOME AN OFFICER IN THE UNITED STATES ARMY!
MORNIN', SIR!
CARRY ON.
I WOULD BE A SECOND LIEUTENANT.
I DECIDED TO TAKE THE TRAIN FROM COLUMBIA, S.C., AND SPEND THE NEXT FIVE DAYS WITH MY PARENTS BACK IN SAVANNAH.
WHILE I SAT IN MY SEAT WAITING FOR THE TRAIN TO LEAVE, I NOTICED A MAN PACING BACK AND FORTH OUT ON THE STATION PLATFORM.
HMMM... HE LOOKS VERY FAMILIAR.
WAIT--! I KNOW THAT MAN!
HEY!
UNCLE BILL!
4207

IT'S ME-- RICKY PARKER!
I-I DIDN'T RECOGNIZE YOU IN THAT UNIFORM...
ARE YOU MEETING SOMEONE?
NO... HA-HA! I'M THE STATION MASTER IN COLUMBIA!
PARKER
WELL... TIME TO GO... IT'S NICE TO SEE YOU AGAIN...
ON THE THREE-HOUR TRIP HOME, I THOUGHT ABOUT MANY THINGS. I THOUGHT ABOUT HOW HAPPY MY MOTHER WAS GOING TO BE WHEN SHE SAW ME... I THOUGHT ABOUT THE GUYS IN THE HOLDOVER PLATOON AND WHAT THEIR LIVES WERE GOING TO BE LIKE ON THE OUTSIDE...
US
PARKER

3

CANDIDATE ZILCH

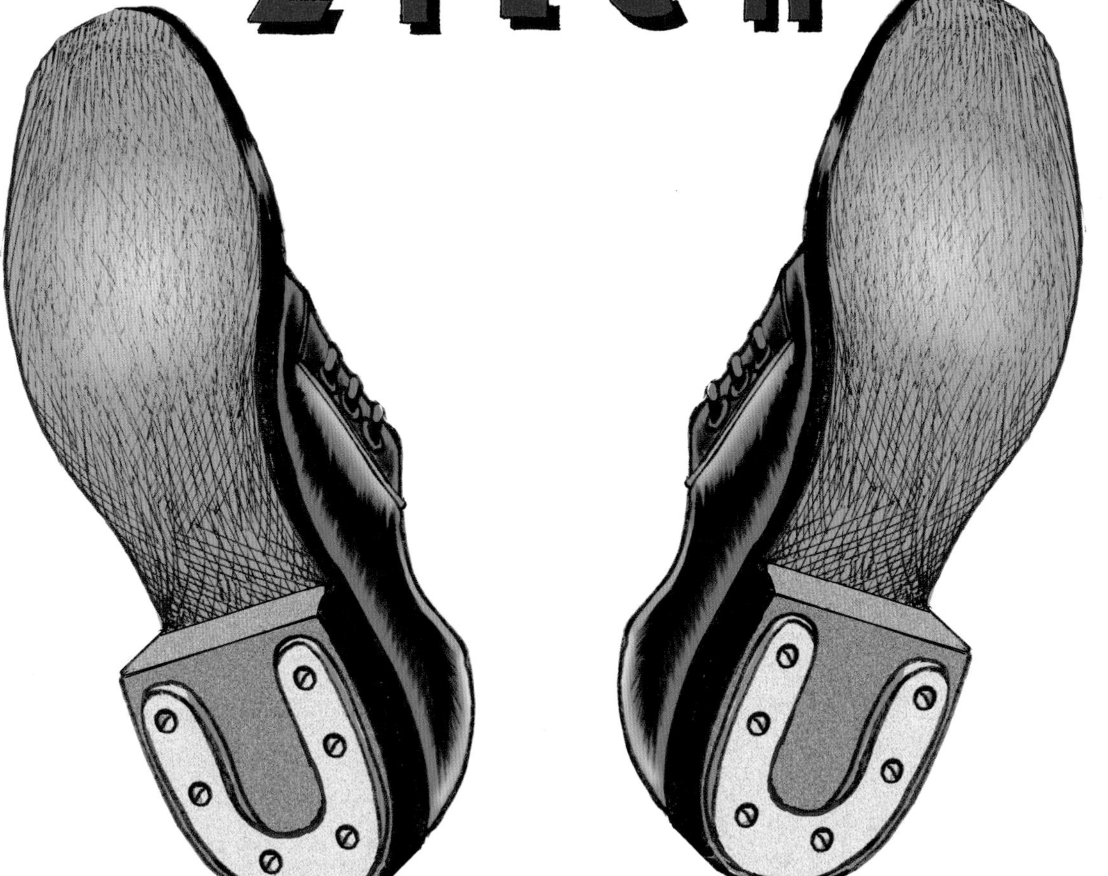

IT WAS GREAT SEEING MY PARENTS, BUT AFTER A COUPLE OF DAYS HANGING AROUND THE HOUSE I BECAME ANXIOUS TO GET ON WITH THE NEXT CHAPTER OF MY LIFE.
I'M MEETING AN OLD FRIEND FOR LUNCH AT JOHNNY HARRIS' TOMORROW-- CARE TO JOIN US?
NO THANKS. I FEEL LIKE I SHOULD GET GOING ALREADY.
EVEN THOUGH I WASN'T DUE TO REPORT TO FORT SILL FOR ANOTHER THREE DAYS, I CONVINCED MYSELF THAT THERE MIGHT BE SOME ADVANTAGE TO ARRIVING AT O.C.S. EARLY.
THE PLANE FROM GEORGIA TO TEXAS WAS NOT AIR-CONDITIONED. STILL I WAS FEELING PRETTY SPIFFY IN MY SLIGHTLY WRINKLED, IF MILDLY SWEAT-STAINED, KHAKI DRESS-UNIFORM BY THE TIME THE PLANE FINALLY TOUCHED DOWN IN DALLAS.
ACTUALLY, I'M DIVORCED...
CHANGING TO A SMALLER PLANE FOR THE SHORT FLIGHT TO LAWTON, I FOUND MYSELF SEATED NEXT TO A LOVELY YOUNG LADY WHO WAS JUST RETURNING HOME FROM VISITING HER GRANDPARENTS.
I'M GOING TO O.C.S.
MY DAD IS PICKING ME UP AT THE AIRPORT.
PARKER

WE CHATTED AMIABLY, AND I CONFESS THAT I BEGAN TO THINK I MIGHT LIKE TO SEE HER AGAIN...
I USED TO LIVE WITH MY GRANDMA.
HAS NO CLUE
HER FATHER, A SERGEANT FIRST-CLASS, GREETED HER WARMLY AT THE GATE. HE LOOKED LESS HAPPY TO SEE ME.
DADDY...
?
UH... CAN I DROP YOU OFF SOMEWHERE...?
NATURALLY, I ACCEPTED.
HE DROVE A BRAND-NEW GOLD TORONADO. I THREW MY DUFFEL BAG IN THE TRUNK AND OFF WE WENT.
NICE CAR!
I WOULD BE ARRIVING IN STYLE!
I'M REPORTING TO THE OFFICER CANDIDATE SCHOOL.
OKAY...
... I THINK I KNOW WHERE THAT IS...
TEN MINUTES LATER, HE DROPPED ME OFF IN FRONT OF YET ANOTHER DRAB WOODEN BUILDING...
BYE-BYE...
SO LONG...
AND THANK YOU!
AND THEN THAT CUTE YOUNG LADY AND HER DADDY DROVE AWAY--
ZOOM
--WITH ALL MY WORLDLY POSSESSIONS IN THE TRUNK OF THEIR FANCY NEW CAR...AND DISAPPEARED FROM MY LIFE FOREVER.

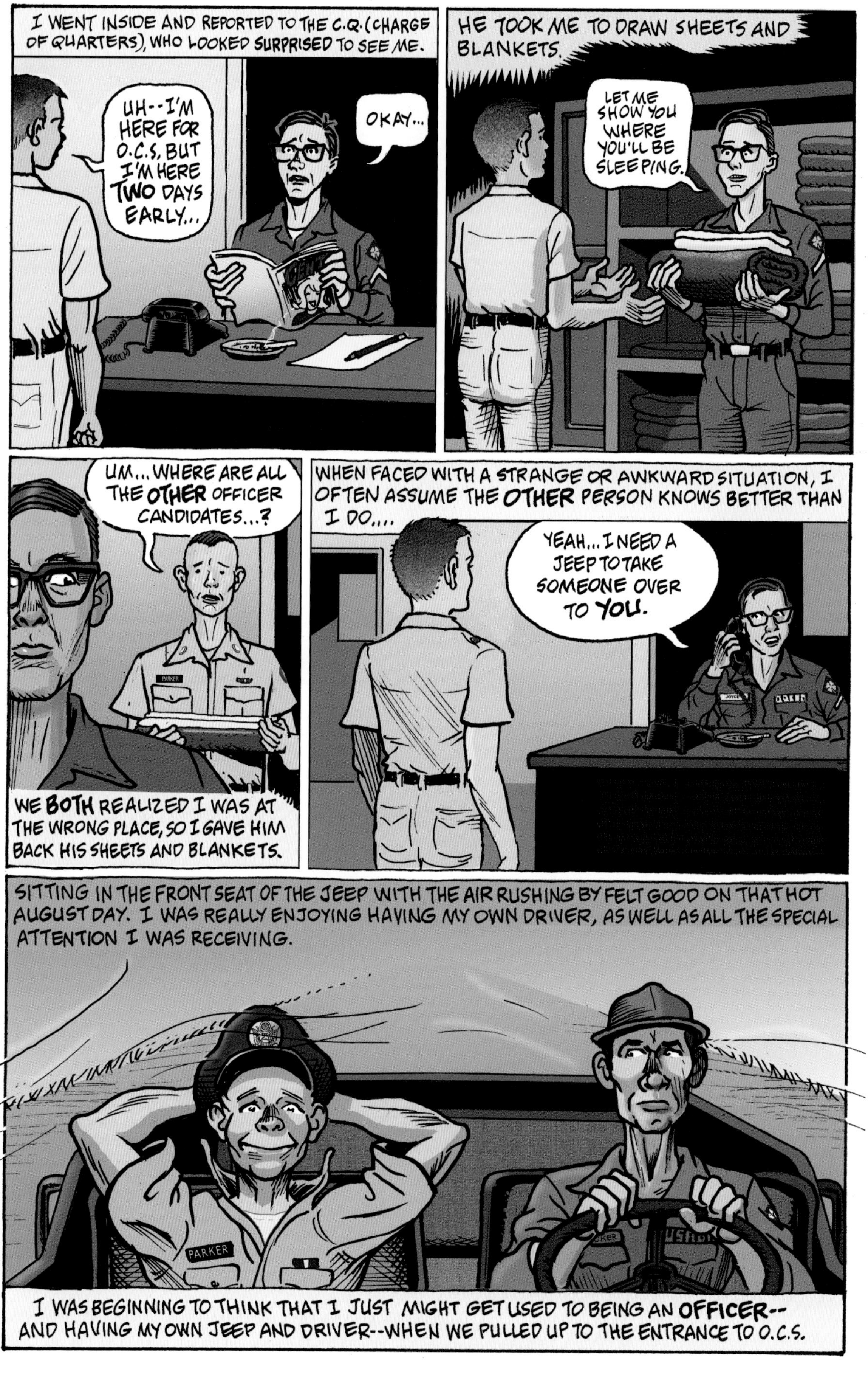

I WENT INSIDE AND REPORTED TO THE C.Q. (CHARGE OF QUARTERS), WHO LOOKED SURPRISED TO SEE ME.
UH--I'M HERE FOR O.C.S. BUT I'M HERE TWO DAYS EARLY...
OKAY...
HE TOOK ME TO DRAW SHEETS AND BLANKETS.
LET ME SHOW YOU WHERE YOU'LL BE SLEEPING.
UM... WHERE ARE ALL THE OTHER OFFICER CANDIDATES...?
PARKER
WE BOTH REALIZED I WAS AT THE WRONG PLACE, SO I GAVE HIM BACK HIS SHEETS AND BLANKETS.
WHEN FACED WITH A STRANGE OR AWKWARD SITUATION, I OFTEN ASSUME THE OTHER PERSON KNOWS BETTER THAN I DO....
YEAH... I NEED A JEEP TO TAKE SOMEONE OVER TO YOU.
JOYCE
SITTING IN THE FRONT SEAT OF THE JEEP WITH THE AIR RUSHING BY FELT GOOD ON THAT HOT AUGUST DAY. I WAS REALLY ENJOYING HAVING MY OWN DRIVER, AS WELL AS ALL THE SPECIAL ATTENTION I WAS RECEIVING.
PARKER
I WAS BEGINNING TO THINK THAT I JUST MIGHT GET USED TO BEING AN OFFICER-- AND HAVING MY OWN JEEP AND DRIVER--WHEN WE PULLED UP TO THE ENTRANCE TO O.C.S.

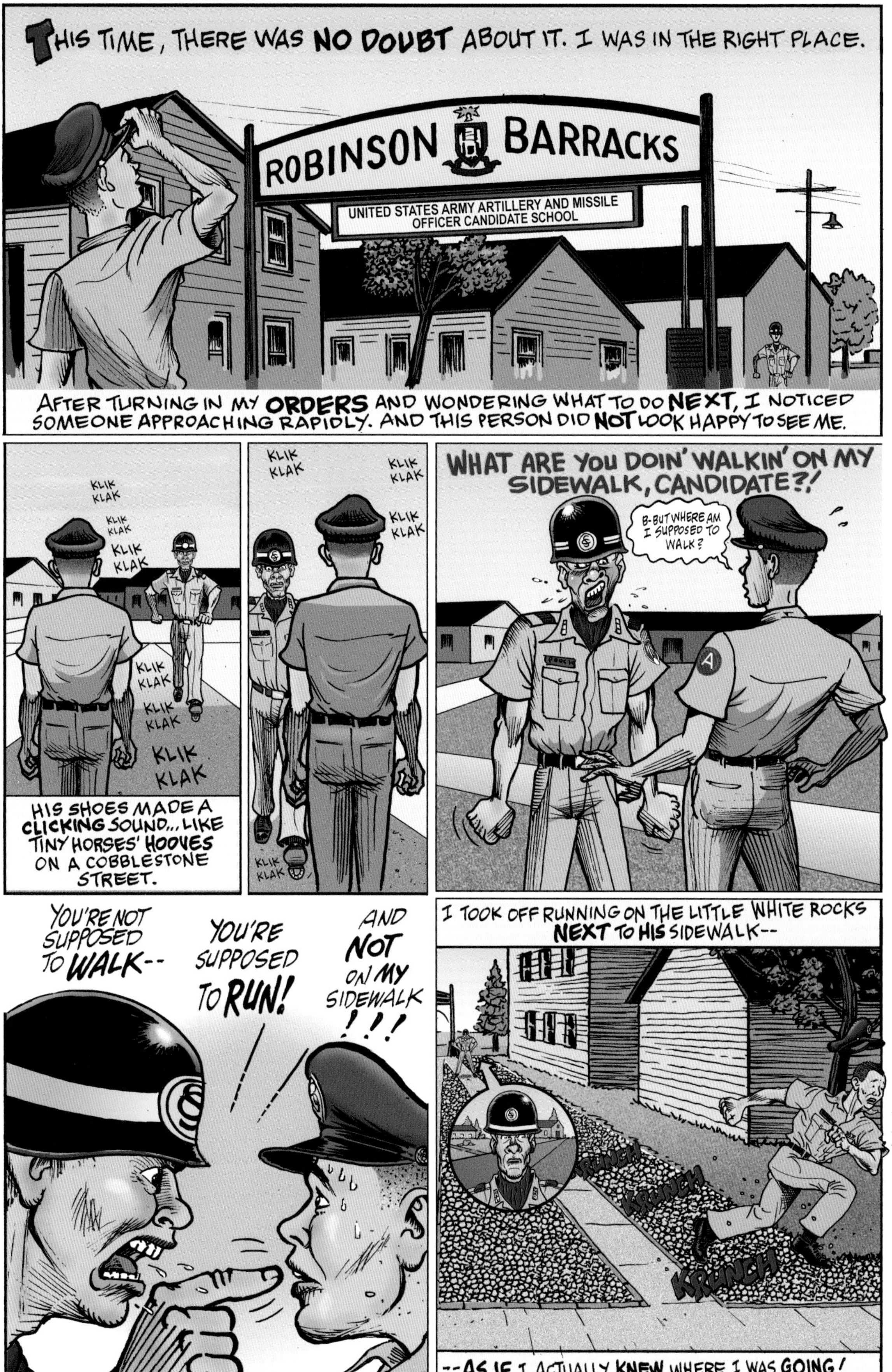
THIS TIME, THERE WAS NO DOUBT ABOUT IT. I WAS IN THE RIGHT PLACE.
ROBINSON BARRACKS
UNITED STATES ARMY ARTILLERY AND MISSILE OFFICER CANDIDATE SCHOOL
AFTER TURNING IN MY ORDERS AND WONDERING WHAT TO DO NEXT, I NOTICED SOMEONE APPROACHING RAPIDLY. AND THIS PERSON DID NOT LOOK HAPPY TO SEE ME.
KLIK KLAK
KLIK KLAK
KLIK KLAK
KLIK KLAK
KLIK KLAK
KLIK KLAK
HIS SHOES MADE A CLICKING SOUND... LIKE TINY HORSES' HOOVES ON A COBBLESTONE STREET.
KLIK KLAK
KLIK KLAK
KLIK KLAK
KLIK KLAK
WHAT ARE YOU DOIN' WALKIN' ON MY SIDEWALK, CANDIDATE?!
B-BUT WHERE AM I SUPPOSED TO WALK?
YOU'RE NOT SUPPOSED TO WALK--
YOU'RE SUPPOSED TO RUN!
AND NOT ON MY SIDEWALK!!!
I TOOK OFF RUNNING ON THE LITTLE WHITE ROCKS NEXT TO HIS SIDEWALK--
KRUNCH
KRUNCH
KRUNCH
--AS IF I ACTUALLY KNEW WHERE I WAS GOING!

IT TURNED OUT THAT ARRIVING AT OFFICER CANDIDATE SCHOOL TWO DAYS EARLY WAS NOT SUCH A SMART IDEA.
CHEW, CANDY-DATE!
KOFF KOFF SPUTTER
SOME POOR, UNFORTUNATE OFFICER CANDIDATE ARRIVED BEFORE I HAD, AND WAS FOUND TO HAVE INCLUDED AMONG HIS PERSONAL POSSESSIONS A GIANT, THREE-POUND BAG OF M&M's!
CHEW, CANDIDATE!
MUMP MUMH MUMP
I WAS ORDERED TO TAKE OVER-- AND TO NOT STOP UNTIL HE HAD EATEN EVERY LAST ONE!
I WOULDN'T MIND HAVING A FEW OF THESE MYSELF.
UPON ENTERING THE SERVICE, I HAD SWORN AN OATH TO "FOLLOW ALL LAWFUL ORDERS," AND I DID SO SOMEWHAT RELUCTANTLY, AS THERE DIDN'T SEEM TO BE ANYTHING ILLEGAL ABOUT IT.
OCS
DODD

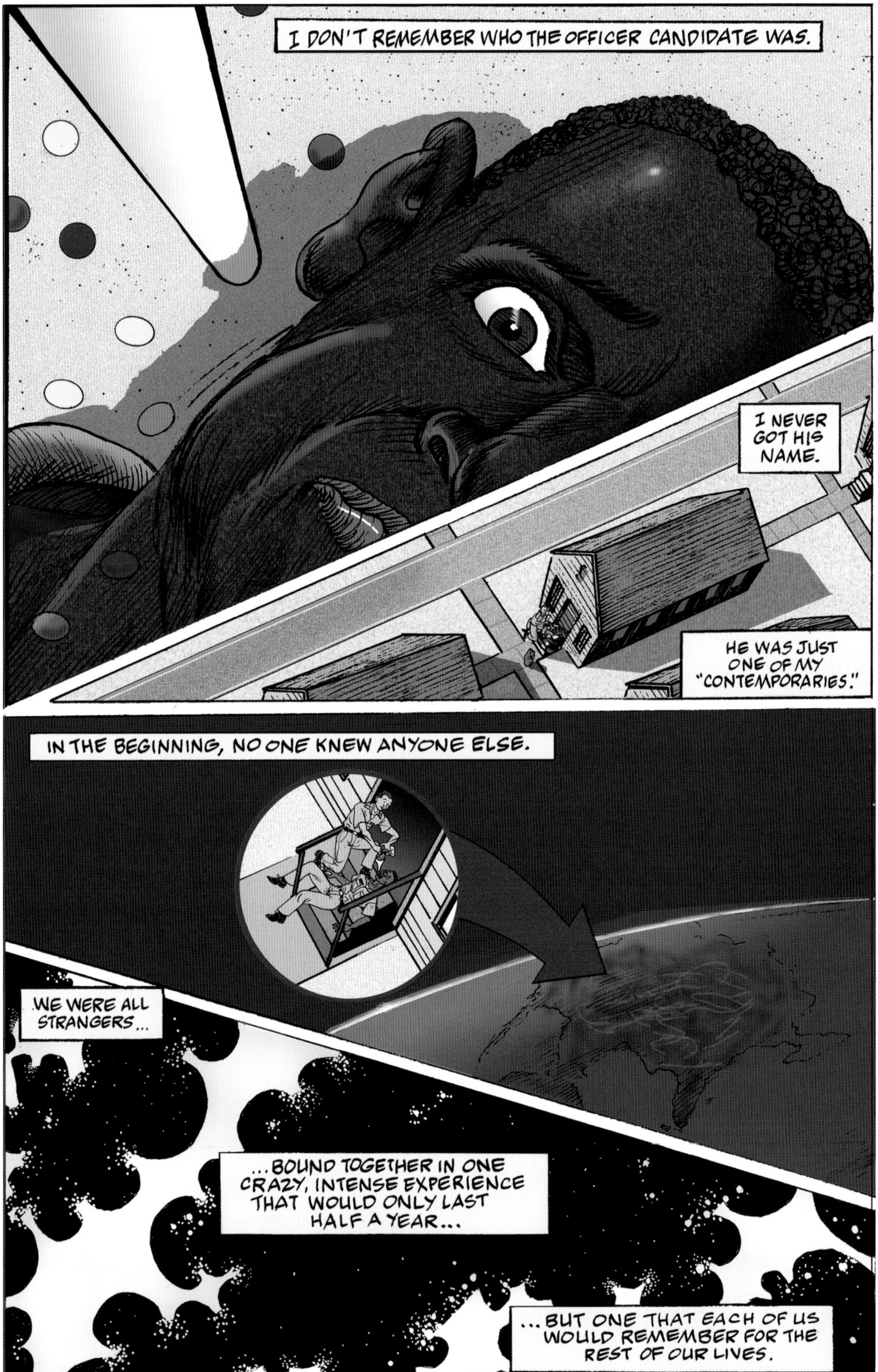
I DON'T REMEMBER WHO THE OFFICER CANDIDATE WAS.
I NEVER GOT HIS NAME.
HE WAS JUST ONE OF MY "CONTEMPORARIES."
IN THE BEGINNING, NO ONE KNEW ANYONE ELSE.
WE WERE ALL STRANGERS...
...BOUND TOGETHER IN ONE CRAZY, INTENSE EXPERIENCE THAT WOULD ONLY LAST HALF A YEAR...
...BUT ONE THAT EACH OF US WOULD REMEMBER FOR THE REST OF OUR LIVES.

TO BE HONEST, I DON'T REMEMBER MUCH ABOUT THE FIRST FEW DAYS...
IS THIS BUNK TAKEN?
OFFICER CANDIDATES WERE STILL ARRIVING AND GETTING SQUARED AWAY...
UHHHHH...
IS THAT YOUR DUFFEL BAG, CANDIDATE--OR YOUR GIRLFRIEND?
IN THE BEGINNING, THERE WERE 66 OF US. I OVERHEARD SOMEONE SAY WE WERE IN "GOLF" BATTERY. "GOLF TWO" TO BE EXACT.
HUT...TWO...THREE...FOUR....
THOMPSON
USARMY
STEVENS
USARMY
I USED TO LIKE TO PLAY GOLF...
USARMY
THERE WAS ALSO ALPHA BATTERY, BRAVO BATTERY, CHARLIE, DELTA, ECHO, FOXTROT, GOLF ONE, AND HOTEL...
ME
THREE-ONE...
THREE-TWO...
THREE-THREE...
THREE-FOUR...
IF I COULD HAVE CHOSEN, I WOULD HAVE PICKED HOTEL BATTERY--
--AS THAT SOUNDED LIKE A NICER BATTERY TO BE IN.

SEPTEMBER 1, 1966: UNITED NATIONS SECRETARY-GENERAL U THANT DECLARED THAT HE WOULD NOT SEEK RE-ELECTION, BECAUSE OF THE FAILURE OF U.N. EFFORTS TO END THE WAR IN VIETNAM. "TODAY IT SEEMS TO ME, AS IT HAS SEEMED FOR MANY MONTHS, THAT THE PRESSURE OF EVENTS IS REMORSELESSLY LEADING TOWARD A MAJOR WAR...IN MY VIEW THE TRAGIC ERROR IS BEING REPEATED OF RELYING ON FORCE AND MILITARY MEANS IN A DECEPTIVE PURSUIT OF PEACE."
AS OUR CONTEMPORARIES CONTINUED ARRIVING, WE WERE KEPT BUSY...
SO MUCH FOR ARRIVING AT O.C.S. EARLY.
SUDDENLY, SOMEONE SHOUTED FROM UP NEAR THE FRONT ENTRANCE.
TEN-CHUT!
FALL OUT FOR A PARKING LOT TOUR!
HOLLAND
U.S. ARMY
WITHIN MINUTES, WE WERE OUTSIDE IN UNIFORM AND FORCED TO RUN AROUND AND AROUND A BIG PARKING LOT.
DAMN!
FUCK THIS SHIT.
WHAT A LOAD OF CRAP.
I'VE GOTTA PISS SO BAD MY BACK TEETH ARE STARTING TO FLOAT!
AFTER A COUPLE OF HOURS, I BEGAN TO WONDER HOW MUCH LONGER I COULD LAST, AS I NOTICED A COUPLE OF MY CONTEMPORARIES BEGIN TO FALTER.
SOON...
WHAT THE HELL IS YOUR PROBLEM, CANDIDATE??
N-NOTHING, SIR... I-I...
FINALLY, WE WERE ORDERED TO HALT-- AND TO TURN IN OUR WEAPONS.
I'LL TAKE THAT, CANDIDATE.
THEN WE WERE ORDERED TO DOUBLE-TIME IT BACK TO THE BARRACKS...
...TO GET READY FOR EVENING MEAL.

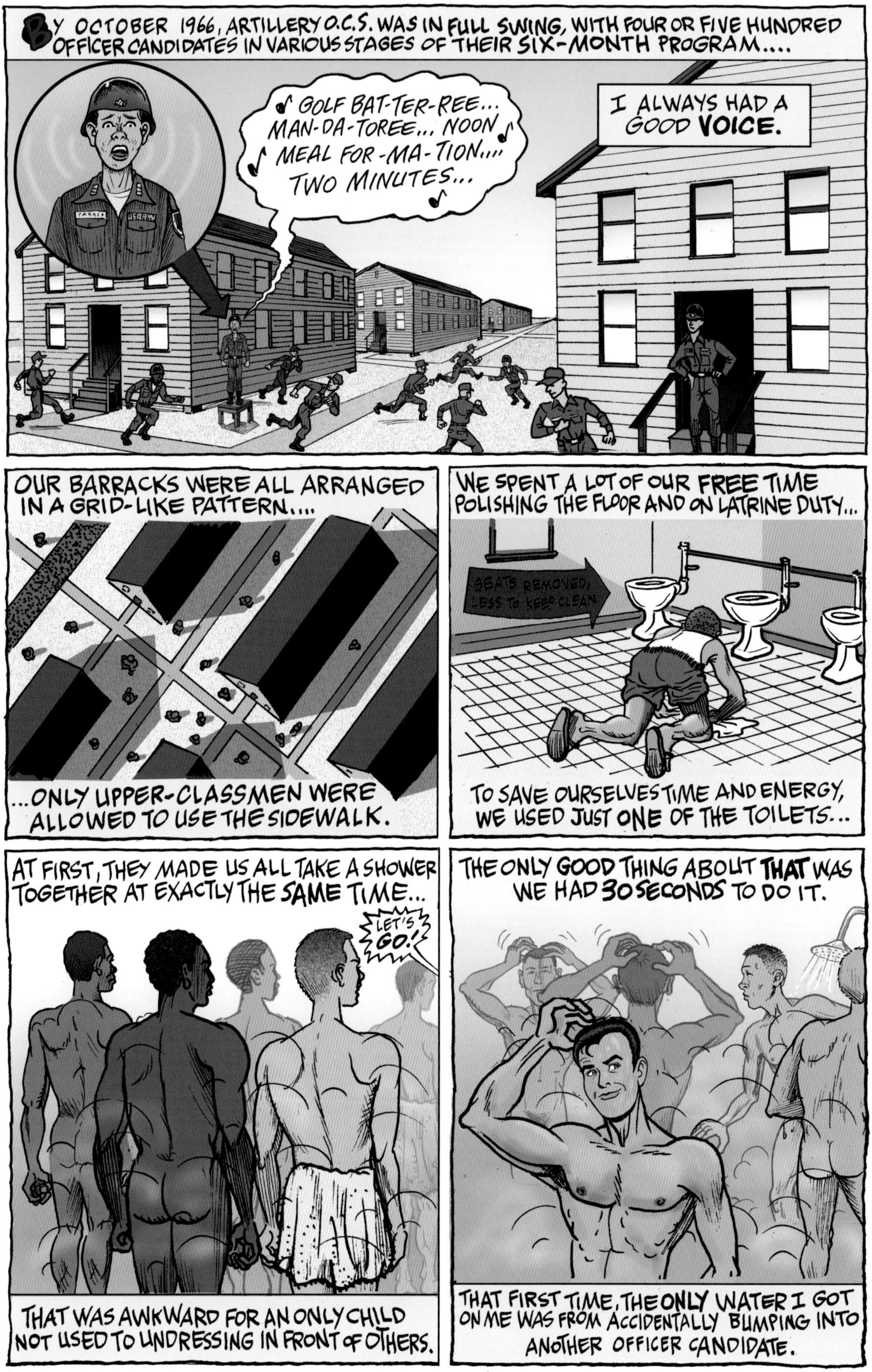
BY OCTOBER 1966, ARTILLERY O.C.S. WAS IN FULL SWING, WITH FOUR OR FIVE HUNDRED OFFICER CANDIDATES IN VARIOUS STAGES OF THEIR SIX-MONTH PROGRAM....
GOLF BAT-TER-REE... MAN-DA-TOREE... NOON MEAL FOR-MA-TION.... TWO MINUTES...
I ALWAYS HAD A GOOD VOICE.
OUR BARRACKS WERE ALL ARRANGED IN A GRID-LIKE PATTERN....
...ONLY UPPER-CLASSMEN WERE ALLOWED TO USE THE SIDEWALK.
WE SPENT A LOT OF OUR FREE TIME POLISHING THE FLOOR AND ON LATRINE DUTY...
SEATS REMOVED: LESS TO KEEP CLEAN
TO SAVE OURSELVES TIME AND ENERGY, WE USED JUST ONE OF THE TOILETS...
AT FIRST, THEY MADE US ALL TAKE A SHOWER TOGETHER AT EXACTLY THE SAME TIME...
LET'S GO!
THAT WAS AWKWARD FOR AN ONLY CHILD NOT USED TO UNDRESSING IN FRONT OF OTHERS.
THE ONLY GOOD THING ABOUT THAT WAS WE HAD 30 SECONDS TO DO IT.
THAT FIRST TIME, THE ONLY WATER I GOT ON ME WAS FROM ACCIDENTALLY BUMPING INTO ANOTHER OFFICER CANDIDATE.

WHEN WE WERE FIRST INDUCTED--IN ADDITION TO OUR UNIFORMS AND A DUFFEL BAG TO PUT EVERYTHING IN--WE WERE ISSUED TWO PAIRS OF COMBAT BOOTS AND ONE PAIR OF LOW QUARTERS. WE WERE EXPECTED TO KEEP THEM POLISHED TO A MIRROR-LIKE FINISH AT ALL TIMES.
THIS WAS NEVER MORE IMPORTANT THAN IT WAS AT O.C.S.
THE LOW QUARTERS WERE FOR WHEN WE WORE OUR DRESS UNIFORM. THE TWO PAIRS OF BOOTS WERE FOR ALL OTHER TIMES.
WE WERE SUPPOSED TO ALTERNATE WEARING EACH PAIR OF BOOTS, AND DUST THE INSIDES OF THE UNWORN PAIR EACH DAY WITH FOOT POWDER.
OUR CUBICLES AND GEAR WERE INSPECTED EACH DAY WHILE WE WERE AWAY IN CLASS, AND WE WERE ISSUED DEMERIT SLIPS FOR "BOOTS, N.S.S." (BOOTS NOT SUFFICIENTLY SHINED) OR UNIFORMS ON HANGERS OUT OF ALIGNMENT OR FACING IN THE WRONG DIRECTION.
IF WE ACCUMULATED **TOO** MANY DEMERITS, WE WERE RESTRICTED TO THE O.C.S. AREA AND REQUIRED TO GO ON A ***"JARK"*** ON SUNDAY.
A ***"JARK"*** IS A FAST-PACED ROUND-TRIP OF 4.2 MILES--SOMEWHERE BETWEEN A FORCED MARCH AND A TROT--FROM THE O.C.S. AREA TO THE OTHER SIDE OF FORT SILL AND UP MEDICINE BLUFF. THE STEP WAS 42 INCHES AND THE PACE WAS 120 STEPS A MINUTE. THE TIME LIMIT WAS **55** MINUTES. THE UNIFORM WAS FATIGUES, BASEBALL CAP, PISTOL BELT WITH A FULL CANTEEN OF WATER, AND AN M-14 CARRIED AT PORT ARMS.
WE WERE ALSO SUBJECTED TO CONSTANT HARRASSMENT BY BOTH MIDDLE AND UPPER-CLASSMEN ANYTIME WE WERE OUTSIDE.
IN THE EVENINGS, WHEN WE WEREN'T ENGAGED IN CLEANING OUR BARRACKS, WE TENDED TO OUR OWN PERSONAL EQUIPMENT.
I ARRIVED AT O.C.S. ON THE AFTERNOON OF AUGUST 30, 1966. THE FIRST TIME I EARNED A PASS TO LEAVE THE O.C.S. AREA AND GO INTO TOWN FOR BEER AND PIZZA WAS IN EARLY DECEMBER.

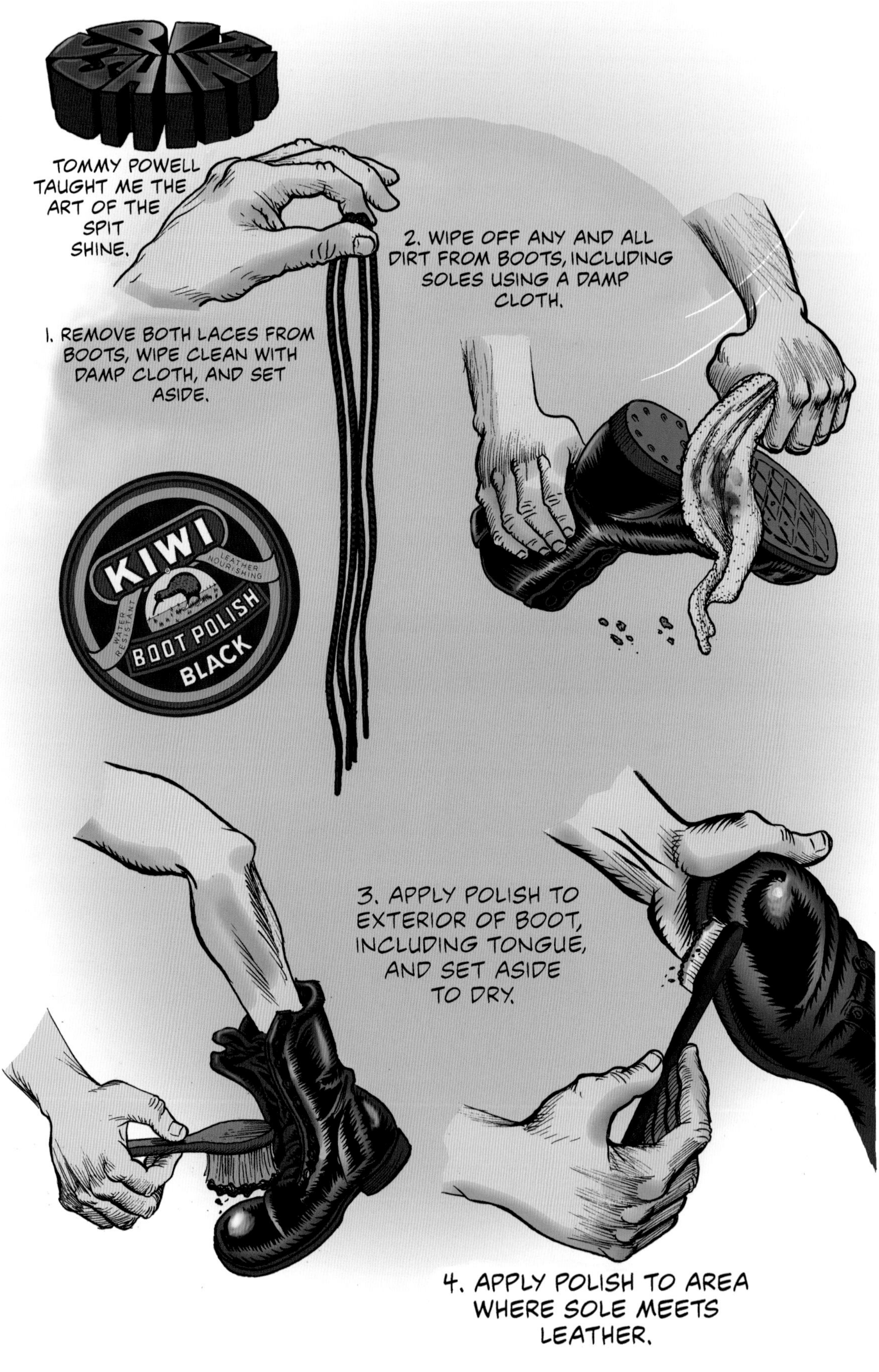
SPIT SHINE
TOMMY POWELL TAUGHT ME THE ART OF THE SPIT SHINE.
1. REMOVE BOTH LACES FROM BOOTS, WIPE CLEAN WITH DAMP CLOTH, AND SET ASIDE.
KIWI
LEATHER NOURISHING
WATER RESISTANT
BOOT POLISH
BLACK
2. WIPE OFF ANY AND ALL DIRT FROM BOOTS, INCLUDING SOLES USING A DAMP CLOTH.
3. APPLY POLISH TO EXTERIOR OF BOOT, INCLUDING TONGUE, AND SET ASIDE TO DRY.
4. APPLY POLISH TO AREA WHERE SOLE MEETS LEATHER.

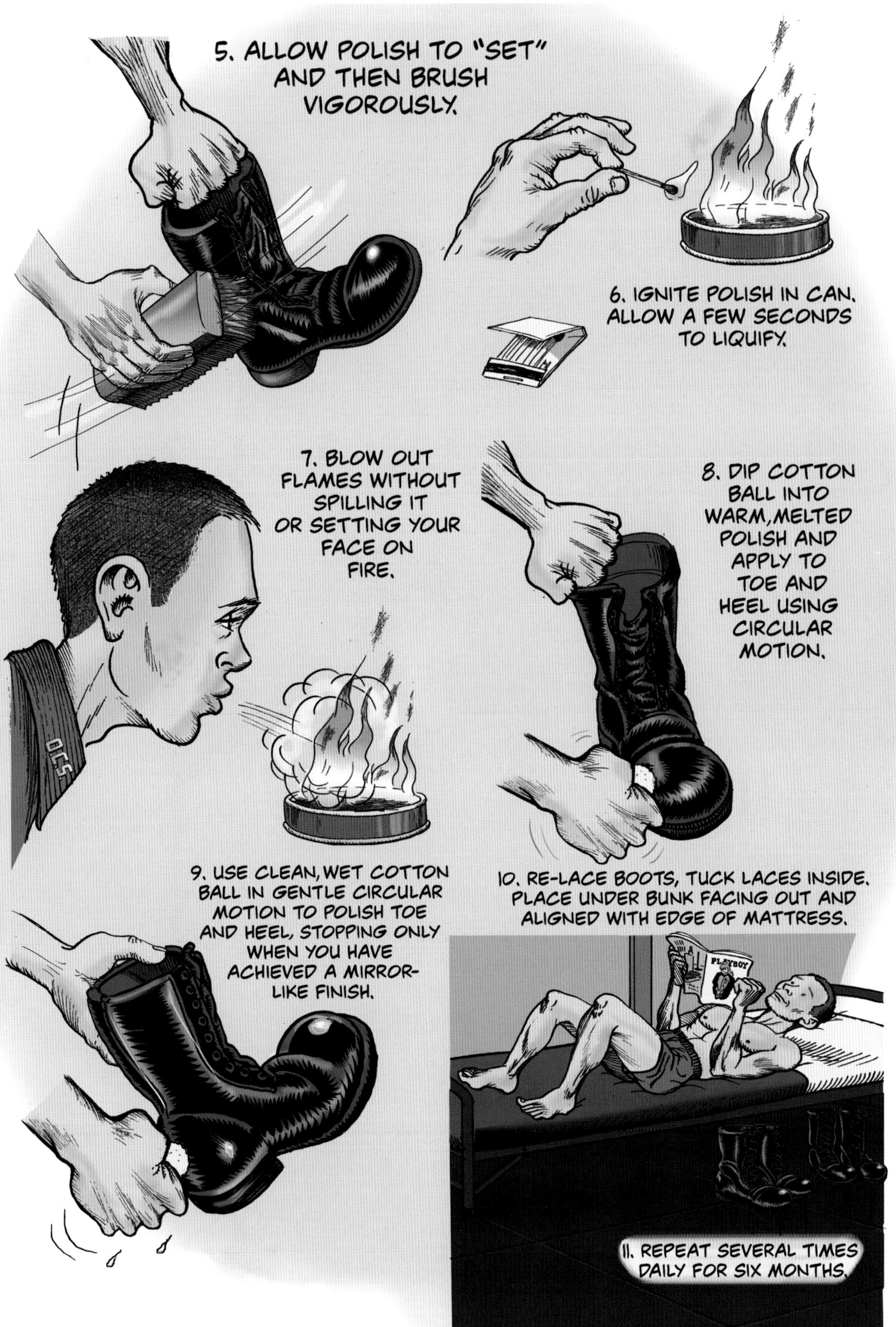
5. ALLOW POLISH TO "SET" AND THEN BRUSH VIGOROUSLY.
6. IGNITE POLISH IN CAN. ALLOW A FEW SECONDS TO LIQUIFY.
7. BLOW OUT FLAMES WITHOUT SPILLING IT OR SETTING YOUR FACE ON FIRE.
O.C.S
8. DIP COTTON BALL INTO WARM, MELTED POLISH AND APPLY TO TOE AND HEEL USING CIRCULAR MOTION.
9. USE CLEAN, WET COTTON BALL IN GENTLE CIRCULAR MOTION TO POLISH TOE AND HEEL, STOPPING ONLY WHEN YOU HAVE ACHIEVED A MIRROR-LIKE FINISH.
10. RE-LACE BOOTS, TUCK LACES INSIDE. PLACE UNDER BUNK FACING OUT AND ALIGNED WITH EDGE OF MATTRESS.
PLAYBOY
11. REPEAT SEVERAL TIMES DAILY FOR SIX MONTHS.

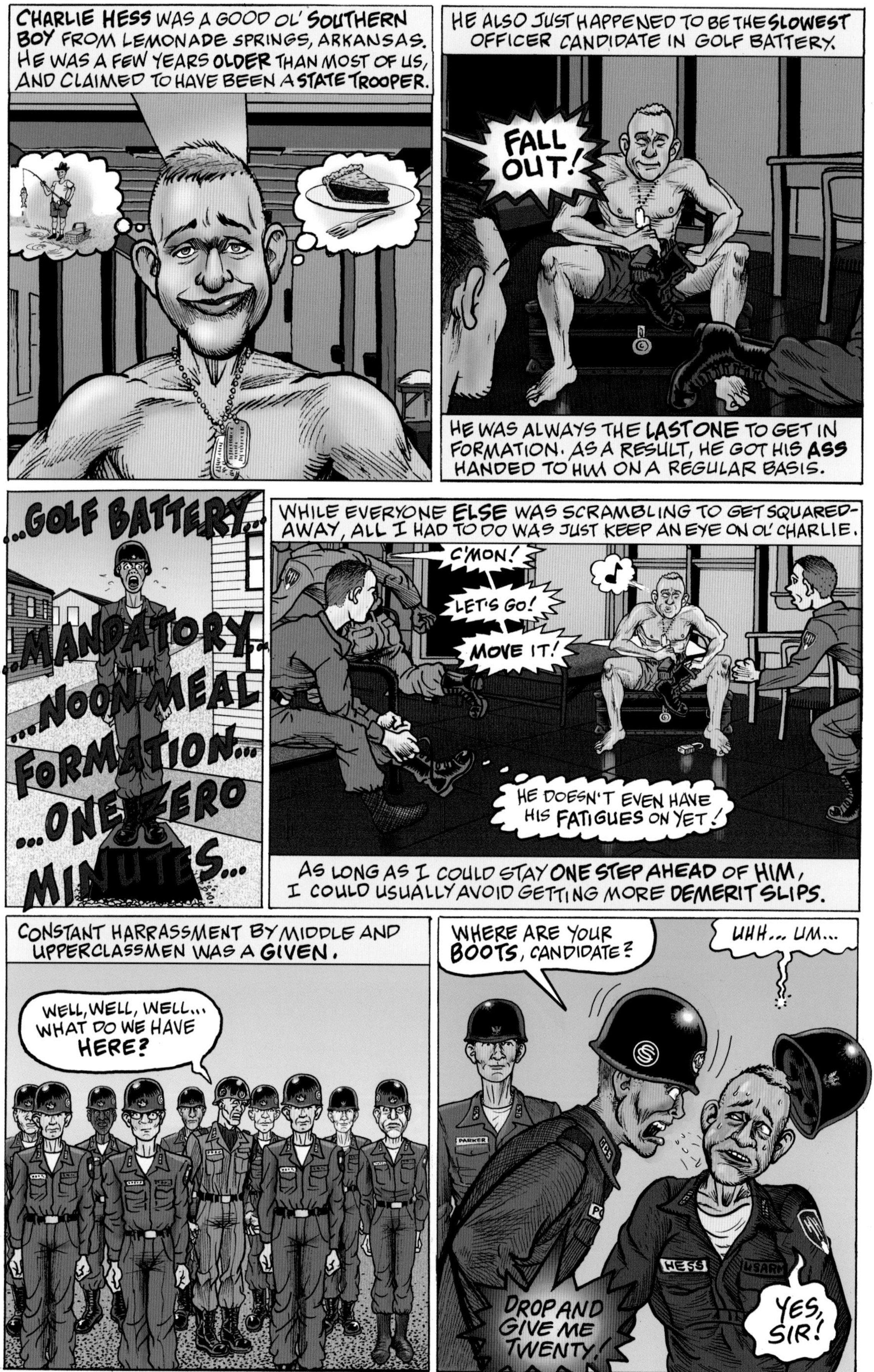
CHARLIE HESS WAS A GOOD OL' SOUTHERN BOY FROM LEMONADE SPRINGS, ARKANSAS. HE WAS A FEW YEARS OLDER THAN MOST OF US, AND CLAIMED TO HAVE BEEN A STATE TROOPER.
HE ALSO JUST HAPPENED TO BE THE SLOWEST OFFICER CANDIDATE IN GOLF BATTERY.
FALL OUT!
HE WAS ALWAYS THE LAST ONE TO GET IN FORMATION. AS A RESULT, HE GOT HIS ASS HANDED TO HIM ON A REGULAR BASIS.
...GOLF BATTERY... ...MANDATORY... ...NOON MEAL FORMATION... ...ONE ZERO MINUTES...
WHILE EVERYONE ELSE WAS SCRAMBLING TO GET SQUARED-AWAY, ALL I HAD TO DO WAS JUST KEEP AN EYE ON OL' CHARLIE.
C'MON!
LET'S GO!
MOVE IT!
HE DOESN'T EVEN HAVE HIS FATIGUES ON YET!
AS LONG AS I COULD STAY ONE STEP AHEAD OF HIM, I COULD USUALLY AVOID GETTING MORE DEMERIT SLIPS.
CONSTANT HARRASSMENT BY MIDDLE AND UPPERCLASSMEN WAS A GIVEN.
WELL, WELL, WELL... WHAT DO WE HAVE HERE?
WHERE ARE YOUR BOOTS, CANDIDATE?
UHH... UM...
PARKER
HESS
DROP AND GIVE ME TWENTY!
YES, SIR!

MEANWHILE, THE REST OF US WERE MARCHED OFF TO THE MESS HALL.

WE FILED IN AND STOOD AT ATTENTION BEHIND OUR CHAIRS UNTIL GIVEN PERMISSION TO BE SEATED.

WE SAT BOLT UPRIGHT IN OUR CHAIRS, WITH BOTH HANDS IN OUR LAP--AND KEPT OUR EYES FIXED ON THE NAMETAG OF THE CANDIDATE SEATED ACROSS FROM US.
CANDIDATES -- BOW YOUR HEADS FOR A MOMENT OF SILENT PRAYER.
GOD BLESS OUR FIGHTING FORCES IN VIETNAM--AND ALL OFFICER CANDIDATES.
YOU MAY BEGIN EATING.
ASSISTANT GUNNER
GUNNER
THE T.C. (TABLE COMMANDANT)
HOLT
CANDIDATE THIRD ON MY RIGHT--HIT A BRACE!
WAIT-- IS HE TALKING TO ME?
FUTCH
THOM
ME

SIR--!
CANDIDATE CURLEY!
CURLEY
US ARMY
CANDIDATE CURLEY...
...DO YOU WANT TO BUY MY MESS HALL--??
FUTCH
EXCUSE ME, SIR...?
CURLEY
US ARMY
YOU WERE DOG-EYEING MY MESS HALL, CANDIDATE!
I SAY AGAIN--
DO YOU WANT TO BUY MY MESS HALL ?
SIR...DO YOU HAVE CHANGE FOR A QUARTER?
CURLEY
US ARMY

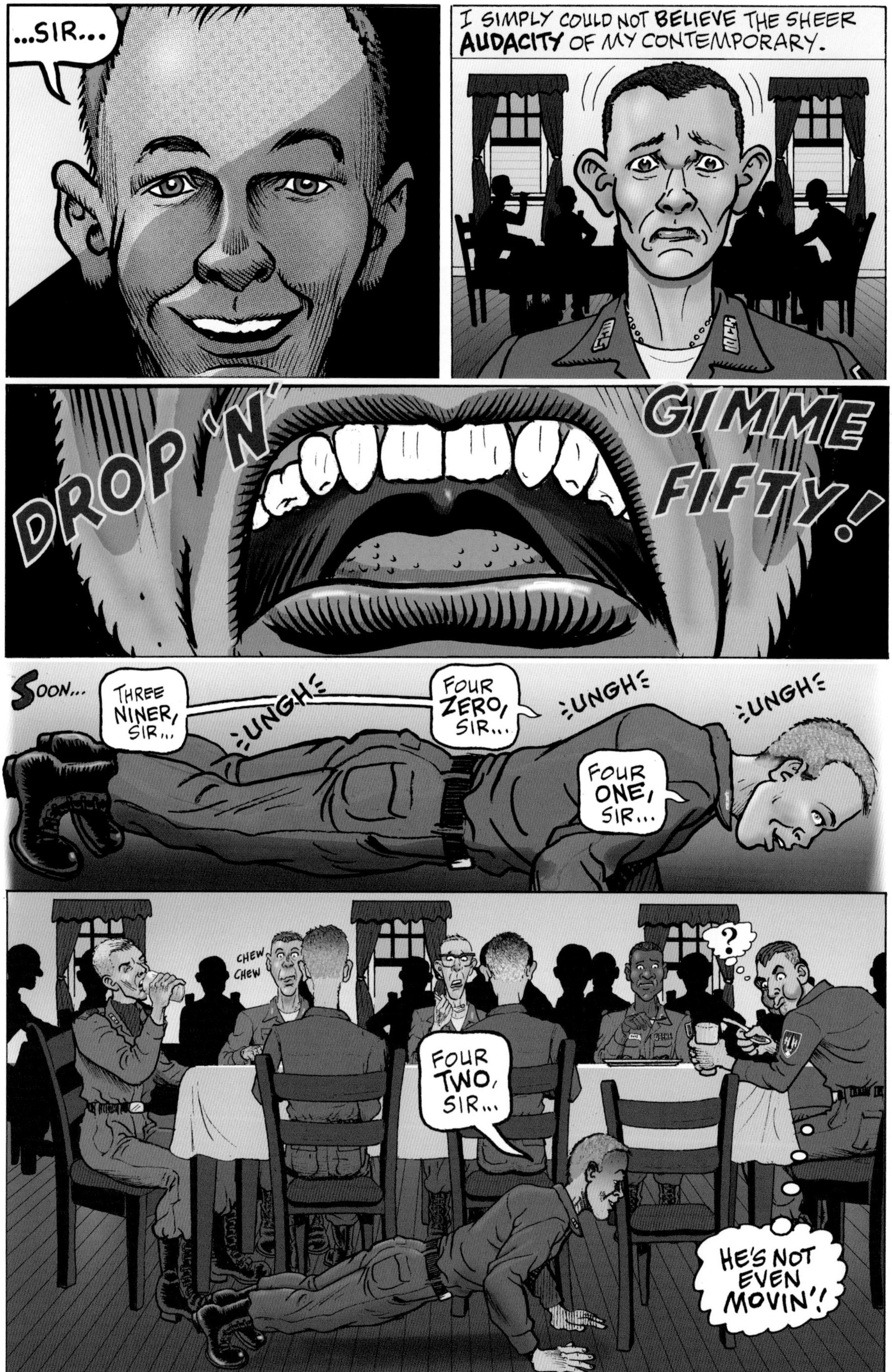
...SIR...
I SIMPLY COULD NOT BELIEVE THE SHEER AUDACITY OF MY CONTEMPORARY.
DROP 'N' GIMME FIFTY!
SOON...
THREE NINER, SIR...
UNGH
FOUR ZERO, SIR...
UNGH
UNGH
FOUR ONE, SIR...
CHEW CHEW
?
FOUR TWO, SIR...
HE'S NOT EVEN MOVIN'!

START AGAIN!
NUDGE
HEH HEH
CANDIDATE CURLEY DID HIS 50 AND SAT BACK DOWN AS ALL MY CONTEMPORARIES TRIED TO EAT AS MUCH AS POSSIBLE ONE TINY MORSEL AT A TIME.
MUNCH MUNCH
!
WE WERE INSTRUCTED TO NOT TAKE BITES BIGGER THAN OUR THUMBNAIL.
CANDIDATE SECOND ON MY RIGHT--
HIT A BRACE!

SWALLOW, CANDIDATE!
STEEVER
SWALLOW!
GULP!
STEEVER
IT IS HARD TO SWALLOW ON COMMAND!
SWALLOW!
YOU TOOK A GROSS BITE, CANDIDATE
NO EXCUSE, SIR.
THERE REALLY WAS NO EXCUSE FOR HIM.
LATER...
YES? WHAT IS IT, CANDIDATE?
SIR, CANDIDATE CURLEY...
REQUEST PERMISSION TO TAKE A GROSS BITE, SIR!
CURLEY
US ARMY

THE VERY NEXT DAY...
YES--? WHAT IS IT, CANDIDATE SECOND ON MY RIGHT?
THE FOOD ALL LOOKS SO GOOD--AN' I'M STARVIN'!
PARKER
U.S.ARMY
SIR-- CANDIDATE PARKER...
SIR--WOULD THE UPPERCLASSMAN AT THIS TABLE CARE FOR ANY POTATOES AT THIS TIME?
...MAYBE IF I CAN EAT SOME POTATOES, IT WILL FILL ME UP...
NO, THANK YOU, CANDIDATE.
SIR--WOULD THE MIDDLE CLASSMAN AT THIS TABLE CARE FOR ANY POTATOES AT THIS TIME?
NO, THANK YOU, CANDIDATE.
MUNCH MUNCH
MUNCH MUNCH
WERST
SIR--WOULD ANY OF MY CONTEMPORARIES CARE FOR ANY POTATOES AT THIS TIME?
ON YOUR FEET, CANDIDATE!
MUNCH CHEW
WHAT DID I DO WRONG?
...AND SAY AGAIN!

SIR... WOULD ANY OF MY CONTEMPORARIES CARE FOR ANY POTATOES AT THIS TIME...?

AFTER YOU, CONTEMPORARY!
I HAD FORGOTTEN TO SAY, "AT THIS TABLE!"
DACEY
TAFT
SMITH
JOYCE
FISK
CHERRY

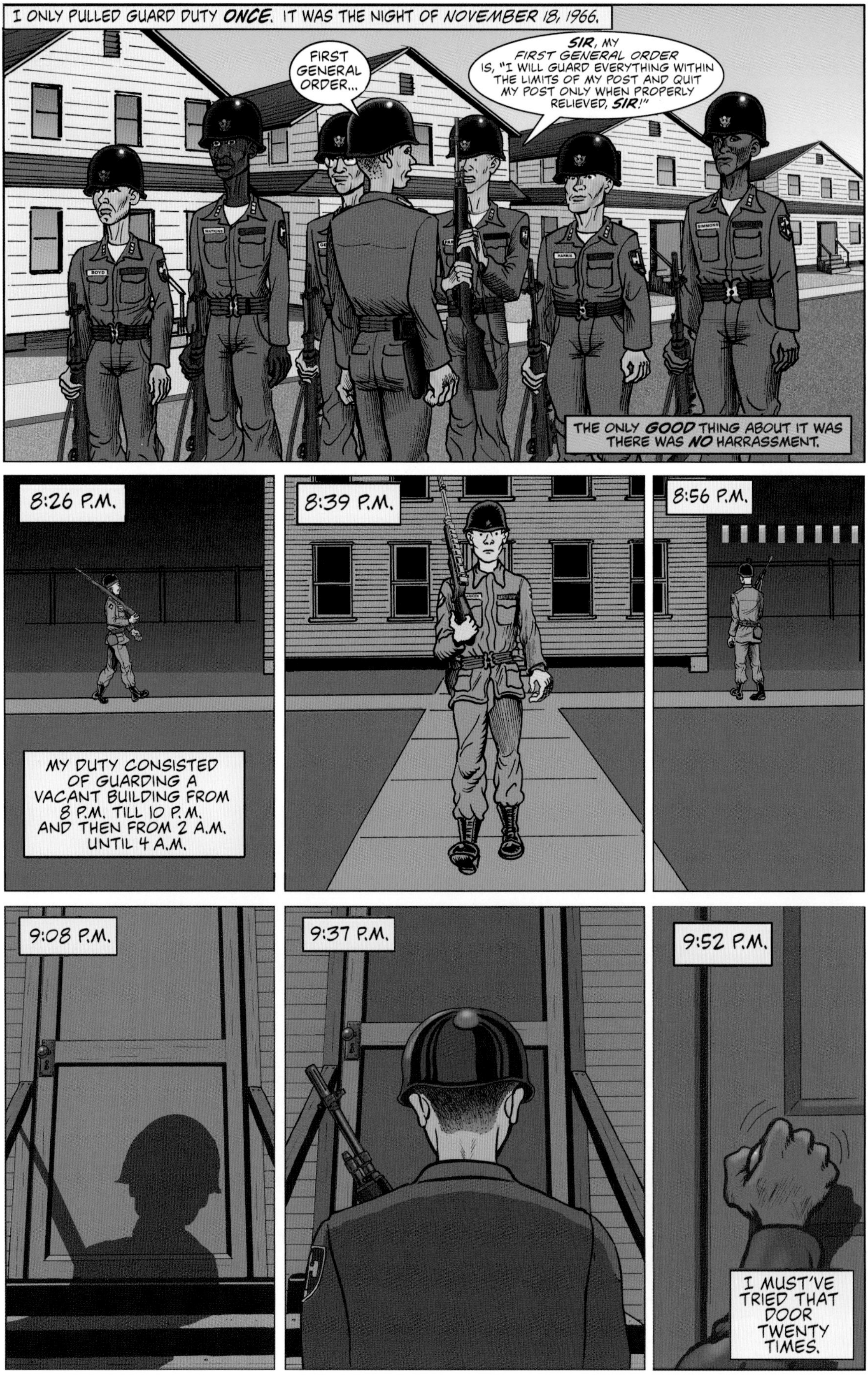
I ONLY PULLED GUARD DUTY ONCE. IT WAS THE NIGHT OF NOVEMBER 18, 1966.
FIRST GENERAL ORDER...
SIR, MY FIRST GENERAL ORDER IS, "I WILL GUARD EVERYTHING WITHIN THE LIMITS OF MY POST AND QUIT MY POST ONLY WHEN PROPERLY RELIEVED, SIR!"
THE ONLY GOOD THING ABOUT IT WAS THERE WAS NO HARRASSMENT.
8:26 P.M.
MY DUTY CONSISTED OF GUARDING A VACANT BUILDING FROM 8 P.M. TILL 10 P.M. AND THEN FROM 2 A.M. UNTIL 4 A.M.
8:39 P.M.
8:56 P.M.
9:08 P.M.
9:37 P.M.
9:52 P.M.
I MUST'VE TRIED THAT DOOR TWENTY TIMES.

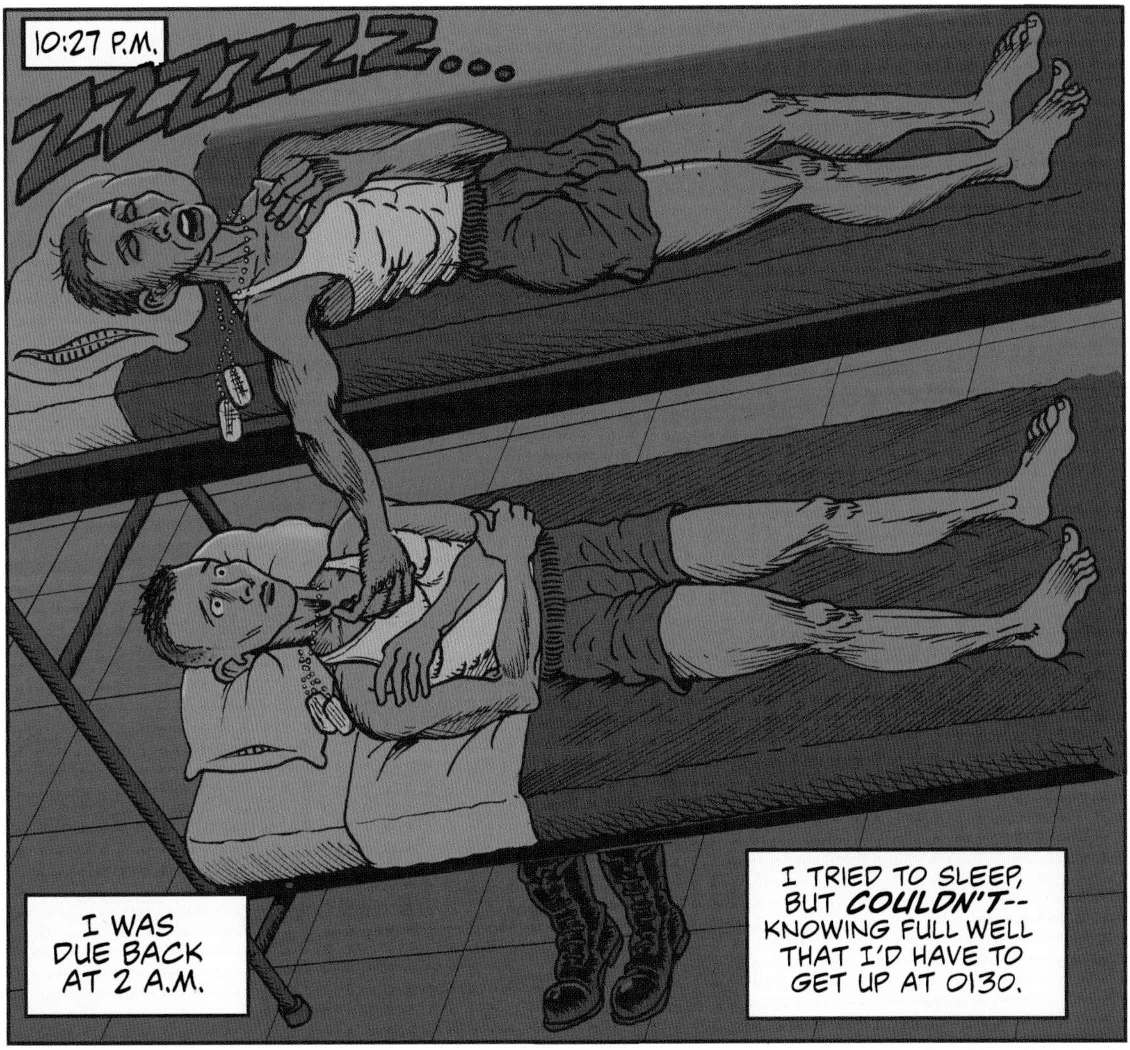
10:27 P.M.
ZZZZZZ...
I WAS DUE BACK AT 2 A.M.
I TRIED TO SLEEP, BUT COULDN'T-- KNOWING FULL WELL THAT I'D HAVE TO GET UP AT 0130.

0215: A COLD, MOONLESS NIGHT WITH A CLOUDLESS SKY.
DETAIL...
WE WERE ORDERED TO HALT-- SO THAT ONE OF US COULD TAKE HIS POST.

...HALT!
I THOUGHT I SAW SOME-THING MOVE OUT OF THE CORNER OF MY EYE.

I LOOKED UP.
U.S.ARMY
WE ALL DID.
U.S.ARMY
THE SKY WAS EXPLODING. SILVER STREAKS WERE SHOOTING IN ALL DIRECTIONS.
ALL AT ONCE...
...IN TOTAL SILENCE.
FOR A MOMENT, WE ALL JUST STOOD THERE AND STARED... KNOWING FULL WELL THAT NONE OF US WOULD SEE ANYTHING REMOTELY LIKE THIS EVER AGAIN.
THEN WE MARCHED OFF TO OUR POSTS IN A MILITARY MANNER.
YO LEFF... YO LEFF... YO LEFF... RIIIGHT, LEFF...
THE LEONID METEOR SHOWER OCCURS EVERY 33 YEARS.

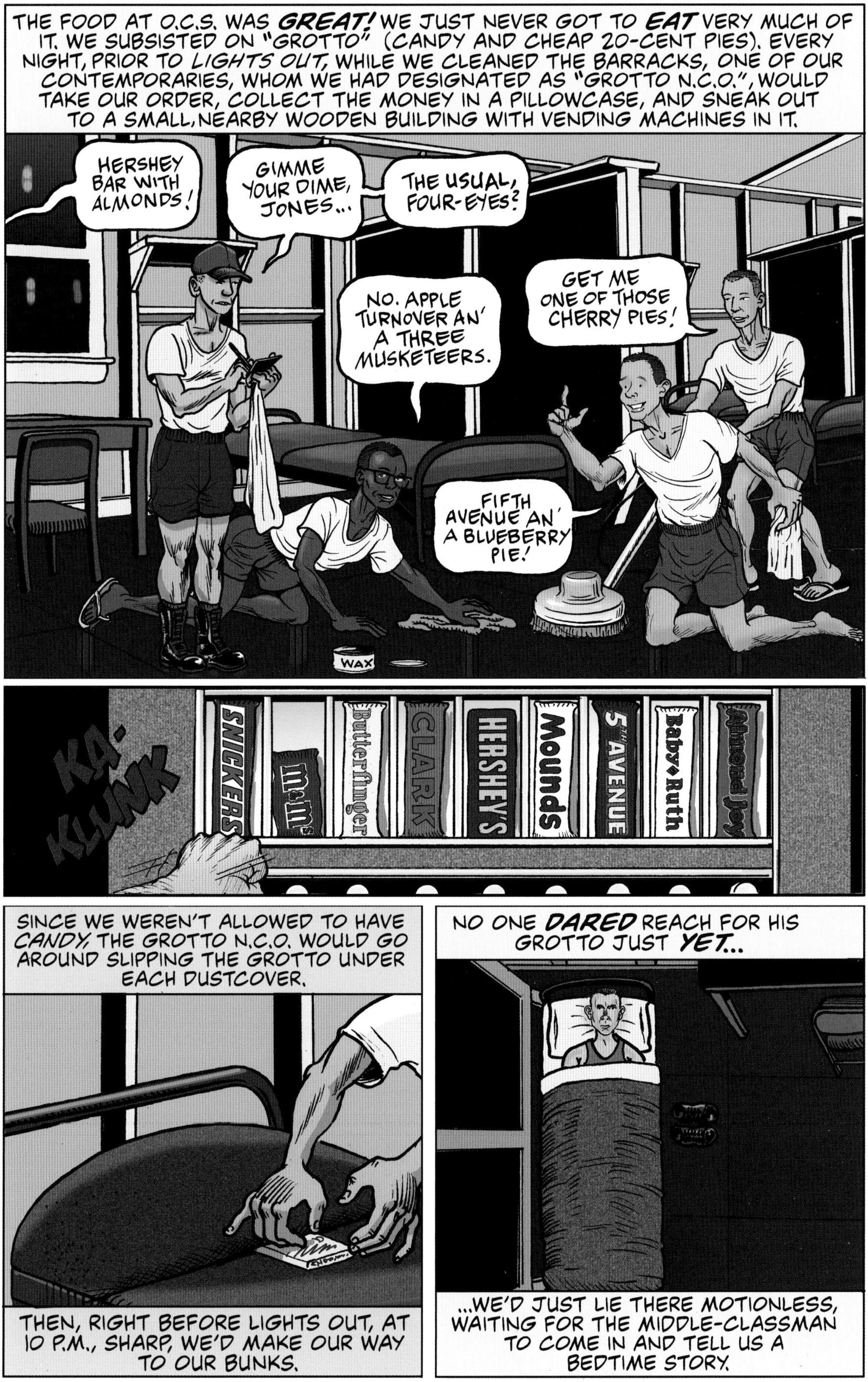
THE FOOD AT O.C.S. WAS GREAT! WE JUST NEVER GOT TO EAT VERY MUCH OF IT. WE SUBSISTED ON "GROTTO" (CANDY AND CHEAP 20-CENT PIES). EVERY NIGHT, PRIOR TO LIGHTS OUT, WHILE WE CLEANED THE BARRACKS, ONE OF OUR CONTEMPORARIES, WHOM WE HAD DESIGNATED AS "GROTTO N.C.O.", WOULD TAKE OUR ORDER, COLLECT THE MONEY IN A PILLOWCASE, AND SNEAK OUT TO A SMALL, NEARBY WOODEN BUILDING WITH VENDING MACHINES IN IT.
HERSHEY BAR WITH ALMONDS!
GIMME YOUR DIME, JONES...
THE USUAL, FOUR-EYES?
NO. APPLE TURNOVER AN' A THREE MUSKETEERS.
GET ME ONE OF THOSE CHERRY PIES!
FIFTH AVENUE AN' A BLUEBERRY PIE!
WAX
KA-KLUNK
SNICKERS
m&m's
Butterfinger
CLARK
HERSHEY'S
Mounds
5th AVENUE
Baby Ruth
Almond Joy
SINCE WE WEREN'T ALLOWED TO HAVE CANDY, THE GROTTO N.C.O. WOULD GO AROUND SLIPPING THE GROTTO UNDER EACH DUSTCOVER.
THEN, RIGHT BEFORE LIGHTS OUT, AT 10 P.M., SHARP, WE'D MAKE OUR WAY TO OUR BUNKS.
NO ONE DARED REACH FOR HIS GROTTO JUST YET...
...WE'D JUST LIE THERE MOTIONLESS, WAITING FOR THE MIDDLE-CLASSMAN TO COME IN AND TELL US A BEDTIME STORY.

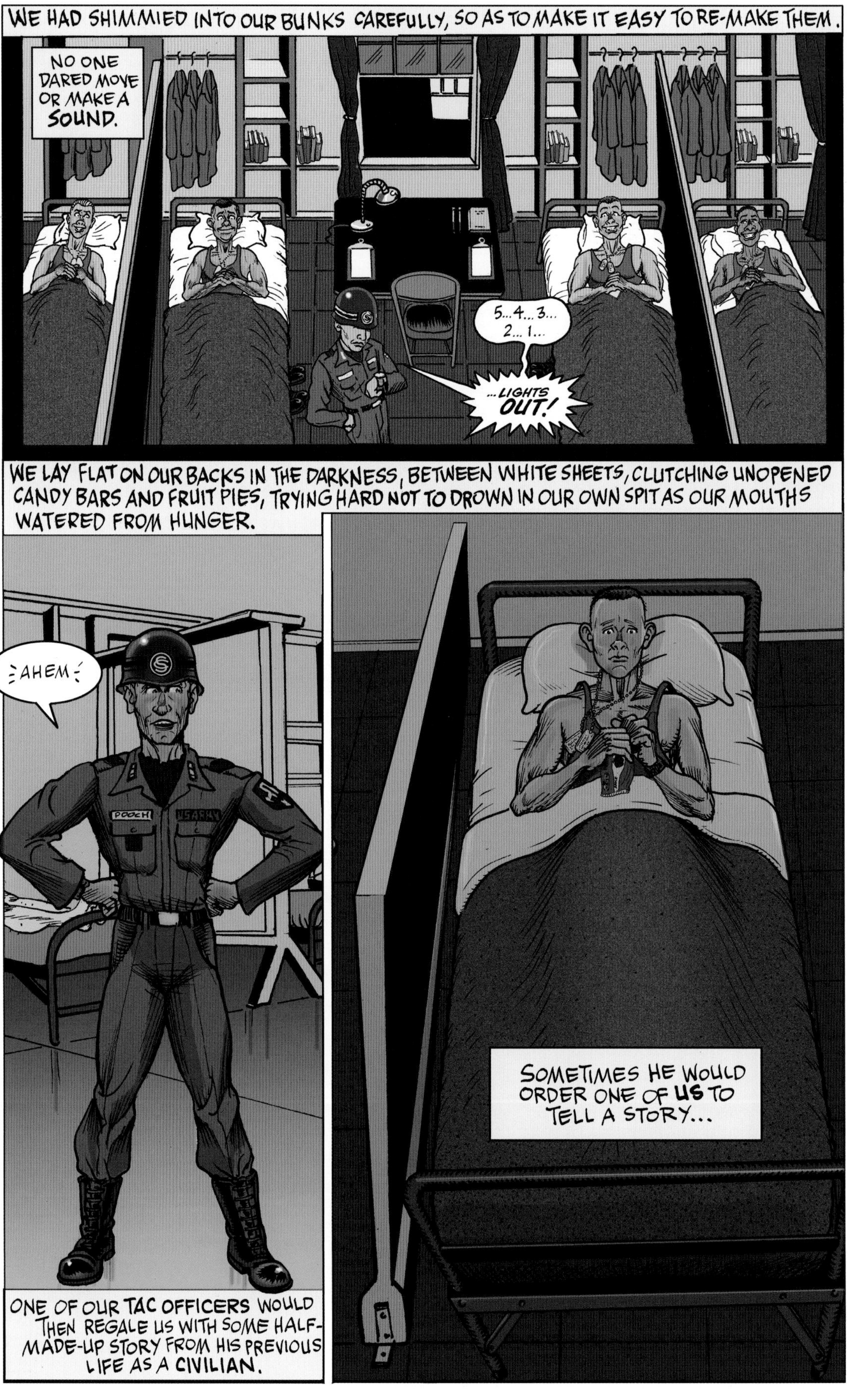
WE HAD SHIMMIED INTO OUR BUNKS CAREFULLY, SO AS TO MAKE IT EASY TO RE-MAKE THEM.
NO ONE DARED MOVE OR MAKE A SOUND.
5...4...3... 2...1...
...LIGHTS OUT!
WE LAY FLAT ON OUR BACKS IN THE DARKNESS, BETWEEN WHITE SHEETS, CLUTCHING UNOPENED CANDY BARS AND FRUIT PIES, TRYING HARD NOT TO DROWN IN OUR OWN SPIT AS OUR MOUTHS WATERED FROM HUNGER.
AHEM
POOCH
U.S.ARMY
ONE OF OUR TAC OFFICERS WOULD THEN REGALE US WITH SOME HALF-MADE-UP STORY FROM HIS PREVIOUS LIFE AS A CIVILIAN.
SOMETIMES HE WOULD ORDER ONE OF US TO TELL A STORY...

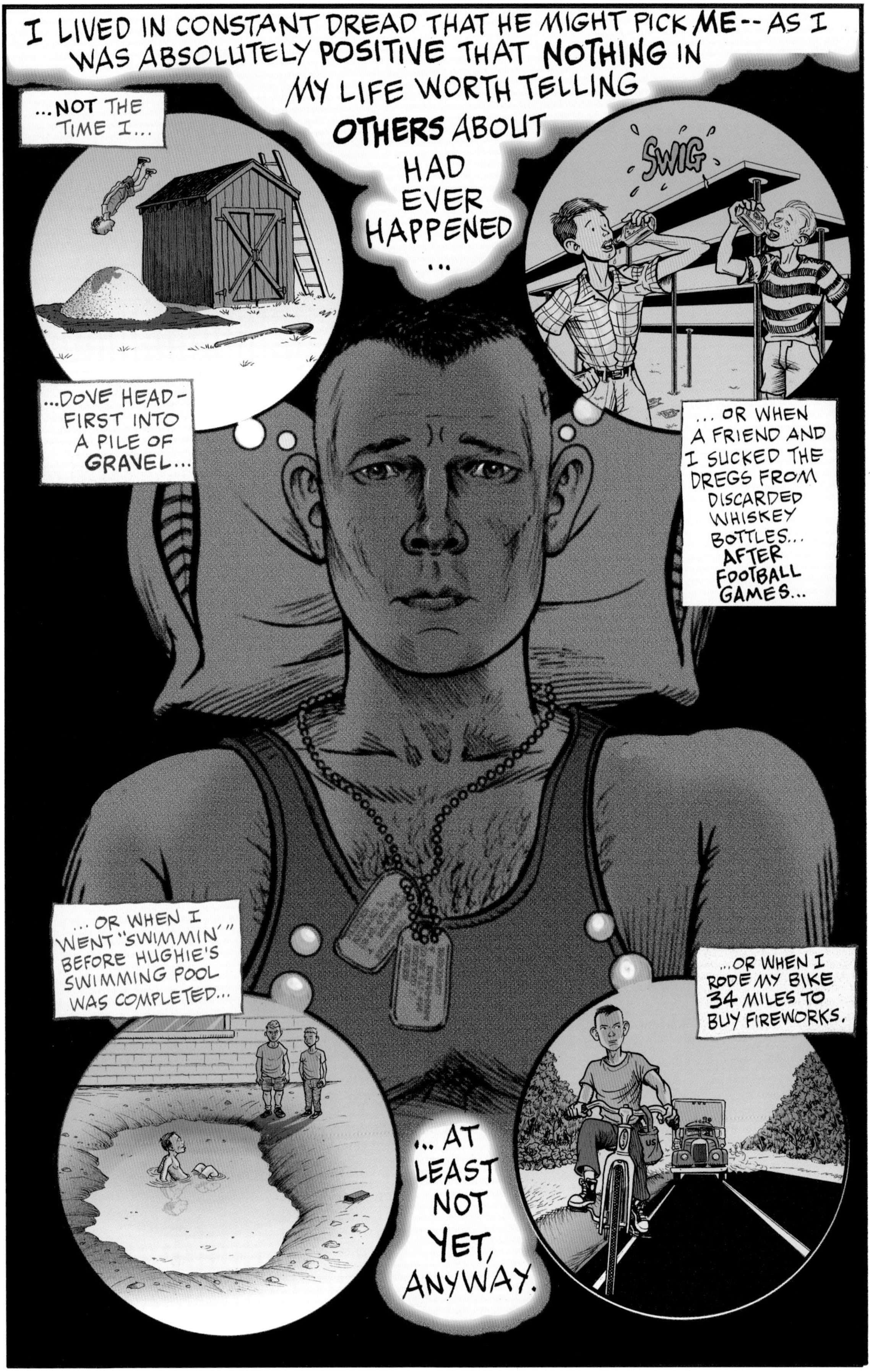
I LIVED IN CONSTANT DREAD THAT HE MIGHT PICK ME-- AS I WAS ABSOLUTELY POSITIVE THAT NOTHING IN MY LIFE WORTH TELLING OTHERS ABOUT HAD EVER HAPPENED ...
...NOT THE TIME I...
...DOVE HEAD-FIRST INTO A PILE OF GRAVEL...
SWIG
... OR WHEN A FRIEND AND I SUCKED THE DREGS FROM DISCARDED WHISKEY BOTTLES... AFTER FOOTBALL GAMES...
... OR WHEN I WENT "SWIMMIN'" BEFORE HUGHIE'S SWIMMING POOL WAS COMPLETED...
...OR WHEN I RODE MY BIKE 34 MILES TO BUY FIREWORKS.
US
... AT LEAST NOT YET, ANYWAY.

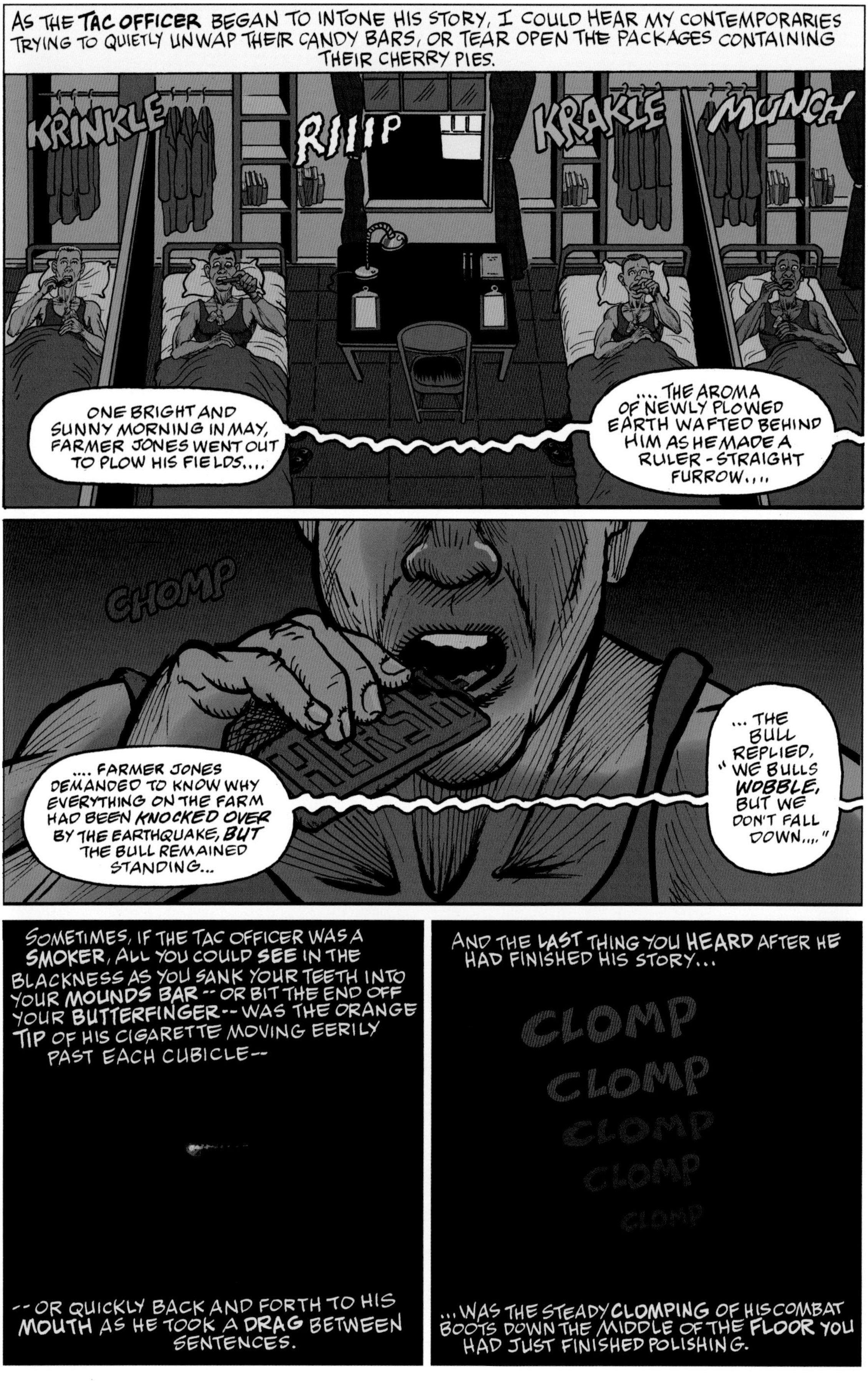
AS THE TAC OFFICER BEGAN TO INTONE HIS STORY, I COULD HEAR MY CONTEMPORARIES TRYING TO QUIETLY UNWAP THEIR CANDY BARS, OR TEAR OPEN THE PACKAGES CONTAINING THEIR CHERRY PIES.
KRINKLE
RIIIP
KRAKLE
MUNCH
ONE BRIGHT AND SUNNY MORNING IN MAY, FARMER JONES WENT OUT TO PLOW HIS FIELDS....
....THE AROMA OF NEWLY PLOWED EARTH WAFTED BEHIND HIM AS HE MADE A RULER-STRAIGHT FURROW....
CHOMP
....FARMER JONES DEMANDED TO KNOW WHY EVERYTHING ON THE FARM HAD BEEN KNOCKED OVER BY THE EARTHQUAKE, BUT THE BULL REMAINED STANDING...
...THE BULL REPLIED, "WE BULLS WOBBLE, BUT WE DON'T FALL DOWN...."
SOMETIMES, IF THE TAC OFFICER WAS A SMOKER, ALL YOU COULD SEE IN THE BLACKNESS AS YOU SANK YOUR TEETH INTO YOUR MOUNDS BAR--OR BIT THE END OFF YOUR BUTTERFINGER--WAS THE ORANGE TIP OF HIS CIGARETTE MOVING EERILY PAST EACH CUBICLE--
--OR QUICKLY BACK AND FORTH TO HIS MOUTH AS HE TOOK A DRAG BETWEEN SENTENCES.
AND THE LAST THING YOU HEARD AFTER HE HAD FINISHED HIS STORY...
CLOMP
CLOMP
CLOMP
CLOMP
CLOMP
...WAS THE STEADY CLOMPING OF HIS COMBAT BOOTS DOWN THE MIDDLE OF THE FLOOR YOU HAD JUST FINISHED POLISHING.

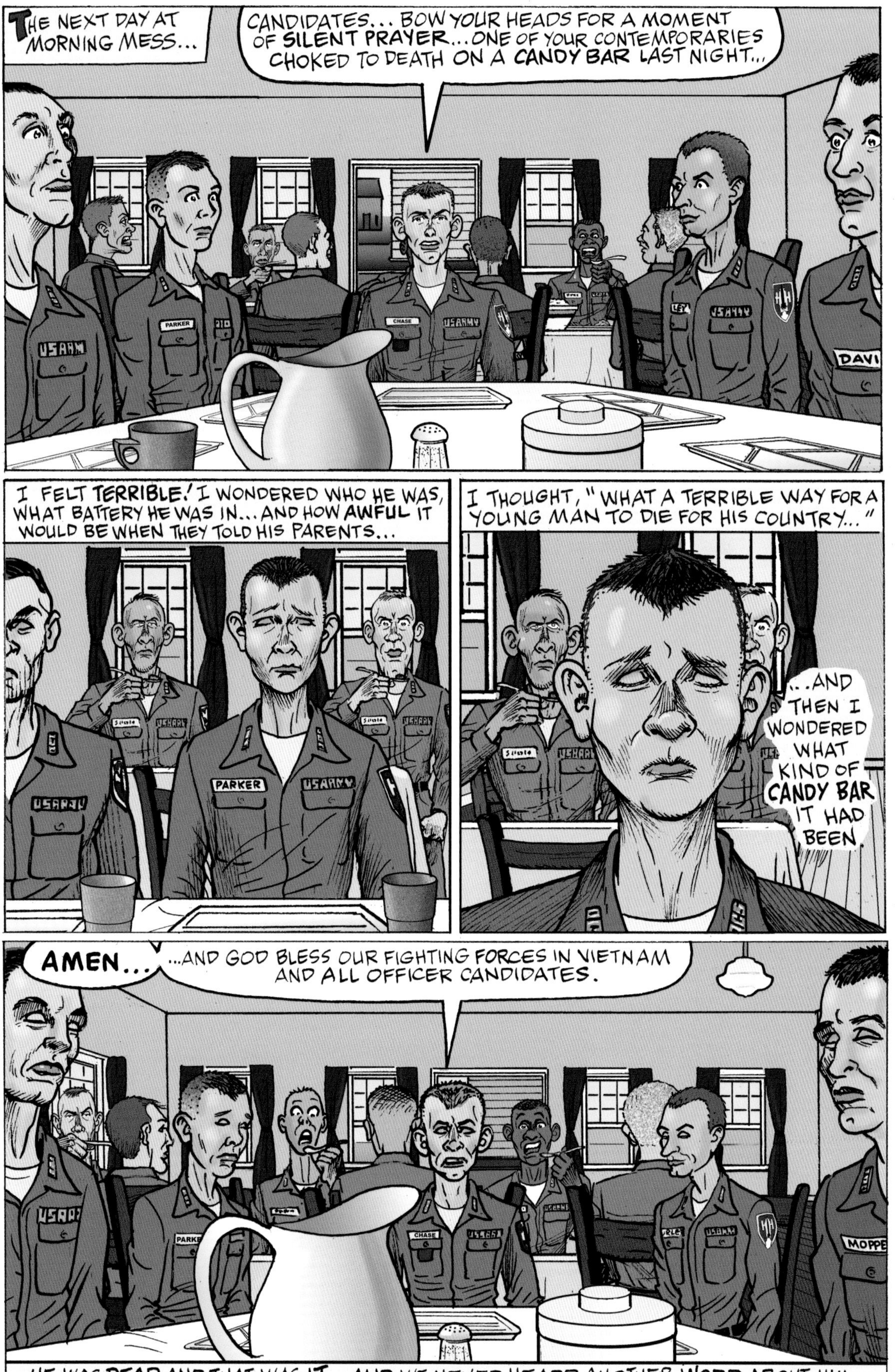

THE NEXT DAY AT MORNING MESS...
CANDIDATES... BOW YOUR HEADS FOR A MOMENT OF SILENT PRAYER... ONE OF YOUR CONTEMPORARIES CHOKED TO DEATH ON A CANDY BAR LAST NIGHT...
I FELT TERRIBLE! I WONDERED WHO HE WAS, WHAT BATTERY HE WAS IN... AND HOW AWFUL IT WOULD BE WHEN THEY TOLD HIS PARENTS...
I THOUGHT, "WHAT A TERRIBLE WAY FOR A YOUNG MAN TO DIE FOR HIS COUNTRY..."
...AND THEN I WONDERED WHAT KIND OF CANDY BAR IT HAD BEEN.
AMEN...
...AND GOD BLESS OUR FIGHTING FORCES IN VIETNAM AND ALL OFFICER CANDIDATES.
HE WAS DEAD AND THAT WAS IT... AND WE NEVER HEARD ANOTHER WORD ABOUT HIM.

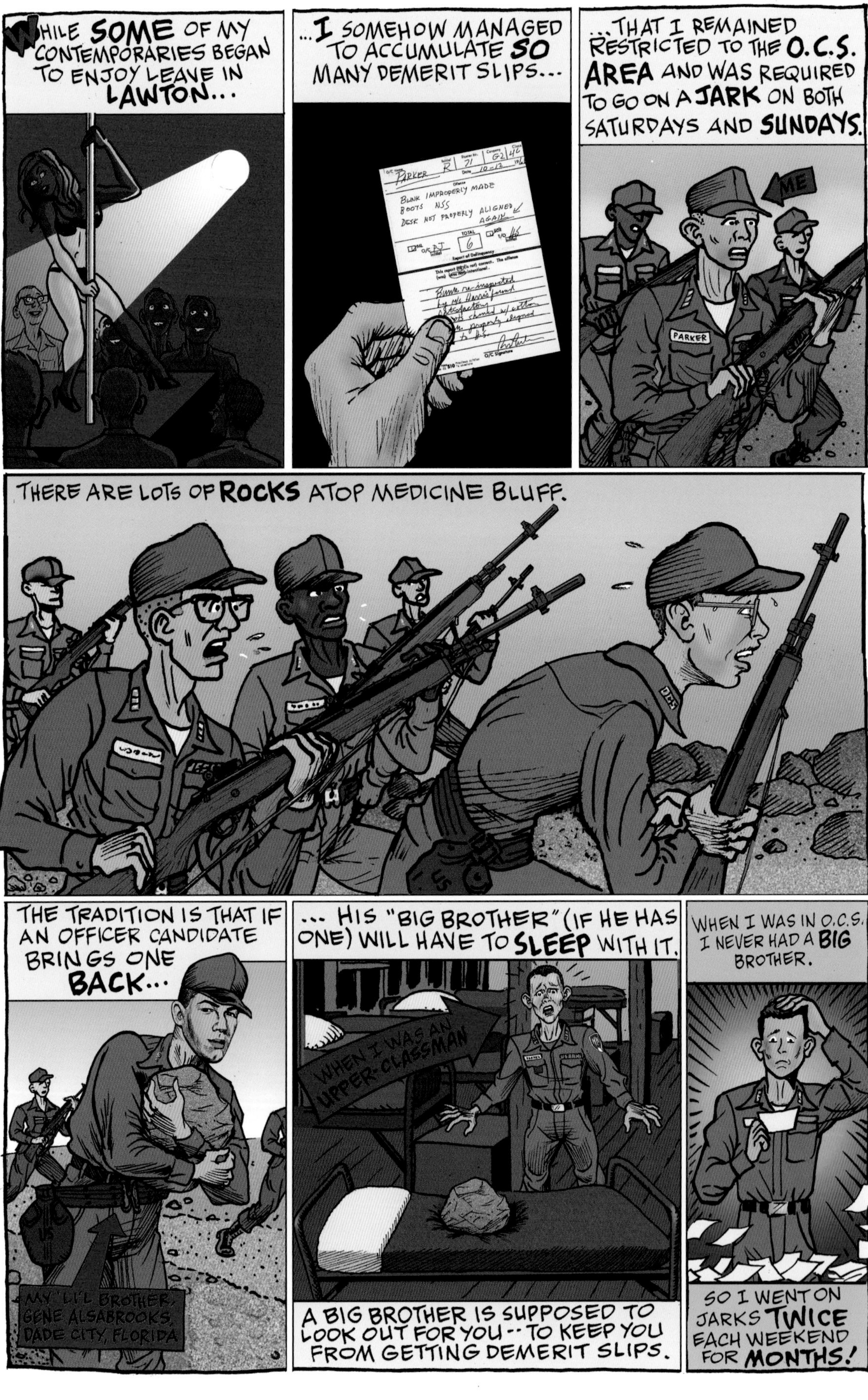
WHILE SOME OF MY CONTEMPORARIES BEGAN TO ENJOY LEAVE IN LAWTON...
...I SOMEHOW MANAGED TO ACCUMULATE SO MANY DEMERIT SLIPS...
PARKER
BUNK IMPROPERLY MADE
BOOTS NSS
DESK NOT PROPERLY ALIGNED AGAIN
...THAT I REMAINED RESTRICTED TO THE O.C.S. AREA AND WAS REQUIRED TO GO ON A JARK ON BOTH SATURDAYS AND SUNDAYS.
ME
PARKER
THERE ARE LOTS OF ROCKS ATOP MEDICINE BLUFF.
THE TRADITION IS THAT IF AN OFFICER CANDIDATE BRINGS ONE BACK...
MY LI'L BROTHER, GENE ALSABROOKS, DADE CITY, FLORIDA
... HIS "BIG BROTHER" (IF HE HAS ONE) WILL HAVE TO SLEEP WITH IT.
WHEN I WAS AN UPPER-CLASSMAN
A BIG BROTHER IS SUPPOSED TO LOOK OUT FOR YOU -- TO KEEP YOU FROM GETTING DEMERIT SLIPS.
WHEN I WAS IN O.C.S. I NEVER HAD A BIG BROTHER.
SO I WENT ON JARKS TWICE EACH WEEKEND FOR MONTHS!

WE DIVIDED OUR TIME BETWEEN THE CLASSROOM AND ACTUAL **FIELD-TRAINING.**

ARTILLERY **ALSO** INVOLVES **TRIGONOMETRY**, A BRANCH OF **MATHEMATICS** THAT STUDIES RELATIONSHIPS BETWEEN THE SIDE LENGTHS AND ANGLES OF TRIANGLES. I WAS **TERRIBLE** IN MATH, AND ALL THOSE LITTLE TIC-MARKS ON THE SLIDE RULES WE USED COULDN'T SAVE ME. I FLUNKED THE CLASSROOM PORTION OF **O.C.S.** AND BECAME A "**SETBACK**." MY CONTEMPORARIES MOVED ON WITHOUT ME, AND I WAS MOVED BACK FOUR WEEKS TO **DELTA** BATTERY AND GIVEN A WHOLE **NEW** GROUP OF CONTEMPORARIES.

I DECIDED TO BECOME AN OFFICER, NOT OUT OF ANY SENSE OF DUTY OR PATRIOTISM--
-- BUT OUT OF SELF-PRESERVATION.
PARKER
I WAS UNDER THE IMPRESSION THAT AS AN OFFICER, WERE I SENT INTO A WAR ZONE, MY CHANCES OF SURVIVAL--
--WOULD BE ENHANCED.
WHEN I SHAMEFULLY CONFESSED THIS TO ONE OF MY CONTEMPORARIES--
--I WAS QUICKLY DISABUSED OF THAT NOTION.
IT'S ACTUALLY QUITE THE OPPOSITE. FORWARD OBSERVERS HAVE ONE OF THE HIGHEST CASUALTY RATES AMONG ALL OUR TROOPS IN THE FIELD!
DUNHAM
USARMY
ODDLY, INSTEAD OF ALARMING ME, THIS MADE ME FEEL SOMEWHAT BETTER AND ACTUALLY RELIEVED MY GUILTY CONSCIENCE.
ALTHOUGH I DIDN'T KNOW IT YET, I WOULD "DIE" THAT VERY DAY, KILLED BY ARTILLERY FIRE--
--WHICH I, MYSELF, HAD DIRECTED ONTO MY OWN POSITION.

OUT ON THE GREAT PLAINS OF OKLAHOMA, JANUARY AND HER TWIN SISTER FEBRUARY ARE COLD, HARSH **BITCHES**, WHOSE WINTER WINDS BLOW STRONG AND HARD, WITH VERY LITTLE IN THEIR PATH BUT THE SHIVERING BODIES OF OFFICER CANDIDATES.
DRESSED IN LONG JOHNS AND WEARING **TWO** PAIRS OF SOCKS INSIDE OUR HIGH, BLACK, TIGHTLY LACED BOOTS--
--WE SUCKED IN SHORT, SHALLOW BREATHS OF COLD, SHARP AIR--
PARKER
--IT ACTUALLY **HURT** TO INHALE--
--THEN WE'D SLOWLY **EXHALE** ONTO THE BACKS OF OUR HALF-FROZEN HANDS--
WHERE ARE YOUR **GLOVES**?
I FORGOT THEM, SIR.

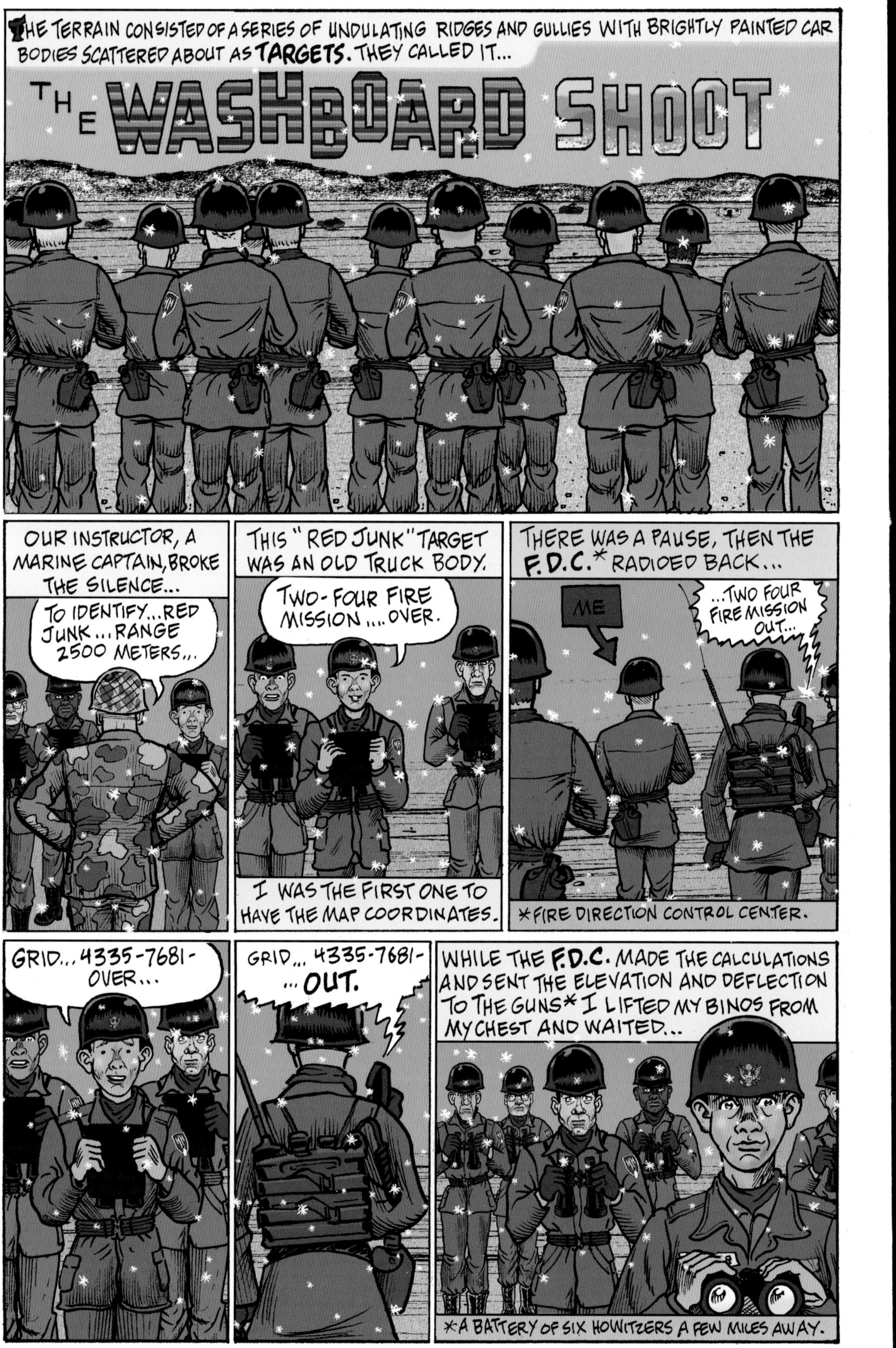
THE TERRAIN CONSISTED OF A SERIES OF UNDULATING RIDGES AND GULLIES WITH BRIGHTLY PAINTED CAR BODIES SCATTERED ABOUT AS TARGETS. THEY CALLED IT...
THE WASHBOARD SHOOT
OUR INSTRUCTOR, A MARINE CAPTAIN, BROKE THE SILENCE...
TO IDENTIFY... RED JUNK... RANGE 2500 METERS...
THIS "RED JUNK" TARGET WAS AN OLD TRUCK BODY.
TWO-FOUR FIRE MISSION.... OVER.
I WAS THE FIRST ONE TO HAVE THE MAP COORDINATES.
THERE WAS A PAUSE, THEN THE F.D.C.* RADIOED BACK...
ME
...TWO FOUR FIRE MISSION OUT...
*FIRE DIRECTION CONTROL CENTER.
GRID... 4335-7681- OVER...
GRID... 4335-7681- ...OUT.
WHILE THE F.D.C. MADE THE CALCULATIONS AND SENT THE ELEVATION AND DEFLECTION TO THE GUNS* I LIFTED MY BINOS FROM MY CHEST AND WAITED...
*A BATTERY OF SIX HOWITZERS A FEW MILES AWAY.

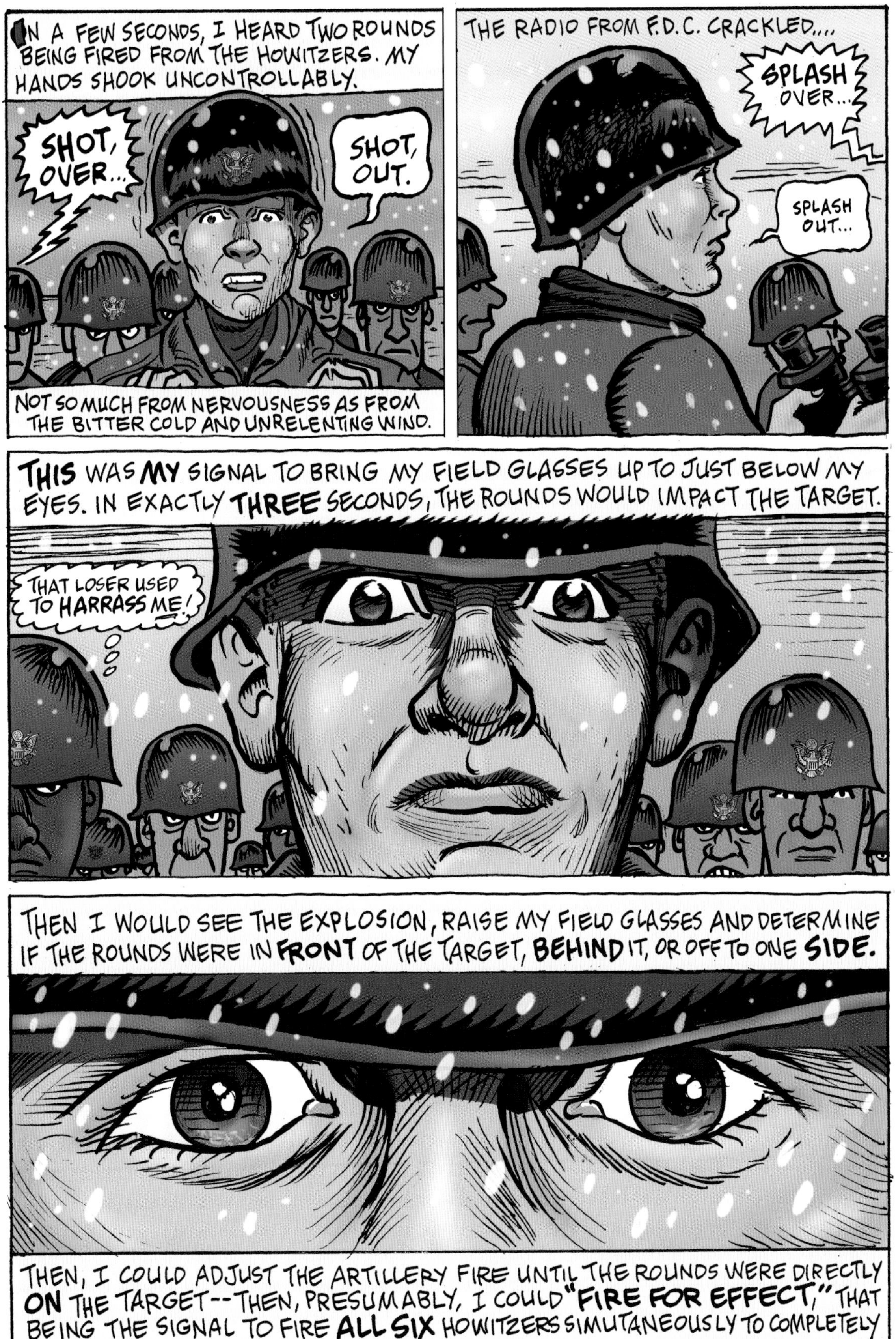
IN A FEW SECONDS, I HEARD TWO ROUNDS BEING FIRED FROM THE HOWITZERS. MY HANDS SHOOK UNCONTROLLABLY.
SHOT, OVER...
SHOT, OUT.
NOT SO MUCH FROM NERVOUSNESS AS FROM THE BITTER COLD AND UNRELENTING WIND.
THE RADIO FROM F.D.C. CRACKLED....
SPLASH OVER...
SPLASH OUT...
THIS WAS MY SIGNAL TO BRING MY FIELD GLASSES UP TO JUST BELOW MY EYES. IN EXACTLY THREE SECONDS, THE ROUNDS WOULD IMPACT THE TARGET.
THAT LOSER USED TO HARRASS ME!
THEN I WOULD SEE THE EXPLOSION, RAISE MY FIELD GLASSES AND DETERMINE IF THE ROUNDS WERE IN FRONT OF THE TARGET, BEHIND IT, OR OFF TO ONE SIDE.
THEN, I COULD ADJUST THE ARTILLERY FIRE UNTIL THE ROUNDS WERE DIRECTLY ON THE TARGET--THEN, PRESUMABLY, I COULD "FIRE FOR EFFECT," THAT BEING THE SIGNAL TO FIRE ALL SIX HOWITZERS SIMUTANEOUSLY TO COMPLETELY DESTROY THE TARGET. AT LEAST, THAT WAS HOW IT WAS SUPPOSED TO WORK ...IN THEORY.

HMM... IT'S BEEN MORE THAN THREE SECONDS... AND I STILL DON'T SEE ANY EXPLOSIONS.
I COULD FEEL THE CAPTAIN'S EYES, LIKE WHITE PHOSPHOROUS, BURNING TWO HOLES THROUGH THE BACK OF MY HELMET... AND I COULD SENSE MY CONTEMPORARIES LOSING WHAT LITTLE RESPECT THEY HAD LEFT FOR ME... IF ANY.
I JAMMED MY FIELD GLASSES CLOSER TO MY WATERY EYES...
AS IF THAT WOULD HELP...
AND THEN... FROM SOMEWHERE VERY FAR AWAY... CAME... A... FAINT... S...O...U...N...D...
POHHHHH...
IT DID NOT SOUND LIKE TWO 105 mm HOWITZER ROUNDS EXPLODING. IT WAS MORE LIKE THE KIND OF SOUND ONE MIGHT CHANCE TO HEAR WERE ONE WALKING PAST A BOWLING ALLEY AFTER MIDNIGHT ON A HOT SUMMER NIGHT-- JUST AS SOMEONE INSIDE MIGHT HAVE OPENED UP A SIDE DOOR TO LET IN SOME FRESH AIR -- JUST AS A BOWLER ROLLED A STRIKE-- AND HAD THE BOWLING ALLEY BEEN SOME DISTANCE AWAY!
LOUSY SETBACK...
THIS IS NOT GOOD.

DROP... 500, OVER...
DROP 500 OUT.
IN ABOUT TEN SECONDS THE VOICE CAME BACK....
SPLASH OVER.
PARKER
U.S. ARMY
SPLASH OUT.
THIS TIME, I SAW SMOKE!
THE SMOKE WAS FOLLOWED BY TWO DISTINCT IMPACT EXPLOSIONS -- ONE ON TOP OF THE OTHER. I COULD SEE THE RED JUNK..., I COULD SEE THE SMOKE... BUT THE WIND WAS BLOWING THE SMOKE!
PUM-BUMP
WAS IT IN FRONT OF THE TARGET-- OR BEHIND THE TARGET? AND IT REALLY DIDN'T HELP THAT THESE LAST TWO ROUNDS LANDED IN THE DEEP GULLEY, OR RAVINE THAT CONSTITUTED THE WASHBOARD-- IN FRONT OF THE RED JUNK --OR WAS IT BEHIND? SO HARD TO TELL...., I GOT BACK ON THE RADIO.
DROP 300!
...OVER...
THIS TIME THERE WAS NO RESPONSE FROM THE F.D.C.
I SAY AGAIN-- DROP 300 ...OVER...
ONCE AGAIN-- DEAD SILENCE.
FORTUNATELY, THE F.D.C. KNEW OUR EXACT COORDINATES, AND WOULD NOT FIRE ON US NO MATTER HOW MANY TIMES I ASKED.
SIT DOWN, CANDIDATE PARKER...
...YOU'RE DEAD.
PARKER
I DID AS I WAS TOLD-- EVEN THOUGH THERE WAS NO CHAIR.

4

XIN LOI

THE O.C.S. ESCAPE & EVASION COURSE WOUND THROUGH EXTREMELY RUGGED TERRAIN OVER A DISTANCE OF TEN MILES. WE WERE DIVIDED INTO TEAMS OF FOUR CANDIDATES EACH. EACH TEAM WAS GIVEN A MAP AND COMPASS AND APPOINTED ITS OWN LEADER... IT WASN'T ME.
WE WERE ADVISED THERE WERE "AGGRESSOR FORCES" OPERATING IN THE AREA, AND TO "AVOID" THEM.
OUR FIRST OBJECTIVE WAS TO MAKE IT TO THE "PARTISAN POINT," INDICATED ON THE MAP, BEFORE NIGHTFALL.
ONCE THERE, WE WOULD BE GIVEN FOOD AND WATER AND ISSUED FURTHER DIRECTIONS.
AS WE STOOD AROUND TRYING TO GET OUR BEARINGS, WE BEGAN TO HEAR MACHINE-GUN FIRE!
RATATATATATATAT!
EVERYONE MADE A MAD DASH TO THE TREE LINE FOR COVER.
IN EMERGENCIES, I HAVE ALWAYS BEEN SORT OF A "DEER-IN-THE-HEADLIGHTS" TYPE OF GUY.

THEY HAD ALL SCATTERED INTO THE WOODS AND ROCKS, AND I FOUND MYSELF ALONE WITH NO MAP OR COMPASS.
REALIZING I WAS BEING LEFT BEHIND, I TRIED TO CATCH UP WITH THE OTHERS.
I HAD GLANCED BRIEFLY AT THE MAP AND BEGAN WALKING IN THE DIRECTION I HOPED WAS THE RIGHT ONE...
AFTER ONLY 15 MINUTES, I WAS CONFRONTED BY A SMALL DETACHMENT OF "AGGRESSORS" AND QUICKLY TAKEN PRISONER.
THEY HAD ALREADY CAPTURED TWO OF MY CONTEMPORARIES.
THEY CONFISCATED OUR EQUIPMENT AND RIPPED OFF OUR NAMETAGS AND U.S. ARMY PATCH.
THEN THEY MADE US UNTIE OUR BOOTS AND TIE THE LACES TOGETHER SO WE COULDN'T RUN AWAY.
THEN THEY HERDED US LIKE LIVESTOCK TO THE SIMULATED P.O.W. CAMP.
WELCOME TO
XIN LOI
XIN LOI-- "SORRY ABOUT THAT."

FIRST WE PASSED THREE OF MY CONTEMPORARIES BEING TORTURED ON THE "INDIAN POLE."
AAAIIII--YOU'RE BREAKIN' MY LEG!
KEEP MOVIN'!
AAII
GET THAT GODDAMN LEG DOWN!

THAT'S MORE LIKE IT...
HEH HEH HEH
I HATE O.C.S.!
I QUIT--!

As we were being marched through the P.O.W. camp, I witnessed other things...
WHAT IN TH--?
GET UP! YOU'RE NOT FINISHED!
CAN I HAVE SOME WATER FIRST?
SOON.
THAT'S DEEP ENOUGH. GET OUT.
SHORTLY...
NOW GET IN...
B-BUT I DON'T WANT TO GET IN...
I SAID GET IN!
WUH--
PLEASE SAVE ME, LORD...
YOU AIN'T AFRAID OF SNAKES, ARE YA?
EEE-YIIIIII!

WE WERE EVENTUALLY TAKEN TO SEE THE CAMP COMMANDANT. I NEVER DID FIND OUT WHAT HAPPENED TO MY OTHER CONTEMPORARY. ONE OF THE CADRE SAID SOMETHING TO HIM THAT I COULDN'T QUITE MAKE OUT OVER ALL THE SCREAMING --AND THEN HE WAS QUICKLY LED AWAY. THE CAMP COMMANDANT LOOKED LIKE A NICE ENOUGH GUY, THOUGH...
UU-MMHHUH!
WHATTA YOU LOOKIN' AT--KEEP MOVING!
GET DOWN, PIG!
UHHHHNNNN...
JEEZUS CHRIST!
I CAN FEEL MY BACK BREAKIN'!
UHHHHNNNN,
WHY ARE YOU TWO WALKIN'?
EXCUSE ME, SIR?
YOU'RE PIGS--!
--AND PIGS CRAWL!
CRAWL, PIGS!
SOMEWHAT LATER...
YOU TWO STINK!
GUARD--TAKE THESE PIGS FOR A BATH!
WAIT--
YOU--IN FRONT--FOLLOW ME!

THE CAMP COMMANDANT TOOK ME OVER TO A FENCED-IN AREA FOR QUESTIONING.
HIS ASSISTANT HELD A FIELD TELEPHONE.
THEY SAID THEY JUST HAD "A FEW QUESTIONS" FOR ME, AND THEN THEY WOULD LET ME GO...
HAVE A SEAT.
THE GUY REMINDED ME A A LITTLE OF JAMES BOND.
WHAT'S YOUR NAME, PIG?
CANDIDATE PARKER, SIR...
HUH-HUH CANDIDATE FARTER.
WHAT UNIT ARE YOU WITH, CANDIDATE FARTER?
UH... SIR...
... I'M NOT ALLOWED TO TELL.
JAMES BOND GAVE THE CRANK ON THE FIELD PHONE A FEW TURNS. IT HURT, BUT ALL I COULD DO WAS LAUGH!
HA HA HA HA HA
PULL UP HIS SHIRT--AND MAKE SURE THE SKIN OF HIS BACK IS MAKING CONTACT WITH THE METAL PLATE ON THE CHAIR.

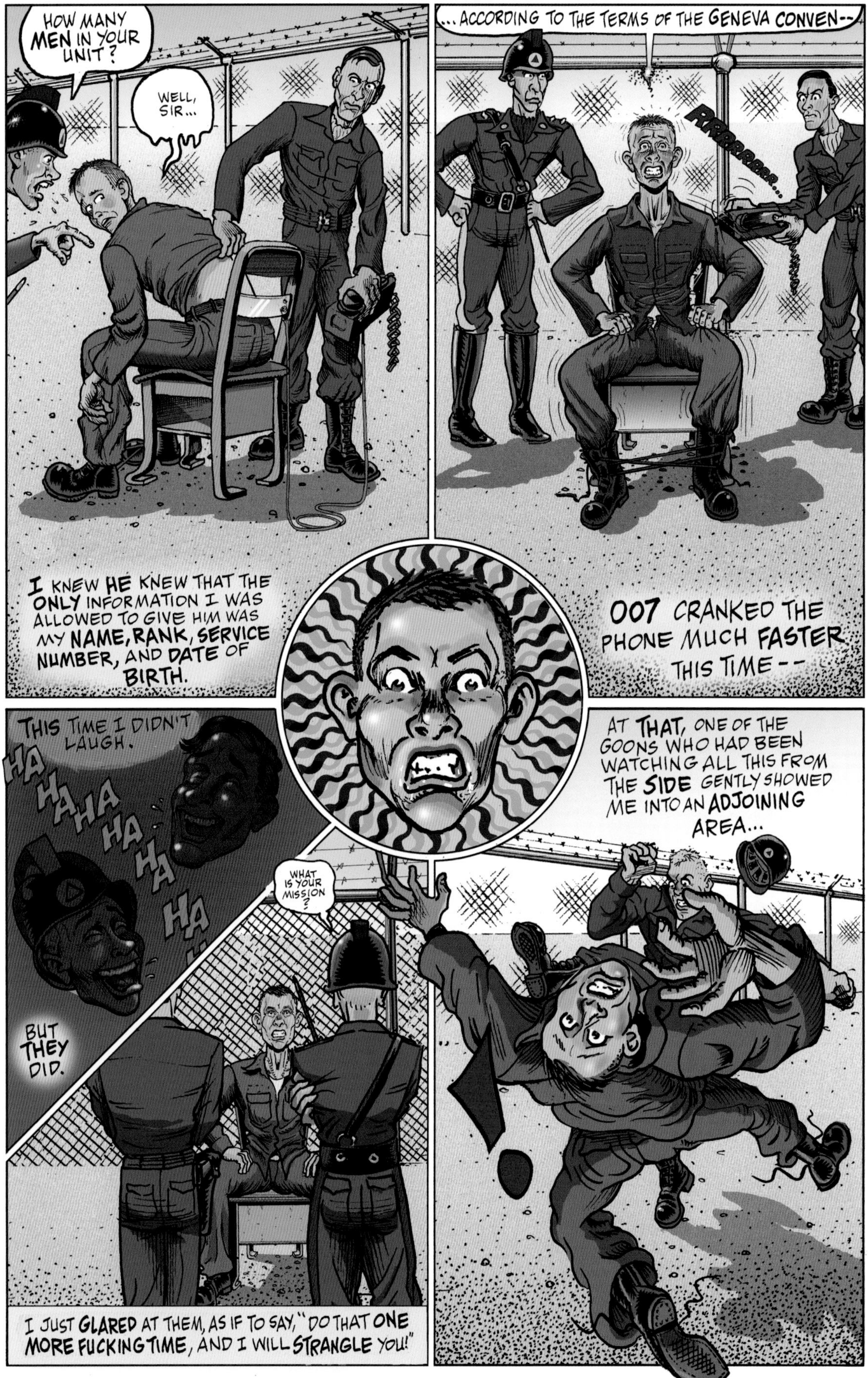
HOW MANY MEN IN YOUR UNIT?
WELL, SIR...
...ACCORDING TO THE TERMS OF THE GENEVA CONVEN--
I KNEW HE KNEW THAT THE ONLY INFORMATION I WAS ALLOWED TO GIVE HIM WAS MY NAME, RANK, SERVICE NUMBER, AND DATE OF BIRTH.
007 CRANKED THE PHONE MUCH FASTER THIS TIME--
THIS TIME I DIDN'T LAUGH.
BUT THEY DID.
WHAT IS YOUR MISSION?
I JUST GLARED AT THEM, AS IF TO SAY, "DO THAT ONE MORE FUCKING TIME, AND I WILL STRANGLE YOU!"
AT THAT, ONE OF THE GOONS WHO HAD BEEN WATCHING ALL THIS FROM THE SIDE GENTLY SHOWED ME INTO AN ADJOINING AREA...

SOON.
WELL... ...WELL... ...WELL.
...LOOKIT WHAT THE CAT DRAGGED IN!
COME WITH ME, PIG!
YOU--! YOU'VE BEEN IN THERE LONG ENOUGH--!
GET OUT!
I WAS STILL TRYING TO RECOGNIZE MY CONTEMPORARIES, WHEN THE GUARD CAME AND TOOK THE FIRST ONE AWAY!
I WONDER HOW HE WILL EVER GET HIS UNIFORM CLEAN?
MY FAMILY BACK HOME WAS IN THE LAUNDRY BUSINESS.
KICK
ME
IT DIDN'T SEEM SO BAD, REALLY.
AND THEN THE GUARD CAME BACK FOR ME!

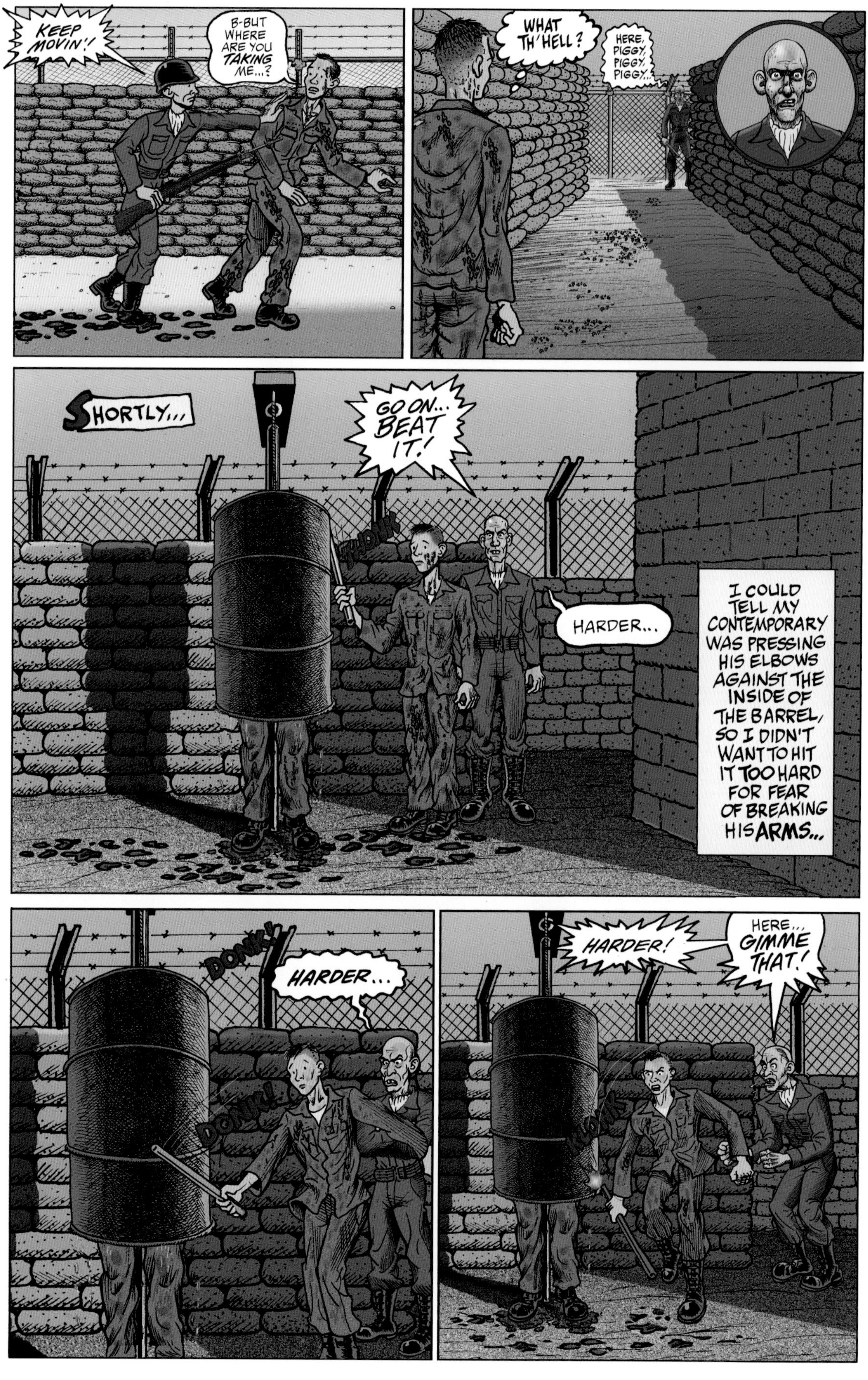

KEEP MOVIN'!
B-BUT WHERE ARE YOU TAKING ME...?
WHAT TH'HELL?
HERE, PIGGY, PIGGY, PIGGY...
SHORTLY...
GO ON... BEAT IT!
THONK
HARDER...
I COULD TELL MY CONTEMPORARY WAS PRESSING HIS ELBOWS AGAINST THE INSIDE OF THE BARREL, SO I DIDN'T WANT TO HIT IT TOO HARD FOR FEAR OF BREAKING HIS ARMS...
DONK!
HARDER...
DONK!
HARDER!
HERE... GIMME THAT!
KLONK

WELL...WHAT ARE YOU LOOKING AT--? GET IN TH' DRUM!
THIRTY SECONDS LATER...
THERE'S TH' WIND-UP...
ME
...AND TH' PITCH--
HOME RUN!
KLONG

SOON...
I USED TO BE IN A BAND, SO I WAS TOLD TO REPORT TO THE DRUM ROOM...
WITH MY EARS STILL RINGING AND A STABBING PAIN IN MY BACK, I DRAGGED MY ASS INTO A NEARBY CAGE-LIKE AREA...
IT WAS CURIOUSLY UNGUARDED, AND MY CONTEMPORARY STOOD NEAR SOME BROKEN TREE LIMBS.
HE HAD JUST DISCOVERED A TUNNEL NEAR ONE CORNER, WHICH SEEMED TO OFFER THE POSSIBILITY OF AN EASY ESCAPE.
IT'S PROBABLY SOME SORT OF TRICK.
NO--THEY WANT US TO ESCAPE...
IT WAS ABOUT EIGHT FEET DEEP.
SNIFF
SNIFF
SOMEBODY HAD PUT A DEAD SKUNK AT THE BOTTOM, AND A FEW DEAD SNAKES, AND THE WHOLE THING SMELLED LIKE PISS.

WITHOUT FURTHER DISCUSSION, MY CONTEMPORARY DESCENDED HEAD FIRST INTO THE HOLE...
THERE'S A TUNNEL AT THE BOTTOM WHICH GOES UNDER THE FENCE AND OUT INTO THE WOODS!
...BUT IT REALLY STUNK DOWN THERE.
FOLLOW ME!
WITH NO DESIRE TO BE LEFT BEHIND AGAIN, I LOWERED MYSELF INTO THE HOLE FEET FIRST...
?
I SOON REALIZED THAT THERE WAS NO ROOM TO TURN AROUND AND I WAS IN TOO DEEP TO CLIMB BACK OUT.
CRAP!
SO I DID THE ONLY THING THAT SOMEONE IN MY SITUATION COULD DO--
SNIFF
SNIFF
--I SHIMMIED INTO THE TUNNEL FEET FIRST!

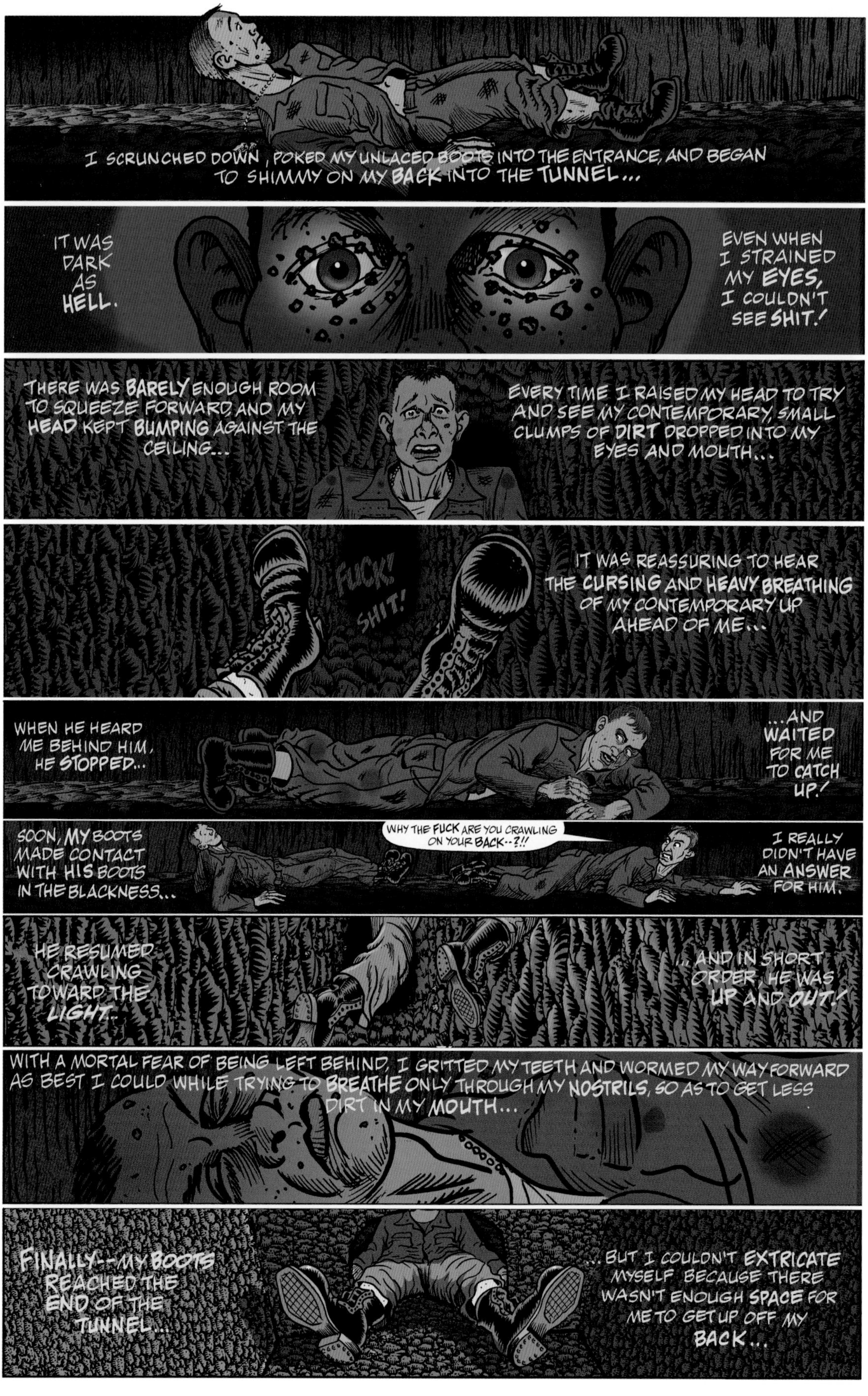
I SCRUNCHED DOWN, POKED MY UNLACED BOOTS INTO THE ENTRANCE, AND BEGAN TO SHIMMY ON MY BACK INTO THE TUNNEL...
IT WAS DARK AS HELL.
EVEN WHEN I STRAINED MY EYES, I COULDN'T SEE SHIT!
THERE WAS BARELY ENOUGH ROOM TO SQUEEZE FORWARD, AND MY HEAD KEPT BUMPING AGAINST THE CEILING...
EVERY TIME I RAISED MY HEAD TO TRY AND SEE MY CONTEMPORARY, SMALL CLUMPS OF DIRT DROPPED INTO MY EYES AND MOUTH...
FUCK!
SHIT!
IT WAS REASSURING TO HEAR THE CURSING AND HEAVY BREATHING OF MY CONTEMPORARY UP AHEAD OF ME...
WHEN HE HEARD ME BEHIND HIM, HE STOPPED...
...AND WAITED FOR ME TO CATCH UP!
SOON, MY BOOTS MADE CONTACT WITH HIS BOOTS IN THE BLACKNESS...
WHY THE FUCK ARE YOU CRAWLING ON YOUR BACK--?!!
I REALLY DIDN'T HAVE AN ANSWER FOR HIM.
HE RESUMED CRAWLING TOWARD THE LIGHT...
...AND IN SHORT ORDER, HE WAS UP AND OUT!
WITH A MORTAL FEAR OF BEING LEFT BEHIND, I GRITTED MY TEETH AND WORMED MY WAY FORWARD AS BEST I COULD WHILE TRYING TO BREATHE ONLY THROUGH MY NOSTRILS, SO AS TO GET LESS DIRT IN MY MOUTH...
FINALLY--MY BOOTS REACHED THE END OF THE TUNNEL...
...BUT I COULDN'T EXTRICATE MYSELF BECAUSE THERE WASN'T ENOUGH SPACE FOR ME TO GET UP OFF MY BACK...

BEFORE I KNEW IT, STRONG HANDS GRABBED ME BY THE ANKLES AND HAULED ME OUT OF THE HOLE.
MY CONTEMPORARY HAD WAITED FOR ME, INSTEAD OF HEADING OFF ON HIS OWN.
THAT WAS KIND OF HEROIC.
I WONDERED WHAT I WOULD HAVE DONE IF THE SITUATION HAD BEEN REVERSED.
THEN I REALIZED NOBODY BUT ME WOULD HAVE BEEN STUPID ENOUGH TO HAVE ENTERED THAT TUNNEL FEET FIRST.

FORTUNATELY, IT WAS BEGINNING TO GET DARK, WHICH SOMEWHAT DIMINISHED MY ANXIETY ABOUT BEING RECAPTURED AND TAKEN BACK TO THE CAMP.
WE HEADED OFF IN THE DIRECTION OF THE SETTING SUN, WITH LITTLE OR NO CONVERSATION.
I ASSUMED MY CONTEMPORARY HAD SOME IDEA ABOUT WHERE WE WERE GOING...
...I KNEW I CERTAINLY DIDN'T.

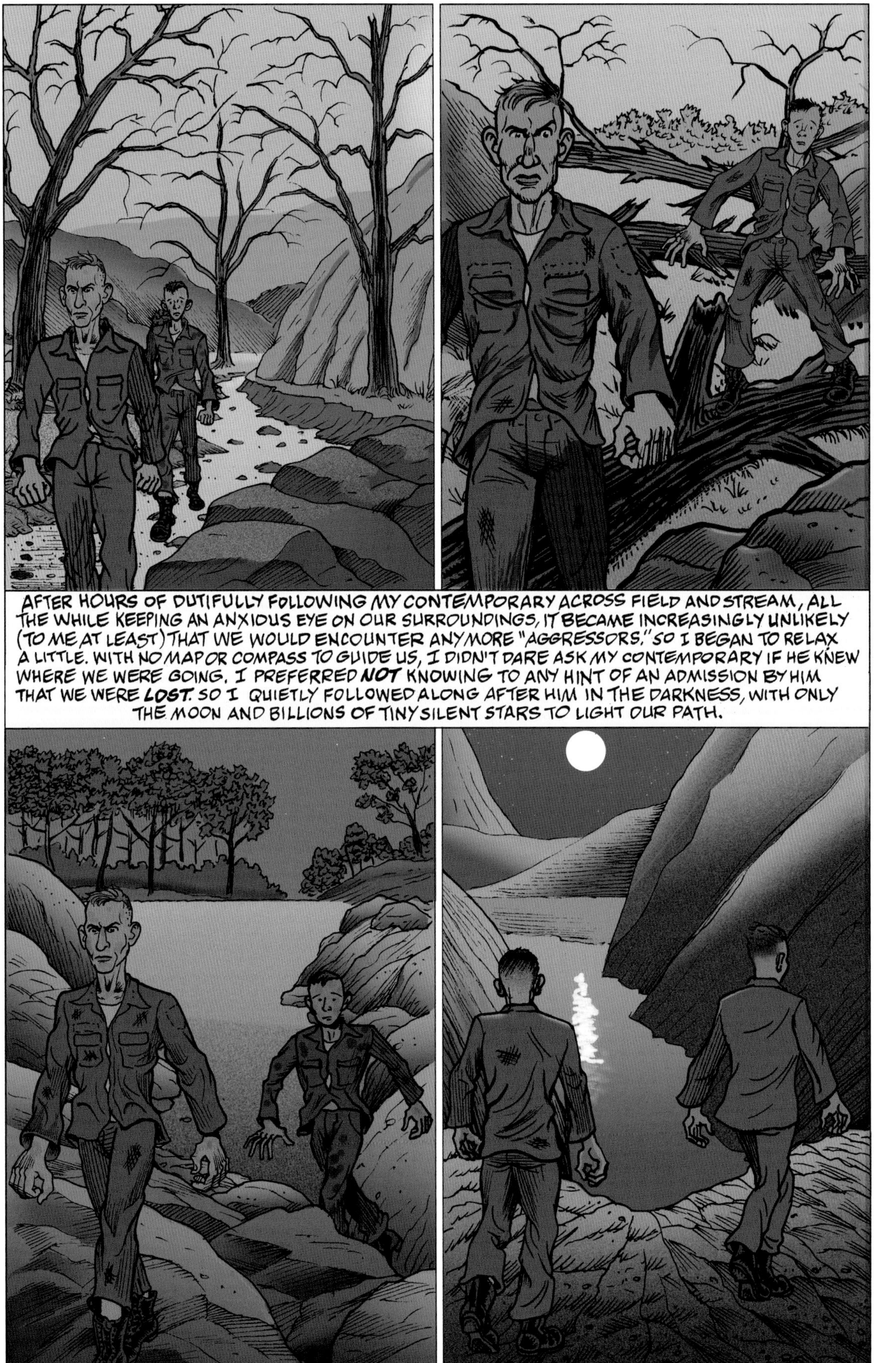
AFTER HOURS OF DUTIFULLY FOLLOWING MY CONTEMPORARY ACROSS FIELD AND STREAM, ALL THE WHILE KEEPING AN ANXIOUS EYE ON OUR SURROUNDINGS, IT BECAME INCREASINGLY UNLIKELY (TO ME AT LEAST) THAT WE WOULD ENCOUNTER ANYMORE "AGGRESSORS," SO I BEGAN TO RELAX A LITTLE. WITH NO MAP OR COMPASS TO GUIDE US, I DIDN'T DARE ASK MY CONTEMPORARY IF HE KNEW WHERE WE WERE GOING. I PREFERRED NOT KNOWING TO ANY HINT OF AN ADMISSION BY HIM THAT WE WERE LOST. SO I QUIETLY FOLLOWED ALONG AFTER HIM IN THE DARKNESS, WITH ONLY THE MOON AND BILLIONS OF TINY SILENT STARS TO LIGHT OUR PATH.

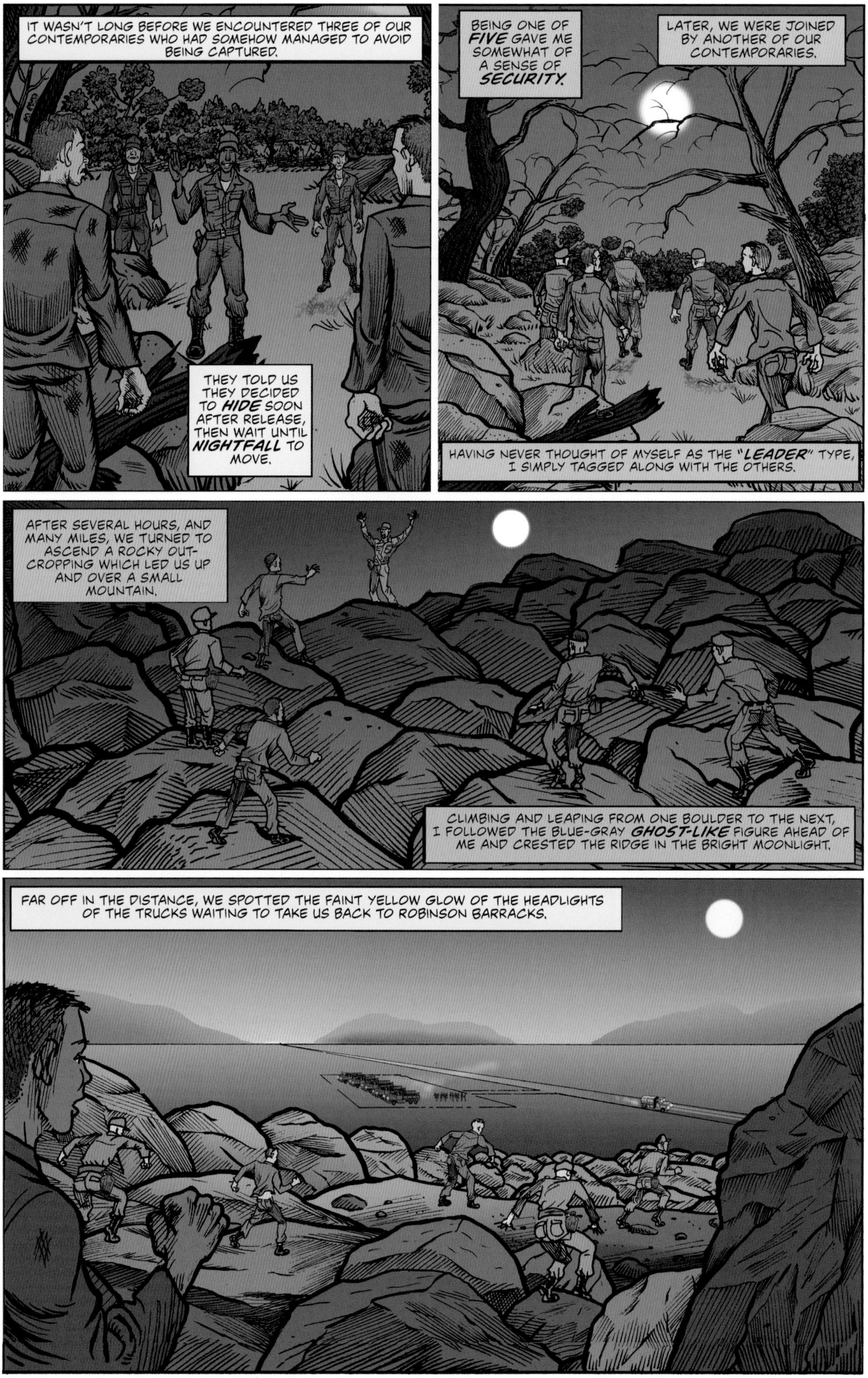
IT WASN'T LONG BEFORE WE ENCOUNTERED THREE OF OUR CONTEMPORARIES WHO HAD SOMEHOW MANAGED TO AVOID BEING CAPTURED.
THEY TOLD US THEY DECIDED TO HIDE SOON AFTER RELEASE, THEN WAIT UNTIL NIGHTFALL TO MOVE.
BEING ONE OF FIVE GAVE ME SOMEWHAT OF A SENSE OF SECURITY.
LATER, WE WERE JOINED BY ANOTHER OF OUR CONTEMPORARIES.
HAVING NEVER THOUGHT OF MYSELF AS THE "LEADER" TYPE, I SIMPLY TAGGED ALONG WITH THE OTHERS.
AFTER SEVERAL HOURS, AND MANY MILES, WE TURNED TO ASCEND A ROCKY OUT-CROPPING WHICH LED US UP AND OVER A SMALL MOUNTAIN.
CLIMBING AND LEAPING FROM ONE BOULDER TO THE NEXT, I FOLLOWED THE BLUE-GRAY GHOST-LIKE FIGURE AHEAD OF ME AND CRESTED THE RIDGE IN THE BRIGHT MOONLIGHT.
FAR OFF IN THE DISTANCE, WE SPOTTED THE FAINT YELLOW GLOW OF THE HEADLIGHTS OF THE TRUCKS WAITING TO TAKE US BACK TO ROBINSON BARRACKS.

AT LAST WE WERE REUNITED.
APPARENTLY, EVERYONE HAD BEEN CAPTURED AND TAKEN TO THE MOCK P.O.W. CAMP EXCEPT FOR THIS ONE OFFICER CANDIDATE.
HE HAD BEEN ONE OF THE ONES WITH A MAP AND COMPASS.
I DID GET SEPARATED FROM MY TEAM--BUT IN LESS THAN THREE HOURS I MADE IT TO THE PARTISAN POINT!
I WAS THE FIRST ONE THERE.
THEY SEEMED SURPRISED TO SEE ME.
TMP 3
TMP 3
THEY CONGRATULATED ME AND TOLD ME IT WAS A REALLY BIG DEAL.
THEY TOLD ME NO ONE IN THE HISTORY OF THE PROGRAM HAD EVER MANAGED TO MAKE IT TO THE PARTISAN POINT WITHOUT GETTING CAPTURED.
THEN THEY DROVE ME STRAIGHT TO THE P.O.W. CAMP SO I COULD TELL THE CAMP COMMANDANT THAT I WAS THE ONLY OFFICER CANDIDATE IN THE HISTORY OF THE PROGRAM EVER TO HAVE DONE SO...
...THEY ACTUALLY OPENED A BOTTLE OF CHAMPAGNE SO WE COULD CELEBRATE.
"THEY EVEN RADIOED AHEAD TO LET HIM KNOW I WAS COMING."
VROOOM
HQ
DE

"...THIRTY MINUTES LATER, HE WAS WAITING FOR US AT THE GATE."
POW COMPOUND
XIN LOI
SIR...WE HAVE THAT CANDIDATE YOU WANTED TO SEE....
GOOD WORK, PRIVATE!
"HE LOOKED HAPPY TO SEE ME."
...SO I WENT RIGHT UP TO HIM AND SAID, "SIR--I DID IT...
...I AM THE ONLY ONE TO EVER MAKE IT TO THE PARTISAN POINT."
NO SHIT.
REALLY?
TMP 3
OH, YEAH...? THEN WHAT HAPPENED AFTER THAT?
"WELL... HE JUST KIND OF SMILED AT ME FOR A MINUTE, AND THEN HE POINTED TO THE GROUND."
AND THEN HE SAID--

CRAWL, PIG!

5 BLAST OFF

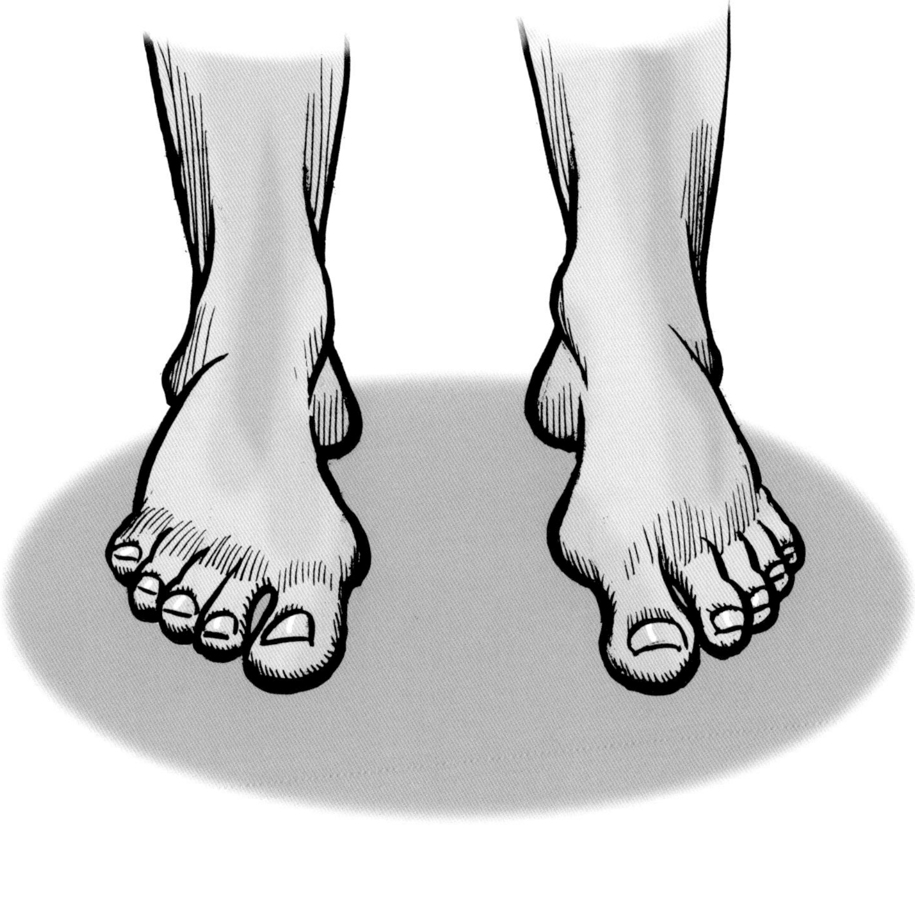

THERE WERE 94 OF US IN CLASS 11-67. ONE THIRD BECAME FORWARD OBSERVERS FOR ARTILLERY UNITS ALREADY IN VIETNAM. A THIRD WENT TO UNITS FORMING TO GO TO VIETNAM--AND ONE THIRD WENT TO OTHER DEPLOYMENTS. I AND A FEW OTHERS WERE HELD FOR ADDITIONAL TRAINING.
VIETNAM.
`NAM.
NAM...
FORT SILL MISSILE SCHOOL...
I UNDERWENT AN ADDITIONAL EIGHT WEEKS TRAINING IN GUIDED MISSILES.
MY PARENTS DROVE OUT TO FORT SILL TO SEE ME GET MY COMMISSION.
THAT NIGHT, THE THREE OF US STAYED IN A MOTEL ON THE OUTSKIRTS OF LAWTON.
THE NEXT DAY...
THANKS FOR COMING!
HAVE A SAFE TRIP HOME.
FOR THE FIRST TIME IN 13 MONTHS, I WAS ALL ALONE.
...I SENT MY PERSONAL BIRTHDAY GREETINGS TO GENERAL WESTMORELAND IN VIETNAM...
THE FOLLOWING DAY, I MOVED INTO THE B.O.Q. (BATCHELOR OFFICER'S QUARTERS).
BOQ

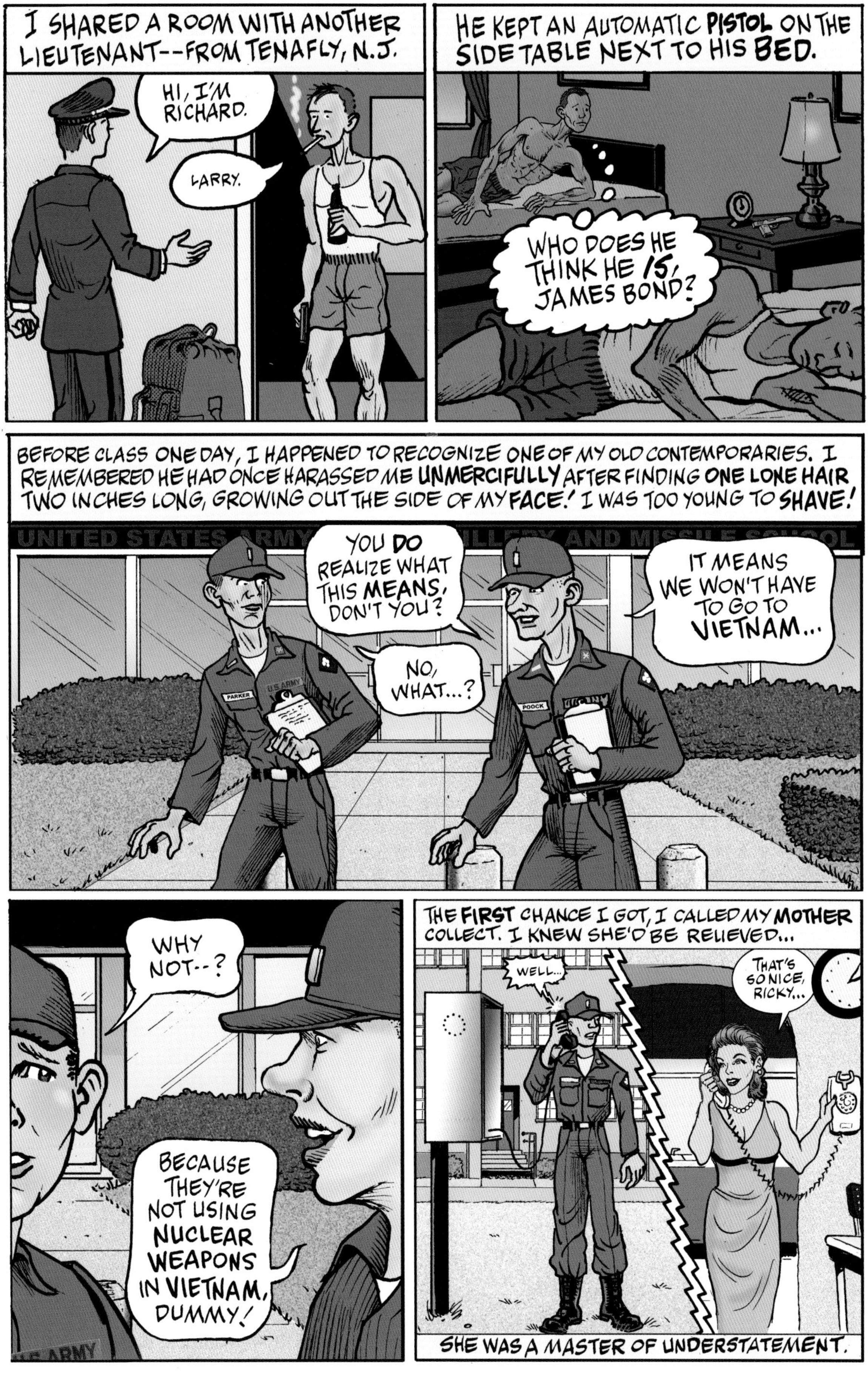
I SHARED A ROOM WITH ANOTHER LIEUTENANT--FROM TENAFLY, N.J.
HI, I'M RICHARD.
LARRY.
HE KEPT AN AUTOMATIC PISTOL ON THE SIDE TABLE NEXT TO HIS BED.
WHO DOES HE THINK HE IS, JAMES BOND?
BEFORE CLASS ONE DAY, I HAPPENED TO RECOGNIZE ONE OF MY OLD CONTEMPORARIES. I REMEMBERED HE HAD ONCE HARASSED ME UNMERCIFULLY AFTER FINDING ONE LONE HAIR TWO INCHES LONG, GROWING OUT THE SIDE OF MY FACE! I WAS TOO YOUNG TO SHAVE!
UNITED STATES ARMY
YOU DO REALIZE WHAT THIS MEANS, DON'T YOU?
NO, WHAT...?
IT MEANS WE WON'T HAVE TO GO TO VIETNAM...
PARKER
POOCK
WHY NOT--?
BECAUSE THEY'RE NOT USING NUCLEAR WEAPONS IN VIETNAM, DUMMY!
THE FIRST CHANCE I GOT, I CALLED MY MOTHER COLLECT. I KNEW SHE'D BE RELIEVED...
WELL...
THAT'S SO NICE, RICKY...
SHE WAS A MASTER OF UNDERSTATEMENT.

LARRY WAS AN OKAY GUY, BUT MADE NO EFFORT TO BE MY FRIEND.
AND I COULD'VE USED A FRIEND.
WHEN I WASN'T ON DUTY, I BEGAN TO SPEND MY EVENINGS IN THE BAR AT THE OFFICER'S CLUB.
LEFT OUT
CHEERS!
WHEN I'D HAD ENOUGH, I'D WALK BACK TO THE B.O.Q. AND CRASH.
GUNS
ONE EVENING, AT THE OFFICER'S CLUB, I RAN INTO A YOUNG LIEUTENANT WHOM I KNEW.
WHY ARE YOU STILL LIVING IN THE B.O.Q.?
GLUG GLUG
TURNS OUT ROGER WAS FROM LAWTON.
STOP WASTING YOUR MONEY IN THE B.O.Q.!
THERE'S THIS NICE OLD COUPLE ACROSS THE STREET FROM ME. THEY HAVE A SPARE BEDROOM
THEY RENT OUT.
PARKER

ROGER DROVE ME OUT TO MEET THEM.
THEY'RE REALLY NICE...
MR. BROOKS, THIS IS RICHARD.
HELLO, RICHARD.
THE FIRST THING MR. BROOKS DID WAS SHOW ME THE ROOM.
VERY NICE.
IF YOU WANT, YOU CAN HAVE IT FOR $30 A MONTH.
OKAY, GREAT!
THEN MR. BROOKS TOOK ME DOWN THE HALL TO MEET MRS. BROOKS.
DARLIN', THIS IS RICHARD.
HELLO, DEAR.
I COULD EASILY AFFORD IT, AND I WAS RIGHT ACROSS THE STREET FROM ROGER!
AND ROGER WAS NICE ENOUGH TO DRIVE ME TO THE POST AND BACK EVERY DAY.

A WEEK LATER.
CAN I CHIP IN FOR GAS?
I'VE GOT A BETTER IDEA.
I WAS REALLY STARTING TO ENJOY HAVING A FRIEND.
WHAT...?
LET'S GET YOU A CAR!
PARKER
LATER.
HOW MUCH IS THIS ONE?
$500!
SHE WAS A '62 CHEVY WITH "THREE ON TH' TREE."
WHAT DO YOU THINK?
I LIKE IT.
IT HAD CHEVY'S CLASSIC STRAIGHT-6 ENGINE.
SO I BOUGHT THE CAR AND ROGER GOT BACK INTO HIS CAR AND DROVE AWAY.
AND THAT WAS PRETTY MUCH THE END OF THAT FRIENDSHIP.
AND ME WITH NOWHERE TO GO.

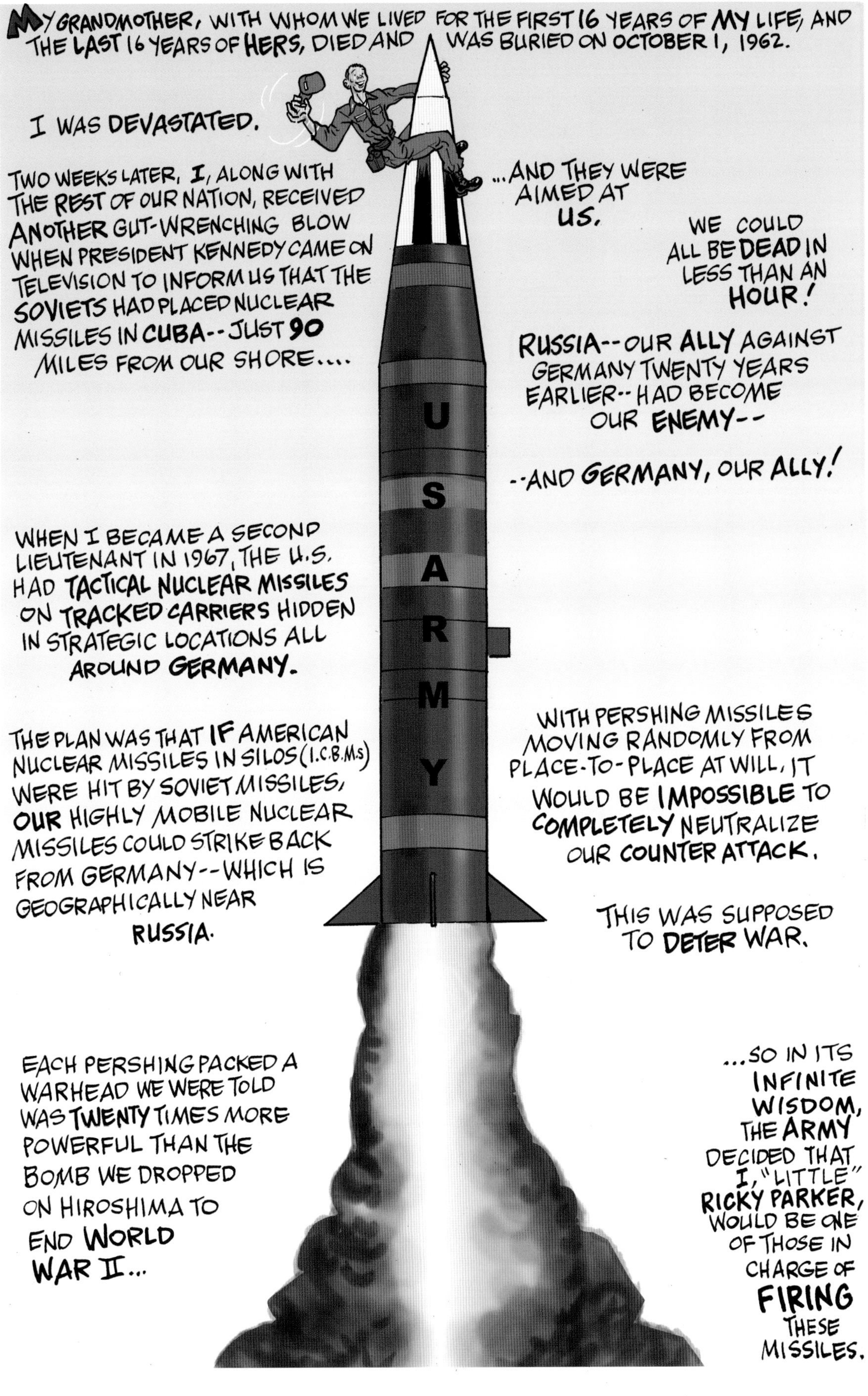

MY GRANDMOTHER, WITH WHOM WE LIVED FOR THE FIRST 16 YEARS OF MY LIFE, AND THE LAST 16 YEARS OF HERS, DIED AND WAS BURIED ON OCTOBER 1, 1962.
I WAS DEVASTATED.
TWO WEEKS LATER, I, ALONG WITH THE REST OF OUR NATION, RECEIVED ANOTHER GUT-WRENCHING BLOW WHEN PRESIDENT KENNEDY CAME ON TELEVISION TO INFORM US THAT THE SOVIETS HAD PLACED NUCLEAR MISSILES IN CUBA--JUST 90 MILES FROM OUR SHORE....
...AND THEY WERE AIMED AT US.
WE COULD ALL BE DEAD IN LESS THAN AN HOUR!
RUSSIA--OUR ALLY AGAINST GERMANY TWENTY YEARS EARLIER--HAD BECOME OUR ENEMY--
--AND GERMANY, OUR ALLY!
U S ARMY
WHEN I BECAME A SECOND LIEUTENANT IN 1967, THE U.S. HAD TACTICAL NUCLEAR MISSILES ON TRACKED CARRIERS HIDDEN IN STRATEGIC LOCATIONS ALL AROUND GERMANY.
THE PLAN WAS THAT IF AMERICAN NUCLEAR MISSILES IN SILOS (I.C.B.M.s) WERE HIT BY SOVIET MISSILES, OUR HIGHLY MOBILE NUCLEAR MISSILES COULD STRIKE BACK FROM GERMANY--WHICH IS GEOGRAPHICALLY NEAR RUSSIA.
WITH PERSHING MISSILES MOVING RANDOMLY FROM PLACE-TO-PLACE AT WILL, IT WOULD BE IMPOSSIBLE TO COMPLETELY NEUTRALIZE OUR COUNTER ATTACK.
THIS WAS SUPPOSED TO DETER WAR.
EACH PERSHING PACKED A WARHEAD WE WERE TOLD WAS TWENTY TIMES MORE POWERFUL THAN THE BOMB WE DROPPED ON HIROSHIMA TO END WORLD WAR II...
...SO IN ITS INFINITE WISDOM, THE ARMY DECIDED THAT I, "LITTLE" RICKY PARKER, WOULD BE ONE OF THOSE IN CHARGE OF FIRING THESE MISSILES.

I WAS ONE OF SIX YOUNG LIEUTENANTS ASSIGNED TO THE 35TH USA MISSILE DETACHMENT--A BRAND-NEW UNIT DESTINED FOR GERMANY--TO WORK WITH OUR NATO ALLIES--THE GERMANS. LIEUTENANT BETINA EXPLAINED OUR MISSION TO US...
ME
...THEY'VE GOT THE MISSILES...
...AND WE'VE GOT THE WARHEADS...
BETINA
USARMY
...AND WE MATE THEM.
YOU'RE FAMILIAR WITH "MATING," RIGHT...?
THERE REALLY WASN'T MUCH TO DO UNTIL OUR C.O. (COMMANDING OFFICER) ARRIVED. CAPTAIN O'CONNOR WAS AN IRISH CATHOLIC FROM BOSTON WHO VOLUNTEERED FOR ACTIVE DUTY FROM THE NATIONAL GUARD.
OUR CAPTAIN'S FIRST DECISION WAS TO CHOOSE AN X-O (EXECUTIVE OFFICER) TO BE HIS ASSISTANT. I DIDN'T REALLY THINK OF MYSELF AS "EXECUTIVE" MATERIAL, BUT STILL, MY FEELINGS WERE HURT WHEN HE DIDN'T PICK ME.
LT. BETINA WILL BE OUR NEW X-O.
ANY QUESTIONS?
I WAS DETERMINED TO PROVE MY TRUE WORTH TO THE CAPTAIN BY PRESENTING HIM WITH A FINE PORTRAIT OF HIMSELF, SURROUNDED BY HIS OFFICERS.
NONE OF THEM COULD DO THAT--BUT THEY WERE ALL NICE ENOUGH TO POSE FOR ME, INCLUDING THE CAPTAIN. CURIOUSLY, I LEFT MYSELF OUT.

WE SPENT THAT SUMMER AND FALL TRYING TO STAY BUSY AS WE AWAITED OUR ORDERS FOR GERMANY.
IBM
IT WAS THE SUMMER OF LOVE IN CALIFORNIA, AND I SPENT MOST OF IT IN BATTERY HQ AS A KIND OF GLORIFIED TYPIST. I WAS TYPING UP "INSERTS"--UPDATES TO ARMY TECHNICAL MANUALS. "BUSY WORK."
TO PASS THE TIME, WHEN I WASN'T ON DUTY, I ENROLLED IN A PUBLIC SPEAKING CLASS AT THE LOCAL COMMUNITY COLLEGE.
SMOKING IS THE LEADING CAUSE OF DEATH...
BLAH BLAH BLAH BLAH...
CAMERON UNIVERSITY OKLAHOMA 1908
IN REALITY, WHEN IT WAS MY TURN, I FROZE LIKE A DEER IN THE HEADLIGHTS.
ON SUNDAYS, I ATTENDED BAPTIST CHURCH SERVICES WITH MR. BROOKS... JUST TO BE SOCIABLE.
...IN THE NAME OF THE FATHER, THE SON, AND THE HOLY GHOST!
AMEN.
AMEN.
ON THE DAY I TURNED 21, I LOOKED IN THE MIRROR TO SEE IF I HAD BECOME A "MAN" LIKE MY FATHER TOLD ME I WOULD--
--BUT I STILL LOOKED PRETTY MUCH THE SAME AS I ALWAYS HAD.
WE FOUND OUT IN THE FALL, THAT, FOR "POLITICAL" REASONS, WE WOULD NOT BE GOING TO GERMANY. INSTEAD, THE GERMANS WOULD BE COMING HERE, TO THE DESERT TO TRAIN WITH US.
PARKER
IN EARLY MARCH, I, ALONG WITH MOST OF THE 2/44TH ARTILLERY AND MISSILE BATTALION, HEADED FOR WHITE SANDS MISSILE RANGE JUST OUTSIDE EL PASO, TEXAS.

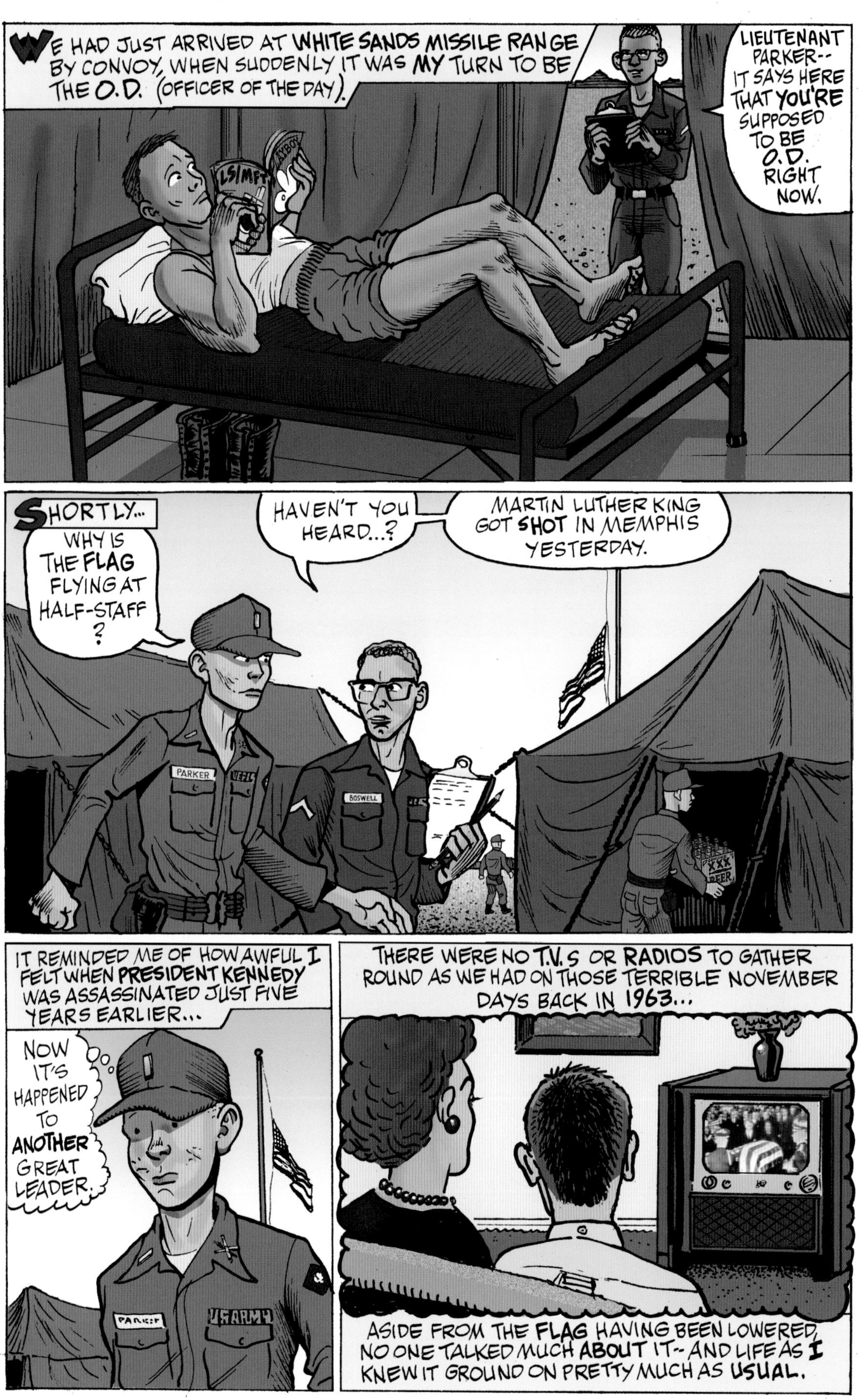
WE HAD JUST ARRIVED AT WHITE SANDS MISSILE RANGE BY CONVOY, WHEN SUDDENLY IT WAS MY TURN TO BE THE O.D. (OFFICER OF THE DAY).
LIEUTENANT PARKER-- IT SAYS HERE THAT YOU'RE SUPPOSED TO BE O.D. RIGHT NOW.
SHORTLY...
WHY IS THE FLAG FLYING AT HALF-STAFF?
HAVEN'T YOU HEARD...?
MARTIN LUTHER KING GOT SHOT IN MEMPHIS YESTERDAY.
PARKER
BOSWELL
XXX BEER
IT REMINDED ME OF HOW AWFUL I FELT WHEN PRESIDENT KENNEDY WAS ASSASSINATED JUST FIVE YEARS EARLIER...
NOW IT'S HAPPENED TO ANOTHER GREAT LEADER.
PARKER
U.S. ARMY
THERE WERE NO T.V.S OR RADIOS TO GATHER ROUND AS WE HAD ON THOSE TERRIBLE NOVEMBER DAYS BACK IN 1963...
ASIDE FROM THE FLAG HAVING BEEN LOWERED, NO ONE TALKED MUCH ABOUT IT-- AND LIFE AS I KNEW IT GROUND ON PRETTY MUCH AS USUAL.

I HAD JUST SAT DOWN BEHIND THE DESK IN HEADQUARTERS TENT AND WAS TRYING TO LOOK "COMMANDING" WHEN THE OTHER BATTERY CLERK, PFC. RANDALL, APPROACHED ME RATHER SHEEPISHLY...
SIR...?
...DO YOU NEED ANY CONDOMS?
EXCUSE ME...?
I JUST CAME FROM FORMATION...
PARKS
U.S. ARMY
IN
OUT
...AND THE FIRST SERGEANT WAS THROWING HANDFULS TO THE TROOPS.
THEY BELONGED TO PFC. KENNET--
--THE GUY WHO WAS KILLED IN THE CONVOY ON MONDAY ON OUR WAY DOWN HERE.
APPARENTLY, HE WAS PLANNING ON HAVING QUITE THE TIME.
RANDALL
ALTHOUGH I WAS STILL A MEMBER OF THE "UNINITIATED," I DIDN'T WANT TO APPEAR "UNMANLY," SO I TOOK ONE AND PROMPTLY PUT IT IN MY WALLET...

THEN RANDALL HELD UP SOMETHING THAT WAS WRAPPED UP IN A SHEET OF NOTEBOOK PAPER WITH A RUBBER BAND TIED AROUND IT.
IT'S KENNET'S GLASSES.
WHAT SHOULD I DO?
SARGE TOLD ME TO GET RID OF THEM.
USARMY
GIVE THEM TO ME.

WANTING TO APPEAR DECISIVE, I TOOK THEM FROM RANDALL.
I OPENED THE TOP DRAWER OF THE DESK AND PUT THEM IN IT.

AND THEN I REMEMBERED THE CAPTAIN TELLING ME HOW THE ACCIDENT HAPPENED...
YAAHOOOOOO...
YA 3519
COLORADO
OLD FORESTER
PFC. KENNET, A MECHANIC, WAS RIDING IN THE BACK OF THE PLL VAN. IT WAS PULLING A TRAILER FULL OF SPARE PARTS. THEY WERE FOLLOWING THE CONVOY AND HAD JUST PULLED OVER BEHIND A DEUCE-AND-A HALF.
THE DRIVER, SPECIALIST BATES, OF NEWARK, NEW JERSEY, GOT OUT AND WENT TO THE BACK TO UNLOCK THE DOUBLE DOORS OF THE VAN TO LET KENNET OUT.
PFC. KENNET WAS IN THE ACT OF JUMPING DOWN OUT OF THE BACK OF THE VAN WHEN A DRUNK DRIVER SLAMMED INTO THE BACK OF THE TRAILER, CRUSHING PFC. KENNET BETWEEN THE TRAILER AND THE PLL VAN.
SPECIALIST BATES SURVIVED, BUT THERE WASN'T ENOUGH LEFT OF PFC. KENNET TO SEND BACK TO HIS FAMILY IN CINCINNATI FOR A DECENT BURIAL.

I HAPPENED TO BE IN THE MOTOR POOL WHEN THE PLL VAN WAS TOWED IN--AND CAPTAIN O'CONNOR APPROACHED ME JUST AS ONE OF THE MEN WENT OVER AND BEGAN HOSING IT DOWN.
AFTERNOON, SIR!
AFTERNOON, LIEUTENANT...
THE CAPTAIN AND I WATCHED AS WATER AND BITS OF FLESH RAN DOWN THE SIDE OF THE TRUCK AND SLOWLY TURNED INTO A BRIGHT PINK POOL ON THE TARMAC.
THE CAPTAIN LOOKED VISIBLY SHAKEN.
I WAS HORRIFIED.
T-THAT POOR B-BOY...
HE SEEMED MORE UPSET THAN I WAS!
AND I WAS PRETTY FREAKED OUT!
MY FIRST THOUGHT WAS MAYBE IT HAD SOMETHING TO DO WITH HIS HAVING COME TO US FROM THE NATIONAL GUARD.
IN BASIC, I HAD HEARD SOME VICIOUS RUMORS ABOUT THE GUARD--
O'CONNOR
US ARMY
PARKER
US ARMY
--LIKE THEY WERE A BUNCH OF WUSSES.
BUT I KNEW CAPTAIN O'CONNOR WAS NO WUSS.
WHAT IS IT, SIR?
AND THEN HE TOLD ME...

"I WAS FOLLOWING THE TRUCK HERE IN MY JEEP, AND AS WE WERE GOING DOWN THE HIGHWAY, I NOTICED SOMETHING GRAY STUCK TO THE BACK BUMPER OF THE TRUCK...
"AT FIRST, I COULDN'T FIGURE OUT WHAT IT WAS..."
OH...MY... GOD!
I JUST LOOKED AT HIM...
HIS VOICE CRACKED AS HE SPOKE.
IT... IT... WAS HIS FACE.
CAPTAIN O'CONNOR RECEIVED ORDERS FOR VIETNAM A WEEK LATER.

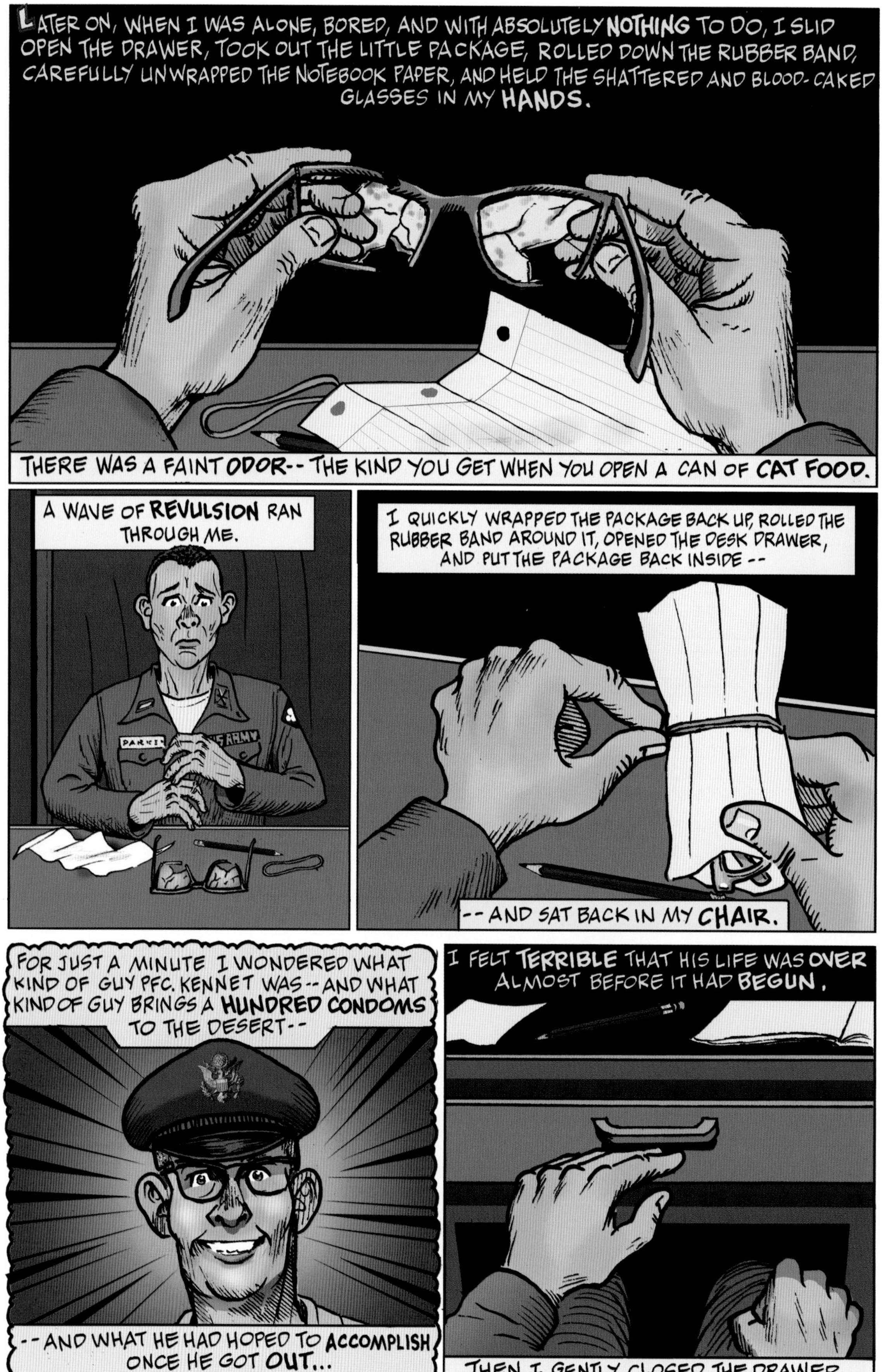
LATER ON, WHEN I WAS ALONE, BORED, AND WITH ABSOLUTELY NOTHING TO DO, I SLID OPEN THE DRAWER, TOOK OUT THE LITTLE PACKAGE, ROLLED DOWN THE RUBBER BAND, CAREFULLY UNWRAPPED THE NOTEBOOK PAPER, AND HELD THE SHATTERED AND BLOOD-CAKED GLASSES IN MY HANDS.
THERE WAS A FAINT ODOR-- THE KIND YOU GET WHEN YOU OPEN A CAN OF CAT FOOD.
A WAVE OF REVULSION RAN THROUGH ME.
I QUICKLY WRAPPED THE PACKAGE BACK UP, ROLLED THE RUBBER BAND AROUND IT, OPENED THE DESK DRAWER, AND PUT THE PACKAGE BACK INSIDE --
-- AND SAT BACK IN MY CHAIR.
FOR JUST A MINUTE I WONDERED WHAT KIND OF GUY PFC. KENNET WAS -- AND WHAT KIND OF GUY BRINGS A HUNDRED CONDOMS TO THE DESERT --
-- AND WHAT HE HAD HOPED TO ACCOMPLISH ONCE HE GOT OUT...
I FELT TERRIBLE THAT HIS LIFE WAS OVER ALMOST BEFORE IT HAD BEGUN.
THEN I GENTLY CLOSED THE DRAWER.

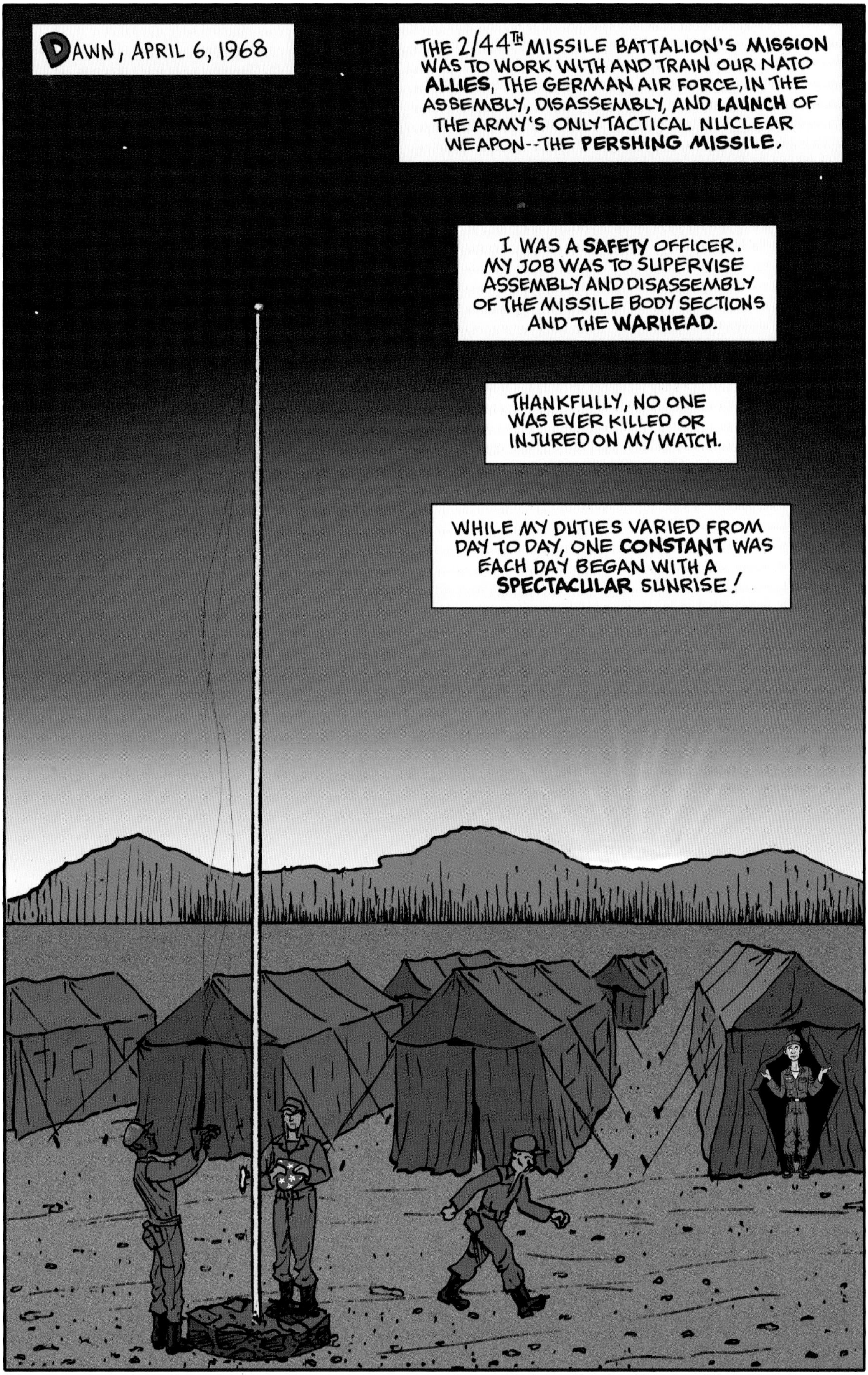
DAWN, APRIL 6, 1968
THE 2/44TH MISSILE BATTALION'S MISSION WAS TO WORK WITH AND TRAIN OUR NATO ALLIES, THE GERMAN AIR FORCE, IN THE ASSEMBLY, DISASSEMBLY, AND LAUNCH OF THE ARMY'S ONLY TACTICAL NUCLEAR WEAPON--THE PERSHING MISSILE.
I WAS A SAFETY OFFICER. MY JOB WAS TO SUPERVISE ASSEMBLY AND DISASSEMBLY OF THE MISSILE BODY SECTIONS AND THE WARHEAD.
THANKFULLY, NO ONE WAS EVER KILLED OR INJURED ON MY WATCH.
WHILE MY DUTIES VARIED FROM DAY TO DAY, ONE CONSTANT WAS EACH DAY BEGAN WITH A SPECTACULAR SUNRISE!

UPON ARRIVAL AT WHITE SANDS MISSILE RANGE, ONE OF THE FIRST ORDERS CAPTAIN O'CONNOR ISSUED INVOLVED SETTING UP A SMALL TENT TO SERVE AS A MAKESHIFT OFFICER'S PUB.
GOD KNOWS, WE COULD ALL HAVE USED A DRINK AFTER WHAT HAD BEEN SUCH A HARROWING CONVOY DOWN FROM FORT SILL.
THOUGH NOT MUCH OF A DRINKER MYSELF, I RELISHED THE THOUGHT OF HAVING A PLACE TO HANG OUT AND BECOME FRIENDS WITH THE OTHERS.
ONE OF THE ENLISTED MEN, PFC. ALBERT, HAD BEEN ASSIGNED TO BE OUR BARTENDER.
THANK YOU...
HEY--
HE WAS SLIGHT OF BUILD, AND WENT ABOUT HIS DUTIES AS BARTENDER WITH VERY FEW WORDS.
EVERYONE KNEW I LIKED TO DRAW, AND HAD SEEN THE DRAWINGS OF MY FELLOW OFFICERS, WHICH I HAD PRESENTED TO CAPTAIN O'CONNOR UPON HIS ASSUMING COMMAND OF THE 35TH USA MISSILE DETACHMENT.
AFTER A DAY OR TWO, ALBERT ASKED ME FOR A FAVOR.
EXCUSE ME, SIR...
...CAN YOU DRAW A FEW DIRTY PICTURES I CAN PUT UP IN HERE?
HOW DIRTY?
MAKE 'EM AS DIRTY AS YOU WANT...
...SHOW EVERYTHING!
ALTHOUGH I HAD NEVER SEEN A NAKED WOMAN-- ONLY A PICTURE OF ONE IN A MAGAZINE-- I OBTAINED SOME POSTER BOARD FROM SOMEWHERE-- AND A SET OF PASTELS--AND DID THREE DIRTY DRAWINGS.
THE DIRTIER I MAKE IT, THE MORE THEY'LL LIKE IT...

THAT EVENING, WHEN I STOPPED IN FOR A BEER, ALBERT HAD THEM HANGING ON THE "WALLS" OF THE TENT.
MY FIRST ART EXHIBIT!
POLK
USARMY
I WOULDN'T EXACTLY SAY THEY CAUSED A "SENSATION" AMONG MY FELLOW OFFICERS. AND, TO MY GREAT DISAPPOINTMENT, NO ONE EVEN SAID A WORD.
BUT, BY THE FOLLOWING DAY, THEY HAD ALL MYSTERIOUSLY DISAPPEARED.
I DON'T GET IT... WHERE ARE MY DRAWINGS?
WHEN I ASKED ALBERT WHERE THEY WERE, HE SEEMED TO SUGGEST THEY HAD BEEN STOLEN!
SIR, ALL I KNOW IS WHEN I GOT HERE TODAY THEY WERE ALL GONE!
PARKER
USARMY
BUT... WHO WOULD HAVE DONE SUCH A THING??
I FEIGNED OUTRAGE AT THE VERY IDEA!
BUT, SIR-- DON'T YOU REALIZE...
...THAT'S THE ULTIMATE COMPLIMENT TO AN ARTIST!
I THOUGHT IT FAR MORE LIKELY THAT CAPTAIN O'CONNOR, AN IRISH-CATHOLIC FROM BOSTON, HAD FOUND THEM TO BE IN VERY POOR TASTE, AND HAD ORDERED THEM DESTROYED.
BOTTOMS UP!
SKETCHBOOK
BOTTOMS
USARMY
I DECIDED IT MIGHT BE BEST TO ACCEPT THE COMPLIMENT.

MAY 7, 1968. A TUESDAY. I WAS 21 YEARS OLD AND STATIONED AT DONA ANA RANGE CAMP, A REMOTE PART OF WHITE SANDS MISSILE RANGE IN NEW MEXICO, ABOUT 90 MILES NORTH OF EL PASO.
I HAD ONLY BEEN THERE FOR A COUPLE OF WEEKS.
A FEW JUNIOR OFFICERS DECIDED TO TAKE THE ARMY BUS TO THE OFFICER'S CLUB IN NEARBY LAS CRUCES. I TAGGED ALONG.
I MIGHT AS WELL GO...
TONIGHT I'M GONNA SCORE!
YEAH, ME TOO!
I DON'T REALLY KNOW ANY OF THESE GUYS...
US ARMY
MAYBE I SHOULD HAVE STAYED IN THE HUT...
DECKED OUT IN MY BEST "CIVVIES," I SAUNTERED UP TO THE BAR--AND ORDERED MYSELF A JACK DANIEL'S ON THE ROCKS -- AND SAT THERE DRINKING IT WHILE TRYING TO LOOK "COOL."
WHAT AM I EVEN DOING HERE?
OF COURSE, NO ONE NOTICED ME, OR PAID ME THE SLIGHTEST ATTENTION.

AS I SLUMPED BACK INTO MY SEAT FOR THE SHORT TRIP BACK TO THE CAMP, I FELT A **HUGE** SENSE OF **RELIEF** WASH OVER ME.
THE PRESSURE TO "**SCORE**" WAS OFF.
ON MY WAY BACK TO THE QUONSET HUT, A WOMAN SITTING BEHIND THE WHEEL OF A CAR SORT OF BECKONED TO ME...
EXCUSE ME--! CAN I ASK YOU SOMETHING?
HMM... I WONDER WHAT **SHE** WANTS?
DO YOU KNOW WHERE LIEUTENANT **BOSTWICK** IS?
IN FACT, I **DID**.
LIEUTENANT BOSTWICK HAS **BEEN** CONFINED TO QUARTERS...
...HE'S BEING PUNISHED FOR BRINGING HIS **P.O.V.** TO EL PASO AND **HIDING** IT THERE.
JUNIOR OFFICERS AREN'T **ALLOWED** TO HAVE VEHICLES HERE.
OH, I **SEE.**
...UM...
WHY DON'T YOU GET IN...?
I **WANTED** TO... BUT I WORRIED LIEUTENANT BOSTWICK WOULD BE **MAD** AT ME.

BUT... IT DOES GET COLD IN THE DESERT AT NIGHT...
...REALLY REALLY COLD...
...THERE'S NOT MUCH TO HOLD THE HEAT ONCE THE SUN GOES DOWN...
SO... I GOT IN...
"WHEN DO YOU THINK LIEUTENANT BOSTWICK WILL BE RELEASED?"
"I DON'T KNOW. IT COULD BE A WHILE."
"I SEE..." I'M PANDY... WHAT DID YOU SAY YOUR NAME WAS?"
"UMM...
DICK..."
WE CHATTED FOR A LITTLE WHILE ABOUT I DON'T REMEMBER WHAT
ALL I COULD THINK ABOUT--
SOK
--WAS WHAT LIEUTENANT BOSTWICK MIGHT DO TO ME
--IF HE EVER FOUND OUT ABOUT THIS!
... I WAS SO NERVOUS, I COULDN'T RECALL WHAT PLAYBOY SAID I WAS SUPPOSED TO DO NEXT...
AFTER A FEW MINUTES, PANDY TOLD ME SHE HAD TO GO.

THE FOLLOWING EVENING, THE C.Q.* CAME TO GET ME...
LIEUTENANT PARKER-- EXCUSE ME, BUT THERE'S A WOMAN HERE TO SEE YOU, SIR...
KNOK KNOK
?
*CHARGE OF QUARTERS
HI! WANT TO GO FOR A RIDE?
I COULDN'T BELIEVE SHE WAS BACK...
...AND TO SEE ME!
WHY DON'T WE DRIVE INTO EL PASO AND SEE A MOVIE?
A COUPLE OF MY MEN WERE OUT BY THE ROAD ON POLICE CALL.
WHAT'S THE STORY WITH LIEUTENANT PARKER?
?
YEAH... LIKE, WHAT'S HE GOT THAT WE DON'T?

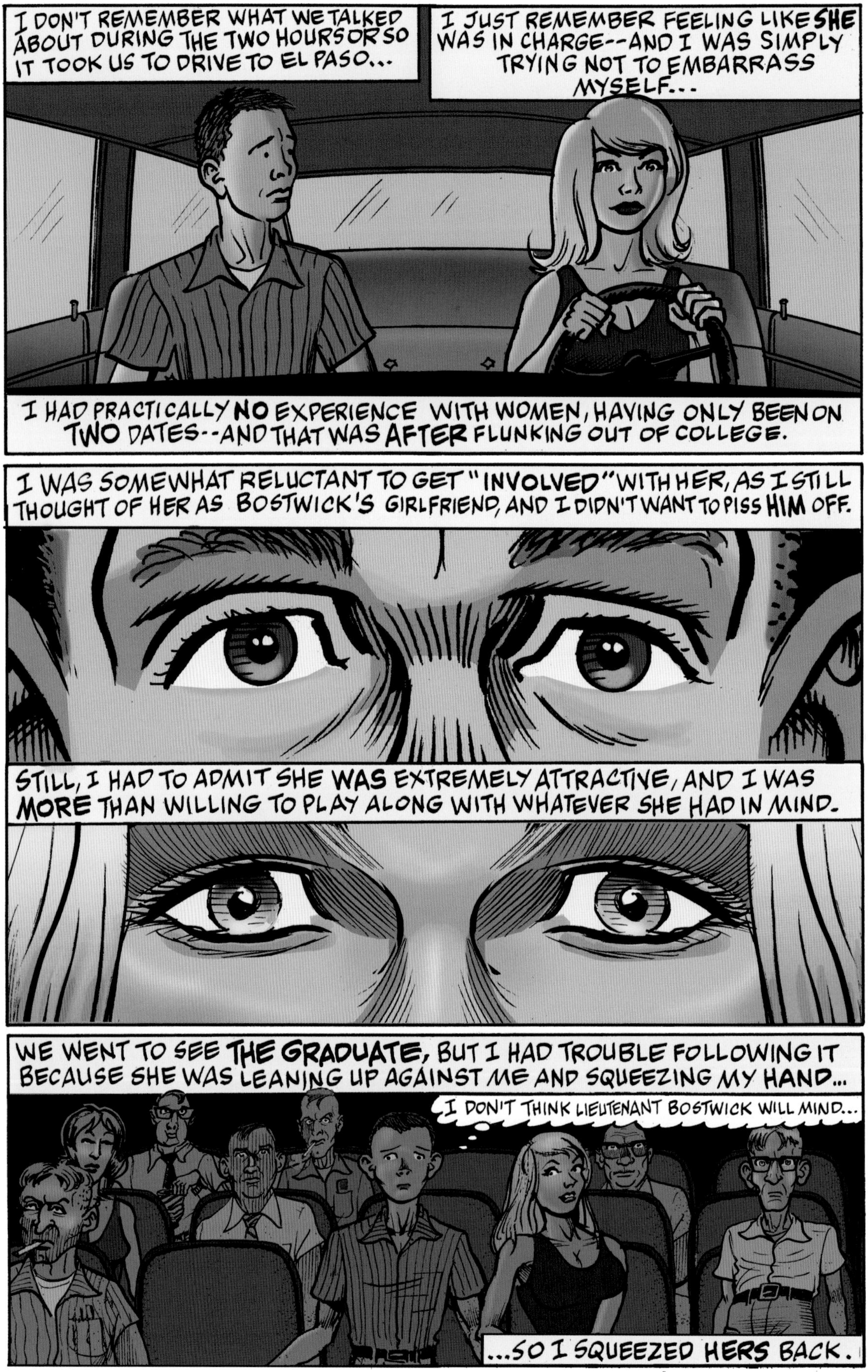
I DON'T REMEMBER WHAT WE TALKED ABOUT DURING THE TWO HOURS OR SO IT TOOK US TO DRIVE TO EL PASO...
I JUST REMEMBER FEELING LIKE SHE WAS IN CHARGE--AND I WAS SIMPLY TRYING NOT TO EMBARRASS MYSELF...
I HAD PRACTICALLY NO EXPERIENCE WITH WOMEN, HAVING ONLY BEEN ON TWO DATES--AND THAT WAS AFTER FLUNKING OUT OF COLLEGE.
I WAS SOMEWHAT RELUCTANT TO GET "INVOLVED" WITH HER, AS I STILL THOUGHT OF HER AS BOSTWICK'S GIRLFRIEND, AND I DIDN'T WANT TO PISS HIM OFF.
STILL, I HAD TO ADMIT SHE WAS EXTREMELY ATTRACTIVE, AND I WAS MORE THAN WILLING TO PLAY ALONG WITH WHATEVER SHE HAD IN MIND.
WE WENT TO SEE THE GRADUATE, BUT I HAD TROUBLE FOLLOWING IT BECAUSE SHE WAS LEANING UP AGAINST ME AND SQUEEZING MY HAND...
I DON'T THINK LIEUTENANT BOSTWICK WILL MIND...
...SO I SQUEEZED HERS BACK.

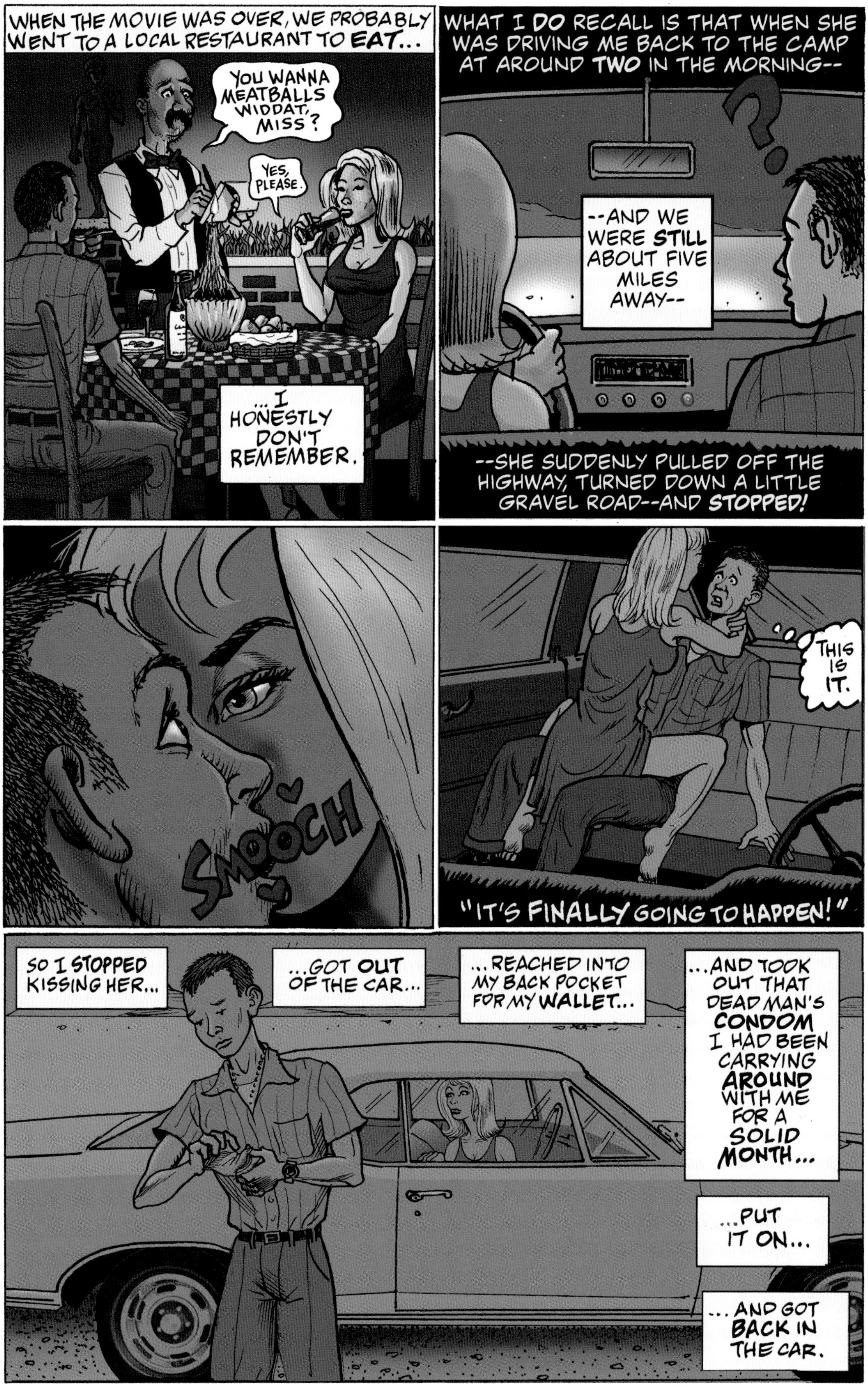
WHEN THE MOVIE WAS OVER, WE PROBABLY WENT TO A LOCAL RESTAURANT TO EAT...
YOU WANNA MEATBALLS WIDDAT, MISS?
YES, PLEASE.
...I HONESTLY DON'T REMEMBER.
WHAT I DO RECALL IS THAT WHEN SHE WAS DRIVING ME BACK TO THE CAMP AT AROUND TWO IN THE MORNING--
?
--AND WE WERE STILL ABOUT FIVE MILES AWAY--
--SHE SUDDENLY PULLED OFF THE HIGHWAY, TURNED DOWN A LITTLE GRAVEL ROAD--AND STOPPED!
SMOOCH
THIS IS IT.
"IT'S FINALLY GOING TO HAPPEN!"
SO I STOPPED KISSING HER...
...GOT OUT OF THE CAR...
...REACHED INTO MY BACK POCKET FOR MY WALLET...
...AND TOOK OUT THAT DEAD MAN'S CONDOM I HAD BEEN CARRYING AROUND WITH ME FOR A SOLID MONTH...
...PUT IT ON...
...AND GOT BACK IN THE CAR.

IT WAS THE DAWN OF A NEW DAY.
IT WAS BEGINNING TO GET LIGHT OUT AS SHE DROVE ME BACK TO WITHIN HALF A MILE OF THE CAMP AND LET ME OUT. SHE SMILED AS SHE DROVE AWAY. I GUESS SHE DIDN'T WANT TO TAKE A CHANCE THAT LIEUTENANT BOSTWICK MIGHT SEE US.
I STOOD AND WATCHED--UNTIL SHE WAS OUT OF SIGHT.
I MUST ADMIT--I WAS PRETTY DAMN PLEASED WITH MYSELF. AND SOON I COULD SEE THE THE CAMP OFF IN THE DISTANCE.
FINALLY... IT HAPPENED...
...NOW I AM A MAN!
AS I APPROACHED THE CAMP, I WAS ELATED TO SEE ALL THE MEN STANDING AT ATTENTION ...WHAT AN HONOR! HOW COULD THEY HAVE POSSIBLY KNOWN WHAT JUST OCCURED?
DOOT DOOT DOODALOOT!
JUST THEN, A BUGLE STARTED TO BLARE THROUGH THE LOUDSPEAKER--AND SUDDENLY I REALIZED, AS THE FLAG RAN UP THE POLE, THAT IT WASN'T FOR ME-- IT WAS REVEILLE!

MY BRIEF ROMANCE CAME TO AN ABRUPT END WHEN WE RECEIVED ORDERS TO CONVOY UP TO UTAH TO JOIN FORCES WITH OUR N.A.T.O. ALLIES--THE GERMAN AIR FORCE.
EACH YEAR, "THE GERRIES" RETURNED TO THE DESERT IN UTAH TO PRACTICE TRANSPORTING, ASSEMBLING, AND FIRING THE U.S. ARMY'S ONLY TACTICAL NUCLEAR WEAPON--THE PERSHING MISSILE.
ACCORDING TO THE TERMS OF THE N.A.T.O. AGREEMENT, THE GERMANS WERE ONLY ALLOWED TO HANDLE THE TWO-STAGE PROPELLANT BODY SECTIONS,--WE'D HANDLE THE NUCLEAR WARHEAD.
I GUESS WE STILL DIDN'T TRUST THEM IN LIGHT OF THEIR ILL-FATED ATTEMPT AT WORLD DOMINATION A MERE 25 YEARS EARLIER--
Mochtest du ein bier, Amerikaner?
DONKEY SHANE!
AND AS AN EXTRA PRECAUTION, THE WARHEAD ITSELF WAS FILLED WITH CONCRETE.
RIGHT... 60-65 FOOT POUNDS OF TORQUE.
I GUESS THE ARMY DIDN'T TRUST US, EITHER!

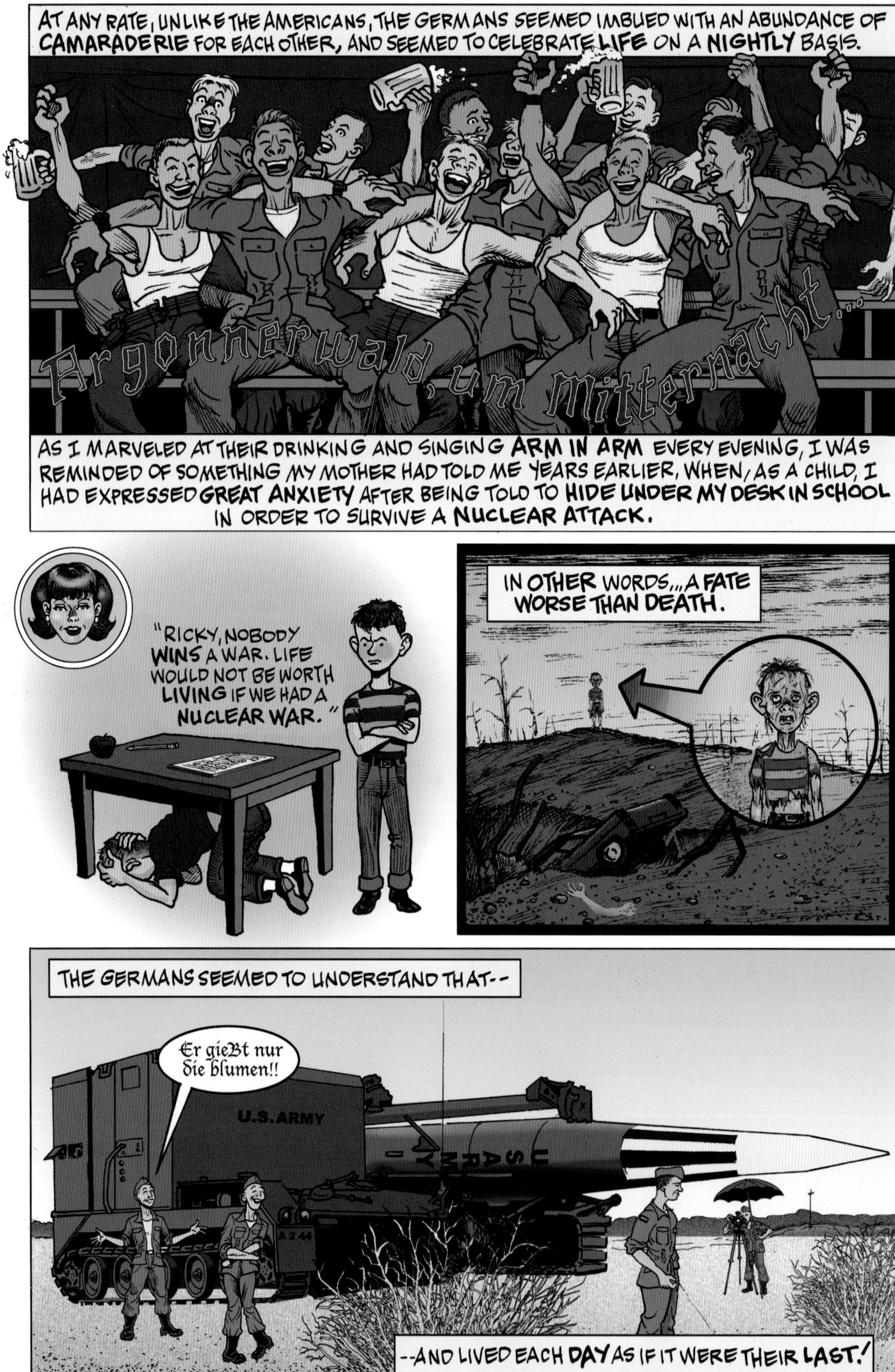
AT ANY RATE, UNLIKE THE AMERICANS, THE GERMANS SEEMED IMBUED WITH AN ABUNDANCE OF CAMARADERIE FOR EACH OTHER, AND SEEMED TO CELEBRATE LIFE ON A NIGHTLY BASIS.
Argonnerwald, um Mitternacht...
AS I MARVELED AT THEIR DRINKING AND SINGING ARM IN ARM EVERY EVENING, I WAS REMINDED OF SOMETHING MY MOTHER HAD TOLD ME YEARS EARLIER, WHEN, AS A CHILD, I HAD EXPRESSED GREAT ANXIETY AFTER BEING TOLD TO HIDE UNDER MY DESK IN SCHOOL IN ORDER TO SURVIVE A NUCLEAR ATTACK.
"RICKY, NOBODY WINS A WAR. LIFE WOULD NOT BE WORTH LIVING IF WE HAD A NUCLEAR WAR."
IN OTHER WORDS,,, A FATE WORSE THAN DEATH.
THE GERMANS SEEMED TO UNDERSTAND THAT--
Er gießt nur die blumen!!
U.S. ARMY
U.S ARMY
A 244
--AND LIVED EACH DAY AS IF IT WERE THEIR LAST!

ONE HOT JULY MORNING, CAPTAIN STARK AND I WERE DRIVEN OUT TO THE LAUNCH SITE. AFTER THE CAPTAIN GOT OUT, I ISSUED SOME INSTRUCTIONS TO THE DRIVER.
COME BACK LATER AND PICK ME UP.
!
WHOA! WHOA! WHOA!
WHAT DO YOU MEAN, "WHOA WHOA WHOA"?
!
LIEUTENANT... THIS IS MY JEEP-- AND MY DRIVER--AND HE TAKES ORDERS FROM ME!
IT WAS MORE OF A REQUEST, ACTUALLY...
I WILL SEE YOU LATER, LIEUTENANT.
I THOUGHT IT WAS "OUR" JEEP.
SO... HAVING BEEN GIVEN NO SPECIFIC RESPONSIBILITIES AT THAT PARTICULAR MOMENT, I DECIDED TO GO OVER TO THE COMMO VAN TO CLEAR MY HEAD AND GET OUT OF THE HOT SUN.

AS I SAT IDLY IN THE BACK OF THE OPEN VAN, MY GAZE FELL UPON AN OPEN WINDOW ON THE SIDE OF THE VAN.
ON THE WIRE MESH OF THE WINDOW SCREEN WERE DOZENS OF DRIED AMBER DROPLETS. I'D NEVER SEEN ANYTHING LIKE IT. I COULD NOT FIGURE OUT WHAT IT WAS...
I TOUCHED ONE WITH MY FINGER...
THEN MY WANDERING EYES CAME TO REST ON THE INSIDE SURFACES OF THE OPEN DOORS OF THE VAN. THERE WERE THOUSANDS OF TINY BROWN DOTS. SUDDENLY, I GOT A SICKENING FEELING IN THE PIT OF MY STOMACH AS I REALIZED WHAT I WAS LOOKING AT.
THE DROPLETS AND TINY BROWN SPOTS WERE NOW ALL THAT REMAINED OF PFC. KENNET, WHO HAD BEEN CRUSHED BETWEEN THE PARTS TRAILER AND THE VAN I WAS SITTING IN FOUR MONTHS EARLIER.
THE NEXT DAY CAPTAIN STARK HAD ME SENT BACK TO FORT SILL.
Cpt. Robert S. Stark
2nd Battalion 34th Artillery
35th U.S.A. Missile Detachment
Gilson Butte, Utah
July 12, 1968
To: Lt. Richard L. Parker
05463386
You are hereby ordered to return to
HQ Battery 2/34th Arty
Fort Sill, Oklahoma
NLT 0600 7/15/68
Robert S. Stark
Cpt. Robert S. Stark
Commanding
WOMMMMMM...

VROMMM
52
US ARMY
52
I NEVER EVEN GOT TO SEE THEM FIRE THE MISSILES!

BEING BACK--AND BEING THE HIGHEST-RANKING OFFICER--MEANT I WAS ACTING BATTERY COMMANDER. IT WAS GOOD FOR MY EGO, NEVER MIND THAT 90% OF THE BATTERY WAS STILL OUT IN THE DESERT FIRING MISSILES.
AFTERNOON, SIR!
CARRY ON, PRIVATE-- I'LL BE IN THE AREA ALL DAY.
I HAD NOWHERE ELSE TO BE.
SERGEANT MYERS PRETTY MUCH RAN THINGS ANYWAY.
WILSON-- GET ME ANOTHER CUP O' COFFEE...
SURE THING, TOP!
MYERS
US ARMY
TOP
I THINK HE WAS NEARING RETIREMENT.
ONE DAY, HE SENT ONE OF THE MEN TO SEE ME... AS A JOKE I GUESS.
SIR, YOU GOTTA HELP ME! THEY KEEP PUTTING CATS IN MY DUFFEL BAG!
AN' THERE'S AN ELEPHANT TRAPPED IN MY FOOTLOCKER!
I CAN'T G-GET HIM OUT--!
P-PLEASE! H-HELP ME!
??
NO CLUE WHAT TO DO
SOMEONE TOLD ME LATER HE WAS ON "SPEED."

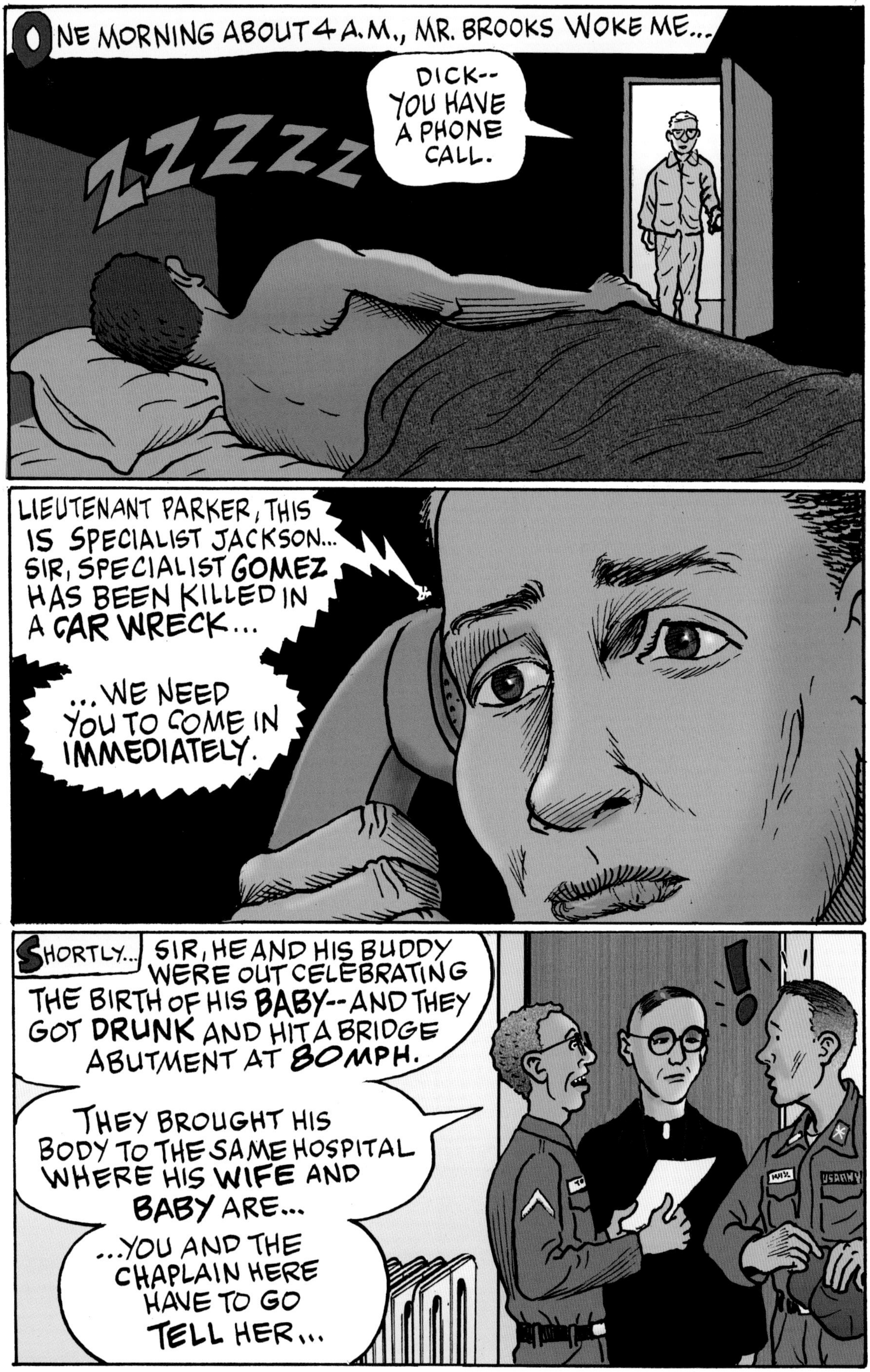
One morning about 4 A.M., Mr. Brooks woke me...
DICK-- YOU HAVE A PHONE CALL.
ZZZZZZ
LIEUTENANT PARKER, THIS IS SPECIALIST JACKSON... SIR, SPECIALIST GOMEZ HAS BEEN KILLED IN A CAR WRECK...
...WE NEED YOU TO COME IN IMMEDIATELY.
Shortly...
SIR, HE AND HIS BUDDY WERE OUT CELEBRATING THE BIRTH OF HIS BABY--AND THEY GOT DRUNK AND HIT A BRIDGE ABUTMENT AT 80MPH.
THEY BROUGHT HIS BODY TO THE SAME HOSPITAL WHERE HIS WIFE AND BABY ARE...
...YOU AND THE CHAPLAIN HERE HAVE TO GO TELL HER...
!

FORTUNATELY, CAPTAIN STARK ARRIVED BACK THAT VERY MORNING.
CLERK-- GET US SOME COFFEE!
YES, SIR!
THANK GOD.
LATER, CAPTAIN STARK ORDERED ME TO THE WRECKING YARD TO WRITE UP AN ACCIDENT REPORT.
OH, MAN...
IT WAS HARD TO BELIEVE THIS WAS THE SAME VEHICLE IN WHICH GOMEZ HAD STOPPED TO GIVE ME A RIDE BACK FROM THE MOTOR POOL ONLY A WEEK BEFORE.
HOP IN, SIR!
SWEET...
GASP
SUFFICE IT TO SAY THAT WHEN I TOOK A LOOK INSIDE THE VEHICLE, I SAW THINGS THE LIKES OF WHICH I HAD NEVER SEEN BEFORE...
...AND WHICH I HOPE TO GOD I NEVER SEE AGAIN.
THOSE POOR GUYS.

ONE FINE AUTUMN DAY, THE CAPTAIN PUT ME IN CHARGE OF SUPERVISING THE ROUTINE MAINTENANCE OF THE VEHICLES IN THE MOTOR POOL.
TO ASSIST ME IN THAT CAPACITY, I WAS ASSIGNED A YOUNG SERGEANT WHOM I DID NOT KNOW. SERGEANT CONRAD SMOKED A PIPE, CARRIED A CLIPBOARD, AND HIS UNIFORM WAS STARCHED AND PRESSED AND HIS BOOTS WELL-POLISHED.
AFTERNOON, SIR!
AFTERNOON, SERGEANT!
CONRAD
US ARMY
I WAS HOPING HE KNEW WHAT HE WAS DOING. I KNEW I CERTAINLY DIDN'T.
I'VE NEVER REALLY DONE THIS BEFORE.
NO SWEAT, SIR. THERE'S NOTHIN' TO IT.
THEY JUST CHECK THE OIL AND THE TIRE PRESSURE, AN' WIPE TH' VEHICLES DOWN WITH AN OILY RAG.
PARKER
US ARMY
CONRAD
US ARMY

WE JUST WALKED UP AND DOWN THE LINE AS THE MEN WORKED! BUT EVERY TIME WE PASSED THIS ONE DEUCE-AND-A-HALF, PRIVATE EPPS CHECKED THE FUNCTIONALITY OF THE HORN.
BEEEEEEP!
I'LL ADMIT, IT WAS FUNNY, IF A BIT JARRING, THE FIRST TIME HE DID IT...
...BUT THEN, TEN MINUTES LATER, WHEN WE PASSED IN FRONT OF HIS TRUCK AND HE BLEW THE HORN AGAIN, SERGEANT CONRAD HAD HEARD ENOUGH.
EPPS-- GET DOWN HERE!
GET YOUR SMART ASS BACK TO THE BARRACKS!
AND START CLEANIN' TH' LATRINE!
WHY YOU ALWAYS GOTTA BE TELLIN' ME WHAT TO DO?

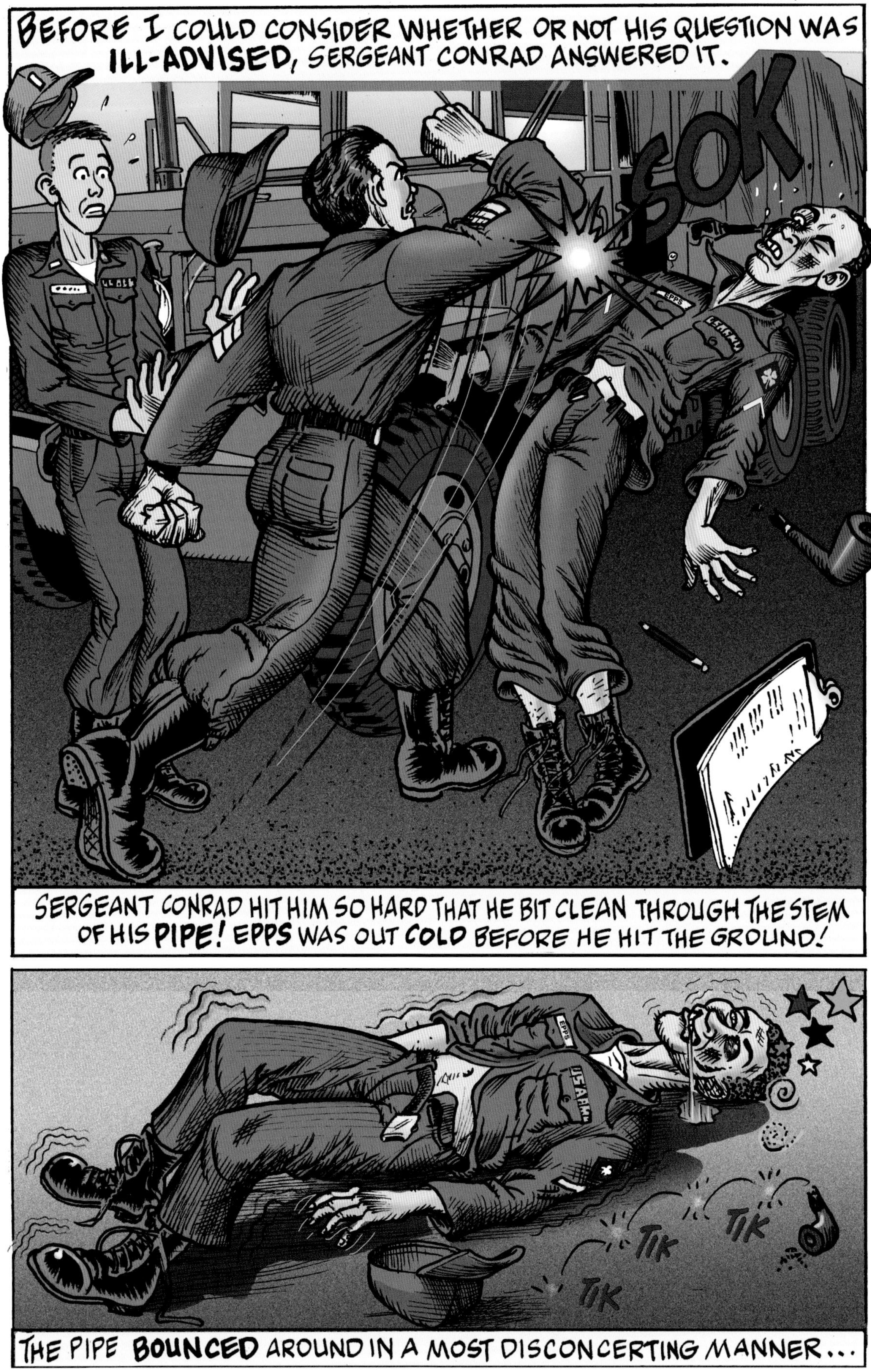
BEFORE I COULD CONSIDER WHETHER OR NOT HIS QUESTION WAS **ILL-ADVISED**, SERGEANT CONRAD ANSWERED IT.
SOK
EPPS
SERGEANT CONRAD HIT HIM SO HARD THAT HE BIT CLEAN THROUGH THE STEM OF HIS **PIPE! EPPS** WAS OUT **COLD** BEFORE HE HIT THE GROUND!
EPPS
TIK
TIK
TIK
THE PIPE **BOUNCED** AROUND IN A MOST DISCONCERTING MANNER...

THEN, SUDDENLY, EPPS STOPPED BREATHING!
USARMY
EPPS
...AND HIS LIPS TURNED BLUE.
LIEUTENANT PARKER...!
...DO SOMETHING!
CONRAD
USARMY
PARKER
USARMY
"DO SOMETHING"?
"DO SOMETHING"...?
WHAT WAS I SUPPOSED TO DO?
WHEN SERGEANT CONRAD REALIZED THAT I WAS TOTALLY AT A LOSS AS TO WHAT TO DO... HE DROPPED TO HIS KNEES AND BEGAN MOUTH-TO-MOUTH RESUSCITATION.
PUFF PUFF

EPPS...
KOFF
GASP
...EPPS... ARE YOU ALL RIGHT?
WH-WHAT HAPPENED?
I HAD BEEN A BOY SCOUT-- I'D TAKEN R.O.T.C. IN HIGH SCHOOL, EVEN TAUGHT FIRST AID CLASSES--BUT WHEN FACED WITH A LIFE-OR-DEATH SITUATION, I FROZE LIKE A DEER IN THE HEADLIGHTS...
THANK GOD HE'S ALIVE-- NO THANKS TO ME.
IF I HARBORED ANY LINGERING THOUGHTS ABOUT STAYING IN THE ARMY, THIS INCIDENT PRETTY MUCH KILLED THEM.

6

GETTING SHORT

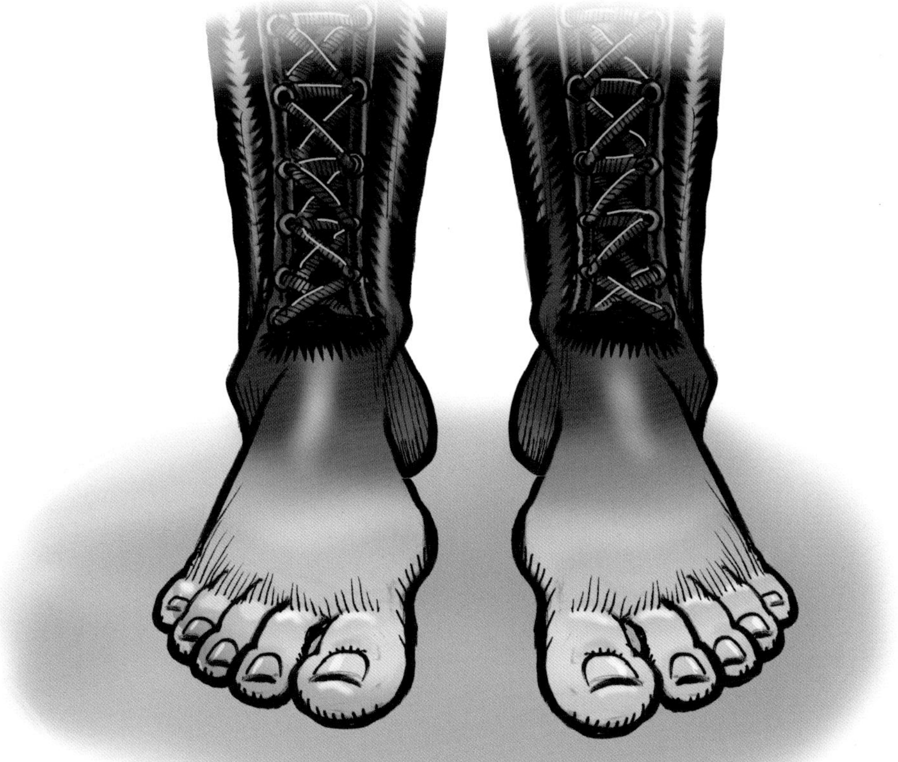

TIME PASSED AND I WAS GETTING "SHORT"-- I ONLY HAD A FEW MONTHS LEFT TO SERVE WHEN I WAS INFORMED BY THE BATTERY CLERK THAT--
OH, SIR--! THE COLONEL WANTS TO SEE YOU...
KLAK-KLAK-KLAKETY KLAK KLAK
? ?
I COULD NOT IMAGINE WHY COLONEL DOYLE WOULD POSSIBLY WANT TO SEE A LOW-RANKING, CLUELESS YOUNG LIEUTENANT LIKE ME.
THAT SINKING FEELING
SO I NERVOUSLY WALKED OVER TO BATTALION HQ, WORRIED THAT SOMEHOW I HAD DONE SOMETHING TERRIBLY WRONG.
THAT SEEMED UNLIKELY SINCE CAPTAIN STARK--THE REAL BATTERY COMMANDER--WAS BACK FROM UTAH, AND I DIDN'T HAVE MUCH RESPONSIBILITY AT ALL....
...AND THEN I REMEMBERED HE HAD APPOINTED ME CBR (CHEMICAL-BIOLOGICAL-RADIOLOGICAL) OFFICER--
--AND RECENTLY, I HAD LED AN ACTUAL FIELD TRAINING EXERCISE INVOLVING THE M-17 GAS MASK.
MAYBE IT HAS TO DO WITH THAT...

AFTER A GOOD BIT OF INSTRUCTION, I HAD THE MEN PUT ON THEIR GAS MASKS AND THEN GO INSIDE A **BIG** ROOM IN A **SMALL** WINDOWLESS BUILDING.

ANY QUESTIONS...?
CBR BUILDING
GOOD!
THEN LET'S GO!

I HAD THEM WALK AROUND WHILE MY **SERGEANT** SET OFF A **TEAR GAS** GRENADE.

OKAY... REMOVE YOUR MASKS!

THE POINT OF THE EXERCISE WAS TO CONVINCE THEM ALL THAT THE GAS MASKS **WORKED**.

I TOOK OFF MY MASK TOO--
--TO SHOW THEM I WASN'T A "WUSS."
GASP
SPUTTER
KOFF
GAK
KOFF
AFTER A MINUTE OR TWO, DURING WHICH WE COULD BARELY SEE OR BREATHE -- I LET THEM RUN OUT INTO THE COOL, BLUE OKLAHOMA AIR TO RECOVER.
MAYBE IT HAD SOMETHING TO DO WITH THAT...

BATTALION HQ WAS A SMALL BRICK BUILDING A SHORT WALK FROM BATTERY HQ.
UPON ENTERING, I WAS GREETED BY THE COLONEL'S CLERK.
GOOD AFTERNOON, SIR.
GOOD AFTERNOON, PRIVATE.
LIEUTENANT PARKER...
...I WAS TOLD THE COLONEL WANTED TO SEE ME.
OH, YES...
...LIEUTENANT PARKER...
...PLEASE FOLLOW ME, SIR.
HE LOOKED A BIT WORRIED-- AND SEEMED TO KNOW WHY I WAS THERE.
THE COLONEL'S DOOR WAS OPEN, BUT I KNOCKED FIRMLY ON IT TWICE...
KNOCK KNOCK
COME IN, LIEUTENANT PARKER.

LIEUTENANT PARKER REPORTING AS ORDERED, SIR.
AT EASE, LIEUTENANT.
RICHARD T. DOYLE
I SEE HERE THAT YOUR E.T.S. IS APPROACHING, AND I WOULD LIKE TO KNOW WHAT YOUR INTENTIONS ARE IN TERMS OF THE SERVICE.
OH--! WHAT A RELIEF!
HAVING HAD AMPLE OPPORTUNITY TO DISCERN THAT I WAS NOT CUT OUT FOR A CAREER IN THE MILITARY, I SPOKE RIGHT UP.
WELL, SIR...
I WOULD LIKE TO GO BACK TO COLLEGE AND FINISH MY EDUCATION...
...SIR!
VERY WELL, LIEUTENANT.
THAT IS ALL.
THANK YOU, SIR.
I SALUTED, TOOK A STEP BACK, DID AN ABOUT-FACE, AND WALKED OVER TO BATTERY HQ.
FRANKLY, MY FEELINGS WERE A LITTLE HURT THAT HE DIDN'T TRY TO TALK ME OUT OF IT.

THE VERY NEXT DAY I WAS RELIEVED OF MY RESPONSIBILITIES WITH RESPECT TO ALPHA BATTERY (SUCH AS THEY WERE) AND PUT IN CHARGE OF THE POST FLAG DETAIL FOR THE ENTIRE MONTH OF OCTOBER.
FLAG DETAIL, EH...?
DON'T SWEAT IT...
...THERE'S NOTHIN' TO IT.
IT'S LIKE YOUR GRANNY'S WASHIN'--IT GOES UP THE LINE IN THE MORNIN'--AN' YOU TAKE IT DOWN IN THE AFTERNOON!
PARK
IN
OUT
AT THE SUGGESTION OF THE FIRST SERGEANT, I HAND-PICKED AN ENLISTED MAN TO ASSIST ME.
WHY DON'T YOU GET SERGEANT BELL?
MYERS
YOU WANTED TO SEE ME, SIR?
AT EASE.
BELL
U.S. ARMY
BUCK SERGEANT ROGER T. BELL HAD BEEN ON THE HONOR GUARD AT THE TOMB OF THE UNKNOWN SOLDIER IN ARLINGTON NATIONAL CEMETERY.
THAT WAS ENOUGH TO CONVINCE ME!
HE STOOD ABOUT 6' 4" AND WAS THIN AS A RAIL.

WITH SERGEANT BELL'S HELP, I SELECTED FOUR OR FIVE ENLISTED MEN FROM THE RANKS AND SPENT A WEEK TRAINING THEM IN D&C (DRILL AND CEREMONIES).
SOON.
FOH-WUDDDD... HARCH!
BELL AND I VISITED POST HQ AT 6 A.M. AND 5 P.M. FOR SEVERAL DAYS TO OBSERVE.
SO THAT'S HOW IT'S DONE...

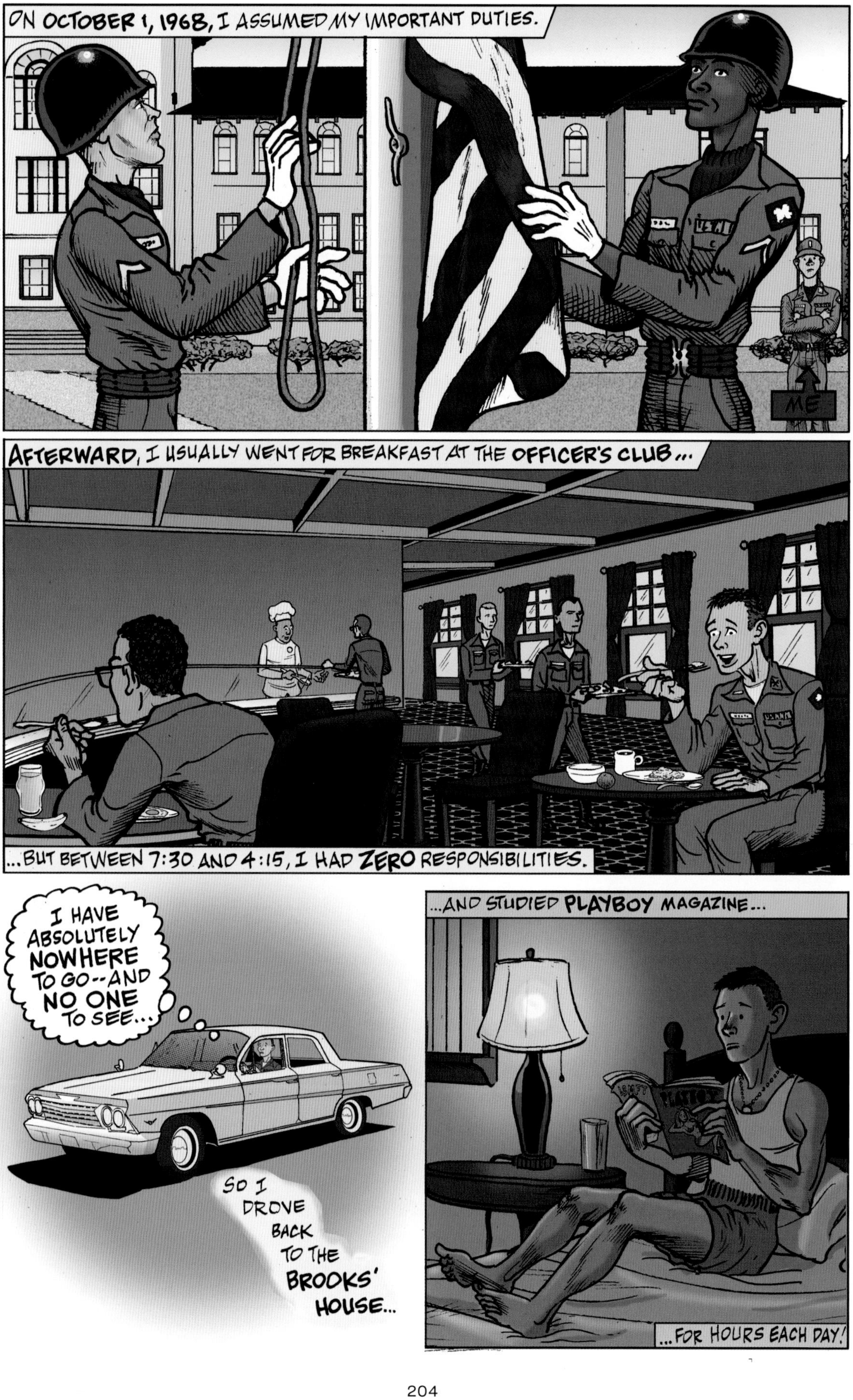
ON OCTOBER 1, 1968, I ASSUMED MY IMPORTANT DUTIES.
ME
AFTERWARD, I USUALLY WENT FOR BREAKFAST AT THE OFFICER'S CLUB...
...BUT BETWEEN 7:30 AND 4:15, I HAD ZERO RESPONSIBILITIES.
I HAVE ABSOLUTELY NOWHERE TO GO--AND NO ONE TO SEE...
SO I DROVE BACK TO THE BROOKS' HOUSE...
...AND STUDIED PLAYBOY MAGAZINE...
PLAYBOY
...FOR HOURS EACH DAY!

AND THEN ONE DAY, I WAS SURPRISED TO DISCOVER THAT WE HAD BEEN BEING RATED BY THE POST COMMANDANT'S ADJUTANT.
" OUTSTANDING..."
7 October 1968
44th Artillery
.....Outstanding
.....Outstanding
.....Outstanding
.....Outstanding
.....Outstanding
.....Outstanding
I LIKE THAT!
Howard T. Hasslebrouck
Howard. T. Hasslebrouck , Majo
Adjutant
SO--I DRILLED THEM EVEN HARDER!
BUT THE FOLLOWING WEEK I WAS OUTRAGED WHEN I NOTED THAT WE HAD BEEN RATED ONLY "EXCELLENT" ON TWO OF THE SEVEN DAYS!
I CANNOT LET THIS STAND!
???
U.S.ARMY
SO I PAID A LITTLE VISIT TO POST HEADQUARTERS.
"EXCELLENT"--?! @★#@!
CAN'T LEAVE WELL ENOUGH ALONE

MORNING, SIR!
YES...? WHAT IS IT, LIEUTENANT?
IT'S ABOUT THE FLAG DETAIL, SIR...
SIR... YOU GAVE US AN "EXCELLENT" INSTEAD OF AN "OUTSTANDING" ON OCTOBER TWELTH AND THIRTEENTH...
YES... SO?
SIR... I SUPERVISED THOSE OPERATIONS--AND I KNOW WE DESERVED AN OUTSTANDING.
LIEUTENANT, ARE YOU ACTUALLY QUESTIONING MY JUDGMENT?
GET OUT OF HERE!
GEEZ! WHAT A GROUCH!
I GUESS HE JUST REALLY DIDN'T WANT TO DISCUSS IT.
NOT CUT OUT FOR A CAREER IN THE ARMY

THE FOLLOWING MONDAY I WAS ORDERED TO REPORT TO POST HEADQUARTERS FOR A BRIEFING...
LIEUTENANT PARKER...
...THE C.O. HAS ANOTHER SHIT DETAIL FOR YA.
THIS WOULD BE THE FIRST OF 13 MILITARY FUNERALS I WOULD BE IN CHARGE OF-- AND THE MOST MEMORABLE.
WE'RE GOING TO POST HEADQUARTERS.
YES, SIR.
SOON...
...THE MILITARY FUNERAL WILL BE FOR PFC. DONALD L. HIGGINS. HE WAS KILLED IN VIETNAM. YOU WILL PRESENT THE FLAG TO HIS NEXT-OF-KIN...
...HIS DAUGHTER...
...A FOUR-YEAR-OLD GIRL.
GULP

I HAD A WHOLE WEEK TO GET A DETAIL TOGETHER AND TRAIN THEM.
I SUGGEST YOU MAKE BELL YOUR HEAD N.C.O.
HE USED TO BE A SENTINEL WITH THE OL' GUARD.
HE TOLD ME THAT A MONTH AGO!
THAT'S THE UNIT THAT GUARDS THE TOMB OF THE UNKNOWN SOLDIER. HE'LL TRAIN YOUR MEN FOR YOU.
THEN WHAT DO I DO?
SERGEANT BELL AND I HAND-PICKED SPEC 4 ARCHIE D. SHEPHERD OF LITTLE ROCK, ARKANSAS, TO BE THE SENIOR PALL BEARER. ONCE WE ARRIVED AT THE CEMETERY, IT WOULD BE HIS JOB AND THAT OF FIVE OTHERS TO CARRY THE BODY OF PFC. HIGGINS FROM THE HEARSE TO THE GRAVE.
OH, SHEPHERD...
STAY IN STEP!
THEY HAVE TO BE PERFECT!
SERGEANT BELL AND I DRILLED THEM ALL DAY FOR A SOLID WEEK.
HE AND I ALSO ASSEMBLED A SEVEN-MAN FIRING PARTY.
KLIK
KLIK
KLIK
KLIK
KLIK
KLIK
KLIK
EACH MAN WOULD FIRE THREE VOLLEYS OF BLANKS FOR THE 21-GUN SALUTE.

AFTER A WEEK OF PRACTICE, WE BOARDED A GREYHOUND FOR FORT KENT, TEXAS, AT 5 A.M. ON A COLD NOVEMBER MORNING...
FORT KENT
1966
GREYHOUND
SCENICRUISER
...IT WAS STILL DARK OUTSIDE.
SOLEMNLY LOST IN OUR OWN THOUGHTS, WE SPOKE NOT A WORD. MOST JUST TRIED TO GO BACK TO SLEEP.
AS THE SUN WAS COMING UP OVER WICHITA FALLS, SOMEONE IN THE BACK TURNED ON A SMALL TRANSISTOR RADIO.
GREYHOUND
GREYHOUND
HEY JUDE...

WE ARRIVED AT THE FUNERAL HOME AND THE FUNERAL DIRECTOR ASKED TO SPEAK WITH ME.
ONE OF THE BEREAVED HAS ASKED ME TO OPEN THE CASKET--BUT IT ARRIVED FROM FORT ORD WITH DIRECTIONS THAT THE BODY WAS NOT "VIEWABLE."
I THINK YOU SHOULD DO WHATEVER THE FAMILY WANTS.
US
US
PARK
?
NO CLUE
PFC. HIGGINS HAD BEEN KILLED IN ACTION IN VIETNAM 33 WEEKS EARLIER.
I LEFT SPECIALIST SHEPHERD IN CHARGE OF THE PALLBEARES AND RE-BOARDED THE BUS TO THE CEMETERY ALONGSIDE THE FIRING PARTY.
ONCE WE ARRIVED AT WALDRING CEMETERY, SERGEANT BELL HAD OVER AN HOUR TO PRACTICE THE 21-GUN SALUTE BEFORE THE FUNERAL PROCESSION ARRIVED.
AIM

FIRE!
KLIK
KLIK
KLIK
KLIK
RENCE
WIL
EACH VOLLEY HAD TO BE IN PERFECT SYNC.

OKAY, PRIVATE HAMPTON-- YOU STAY HIDDEN BEHIND THESE TREES...
DOESN'T HE REALIZE I DO THIS ALL THE TIME?
...AND AS SOON AS THE SOUND FROM THE LAST VOLLEY OF SHOTS HAS FADED AWAY...
YES, SIR. UNDER-STOOD!
...THAT'S WHEN YOU BLOW TAPS.
DAVIS RONNIE 1935-1961
DAVIS MARY 1911-195
DAVIS JOHN 1907-1952
INRI

THE WIND WAS PICKING UP JUST AS THE FUNERAL PROCESSION ARRIVED AND PRIVATE HIGGINS'S FAMILY AND FRIENDS HUDDLED TOGETHER UNDER A LITTLE TENT.
PIRO FUNERAL HOME

SPECIALIST SHEPHERD AND HIS MEN SLOWLY CARRIED THE SILVER CASKET CONTAINING THE REMAINS OF PFC. HIGGINS AND PLACED IT GENTLY ATOP HIS FRESHLY DUG GRAVE.

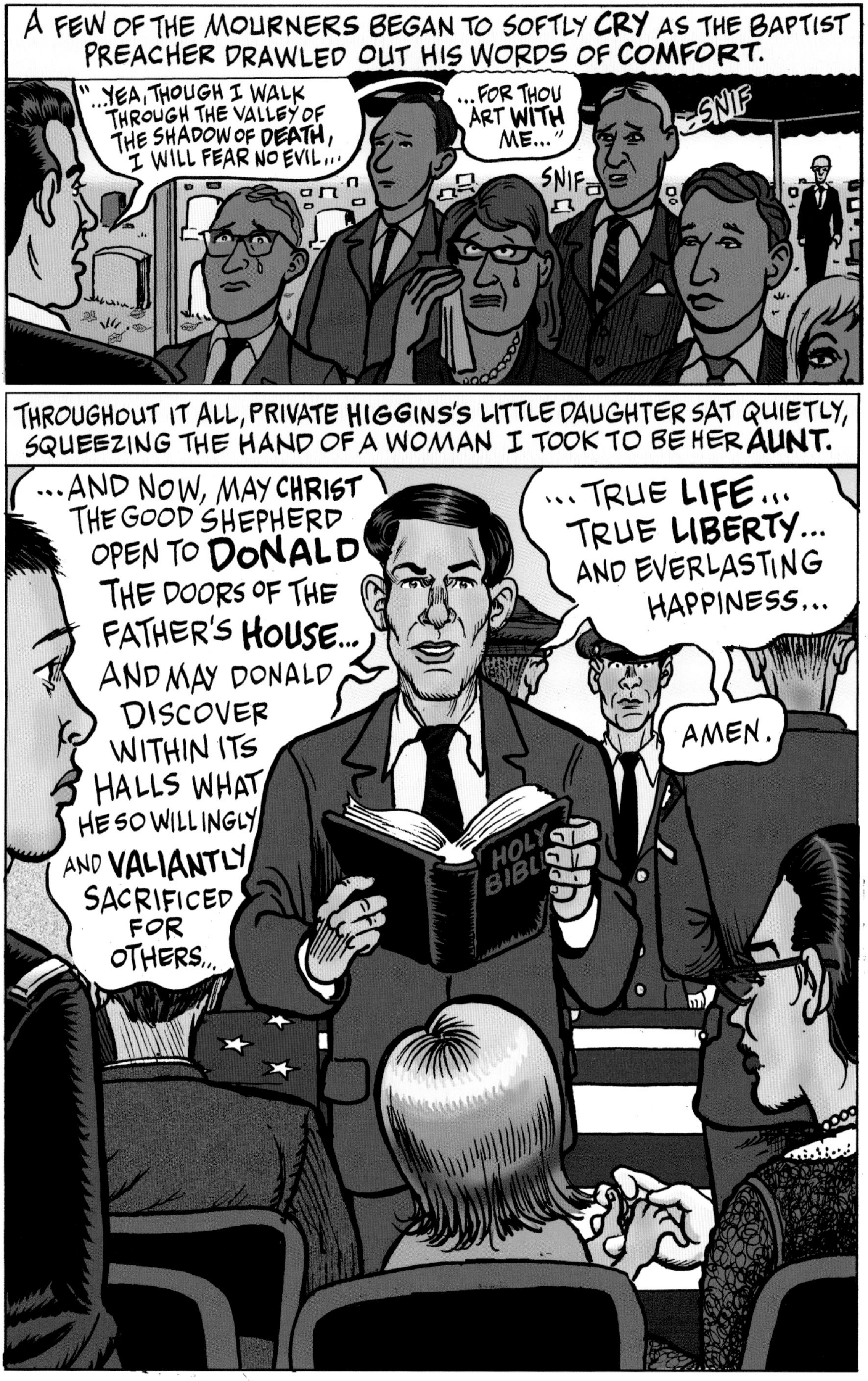
A FEW OF THE MOURNERS BEGAN TO SOFTLY CRY AS THE BAPTIST PREACHER DRAWLED OUT HIS WORDS OF COMFORT.
"...YEA, THOUGH I WALK THROUGH THE VALLEY OF THE SHADOW OF DEATH, I WILL FEAR NO EVIL...
...FOR THOU ART WITH ME..."
SNIF
SNIF
THROUGHOUT IT ALL, PRIVATE HIGGINS'S LITTLE DAUGHTER SAT QUIETLY, SQUEEZING THE HAND OF A WOMAN I TOOK TO BE HER AUNT.
...AND NOW, MAY CHRIST THE GOOD SHEPHERD OPEN TO DONALD THE DOORS OF THE FATHER'S HOUSE... AND MAY DONALD DISCOVER WITHIN ITS HALLS WHAT HE SO WILLINGLY AND VALIANTLY SACRIFICED FOR OTHERS...
...TRUE LIFE... TRUE LIBERTY... AND EVERLASTING HAPPINESS...
AMEN.
HOLY BIBLE

THE PREACHER CLOSED HIS BIBLE WITH A RESOUNDING THUMP AND TOOK ONE STEP BACK. THAT WAS MY SIGNAL TO INITIATE THE 21-GUN SALUTE.
THUMP
WILSON
I NODDED TO SERGEANT BELL.
FIRING PARTY...
UH-TEN-
SHUN!
READY...

... AIM...
CAVI
...FIRE!
KRAK
... AIM...
...FIRE!
KRAK
... AIM...
...FIRE!
KRAK

THE LOUDNESS OF THE SHOTS STARTLED ME -- EVEN THOUGH I KNEW THEY WERE COMING.
PARKER
THEY HAD STARTLED THE PREACHER, ALTHOUGH I WAS SURE HE HAD HEARD IT ALL MANY TIMES BEFORE.
THE SHOTS STARTLED THE CROWD...
... AND THE SHOTS STARTLED PRIVATE HIGGINS'S LITTLE DAUGHTER, WHO HELD ON EVEN TIGHTER TO HER AUNT'S GLOVED HAND.

JUST AS THE LAST VOLLEY OF SHOTS WAS ECHOING INTO THE DISTANCE, PRIVATE HAMPTON BEGAN TO SOFTLY BLOW TAPS ON HIS GOLDEN HORN.
DOOO-DOOO-DOOO-DOOO
THOSE WHO HAD BEEN SOFTLY CRYING BEFORE, NOW BEGAN TO SOB AND WEEP UNCONTROLLABLY.
AND TEARS FILLED THE EYES OF MOST OF THE OTHERS.
SUDDENLY, I FELT A LUMP IN MY OWN THROAT--AND MY VISION BECAME BLURRY.
PARK
I KEPT THINKING, "HE WAS ONLY 20 YEARS OLD--YOUNGER THAN I AM!" AND HIS LIFE IS OVER ALREADY! AND FOR WHAT--? "MOTHERHOOD AND APPLE PIE"?

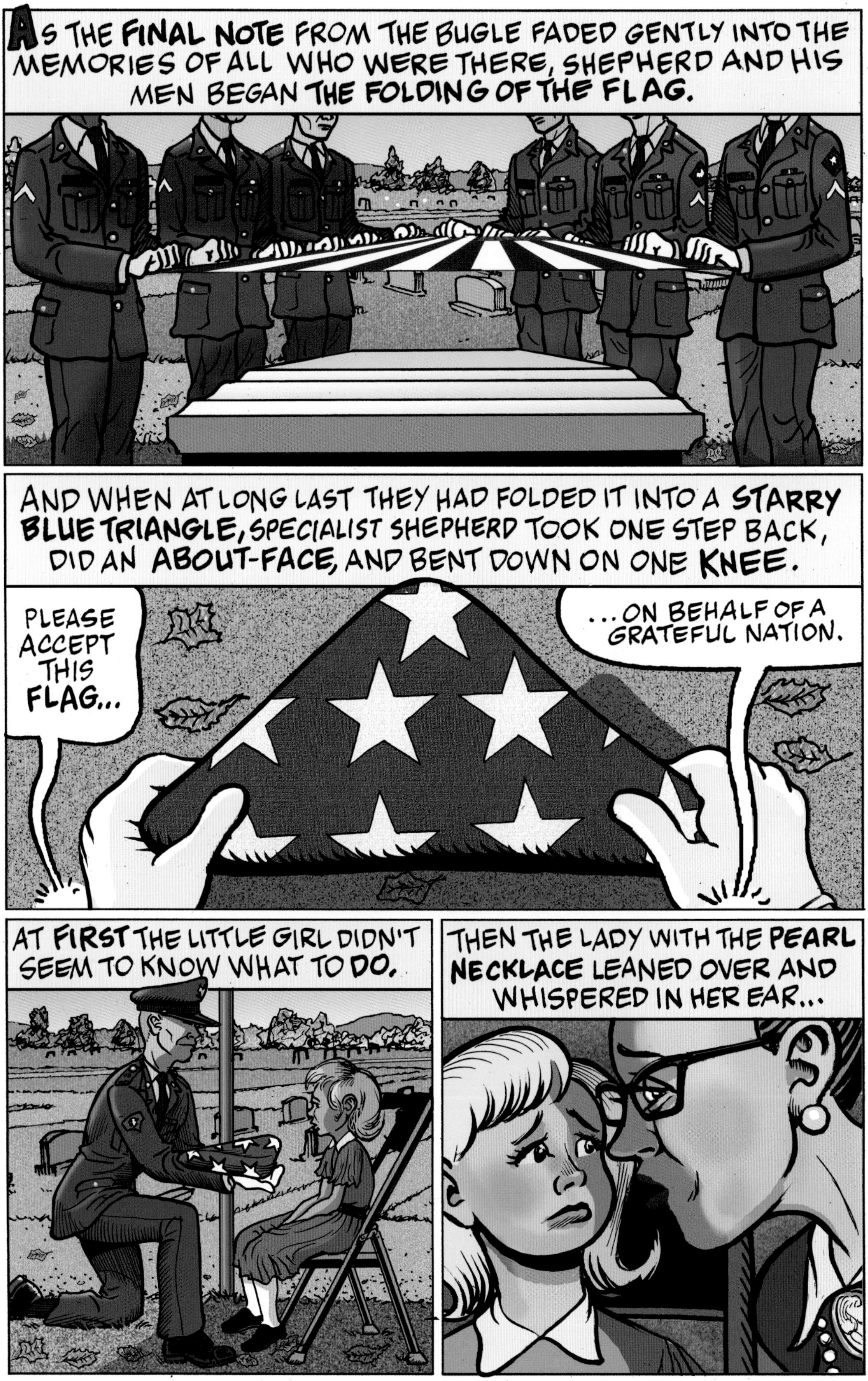
AS THE FINAL NOTE FROM THE BUGLE FADED GENTLY INTO THE MEMORIES OF ALL WHO WERE THERE, SHEPHERD AND HIS MEN BEGAN THE FOLDING OF THE FLAG.
AND WHEN AT LONG LAST THEY HAD FOLDED IT INTO A STARRY BLUE TRIANGLE, SPECIALIST SHEPHERD TOOK ONE STEP BACK, DID AN ABOUT-FACE, AND BENT DOWN ON ONE KNEE.
PLEASE ACCEPT THIS FLAG...
...ON BEHALF OF A GRATEFUL NATION.
AT FIRST THE LITTLE GIRL DIDN'T SEEM TO KNOW WHAT TO DO.
THEN THE LADY WITH THE PEARL NECKLACE LEANED OVER AND WHISPERED IN HER EAR...

THE LITTLE GIRL REACHED OUT, TOOK THE FLAG-- AND HELD IT TO HER CHEST.
IT STRUCK ME THAT IN MUCH THE SAME WAY, PRIVATE HIGGINS MUST HAVE HELD HER TO HIS JUST A FEW YEARS BEFORE.
THE FUNERAL DIRECTOR WALKED OVER AND RELEASED A LITTLE LEVER, AND THE SILVER CASKET CONTAINING ALL THAT REMAINED OF PRIVATE HIGGINS BEGAN TO SLOWLY AND SILENTLY DESCEND FROM VIEW...
KREEK
KREEK
DADDY...
DADDY...
HIS LITTLE DAUGHTER BEGAN TO CRY OUT...
DADDY...
FAR BELOW, DOWN ON THE HIGHWAY, A PASSING TRUCK LET OUT A LONG LOW MOAN, AND CONTINUED ON ITS WAY AS IF NOTHING WAS HAPPENING.
DADDY...
I COULDN'T BELIEVE THAT TRUCK JUST KEPT ON GOING!
...IT SEEMED TO ME THE WHOLE WORLD SHOULD STOP!
DADDY...
DADDY...
DADDY...

CREE...
DADDY...
CREEEAK
DADDY...
CREEEAK
CREEEAK
CREEEAK
DADDY...

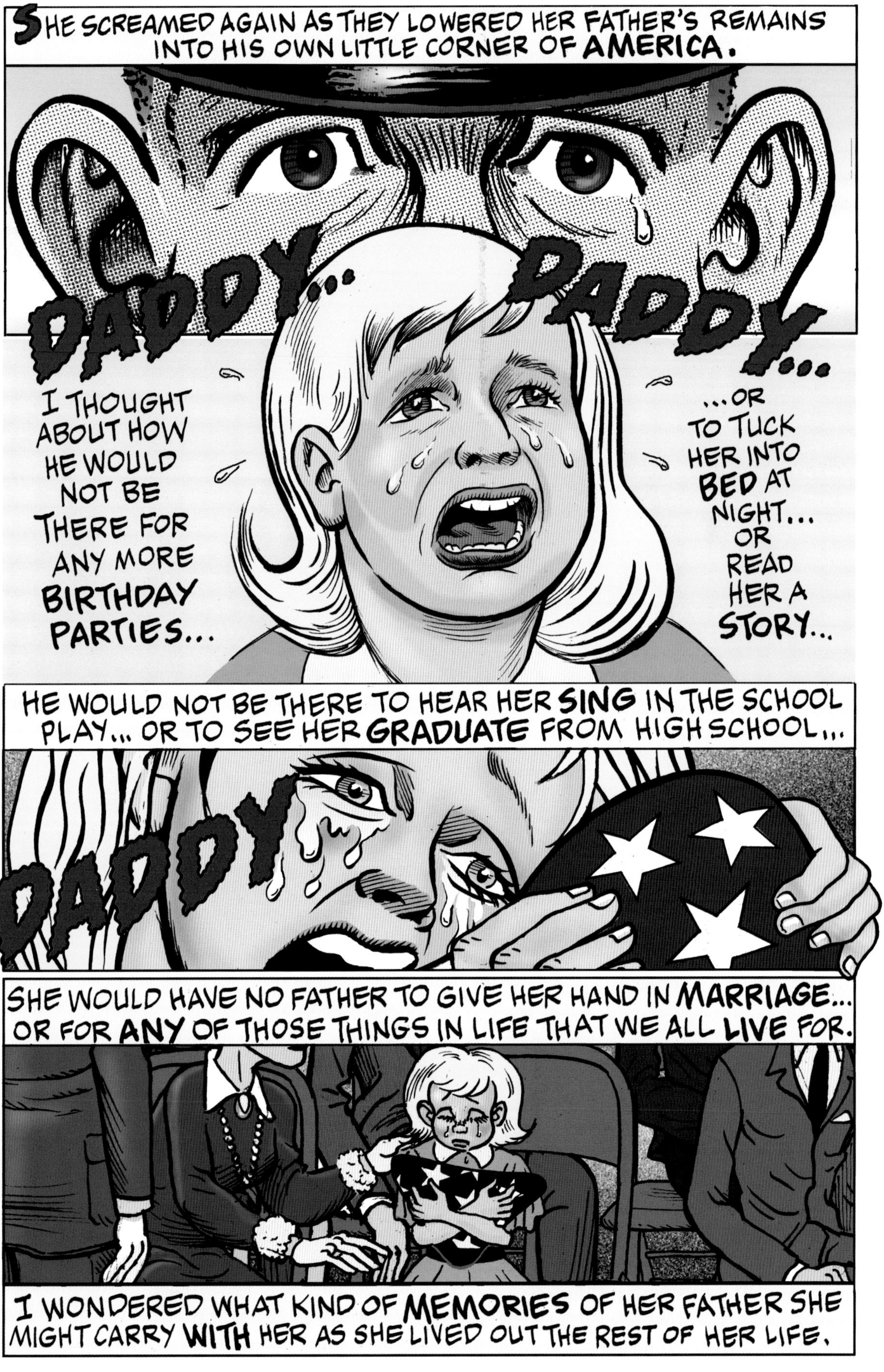
SHE SCREAMED AGAIN AS THEY LOWERED HER FATHER'S REMAINS INTO HIS OWN LITTLE CORNER OF AMERICA.
DADDY... DADDY...
I THOUGHT ABOUT HOW HE WOULD NOT BE THERE FOR ANY MORE BIRTHDAY PARTIES...
...OR TO TUCK HER INTO BED AT NIGHT... OR READ HER A STORY...
HE WOULD NOT BE THERE TO HEAR HER SING IN THE SCHOOL PLAY... OR TO SEE HER GRADUATE FROM HIGH SCHOOL...
DADDY
SHE WOULD HAVE NO FATHER TO GIVE HER HAND IN MARRIAGE... OR FOR ANY OF THOSE THINGS IN LIFE THAT WE ALL LIVE FOR.
I WONDERED WHAT KIND OF MEMORIES OF HER FATHER SHE MIGHT CARRY WITH HER AS SHE LIVED OUT THE REST OF HER LIFE.

SERGEANT BELL CALLED THE FIRING PARTY TO ATTENTION, AND MARCHED THEM IN A COLUMN OF SEVEN DOWN THE GRAVEL PATHWAY TOWARD THE WAITING BUS.
KRUNCH
KRUNCH
THE CRIES OF THE LITTLE GIRL SOFTENED, AND THE LADY WITH THE PEARL NECKLACE GENTLY TOOK HER BY THE HAND AND LED HER AWAY, FOLLOWED BY ALL THE MOURNERS.
PIRO FUNERAL HOME
REINECKE
SPECIALIST SHEPHERD LED THE PALLBEARERS AWAY WHILE I WENT OVER TO GET HAMPTON, THE BUGLER, WHO WAS STILL HIDDEN BEHIND SOME TALL TREES.
HUT TWO THREE FOUR...
SEXTON
KRUNCH
KRUNCH
KRUNCH

HE LOOKED RELIEVED TO SEE ME.
THAT WAS BEAUTIFUL.
TH-THANK YOU, SIR.
HE MAY HAVE BEEN WORRIED THAT I HAD FORGOTTEN ABOUT HIM AND THAT WE MIGHT DRIVE AWAY AND ACCIDENTALLY LEAVE HIM BEHIND.
ALL IN ALL, I WAS EXTREMELY PLEASED WITH THE WAY THE MEN MAINTAINED THEIR BEARING THROUGHOUT THE ENTIRE MILITARY FUNERAL.
MOTHER
NO ONE SO MUCH AS BLINKED AN EYE--OR COUGHED-- DURING THE WHOLE SAD ORDEAL.

ONCE BACK ON THE BUS, THE MEN THREW OFF THEIR HELMETS AND PISTOL BELTS.
SOME EVEN TOOK OFF THEIR BOOTS.
OTHERS REACHED INTO OVERNIGHT BAGS AND PULLED OUT BIG BOTTLES OF LIQUOR THEY HAD STASHED AWAY.
NO ONE OFFERED ME A DRINK.
PARKER
BELL
BEFORE THEY GOT TOO DRUNK, I PERSUADED THE DRIVER TO STOP AND EVERYONE BUT ME BOUGHT CRACKERS, PEANUTS, SLIM JIMS, GUM, CIGARETTES, AND OF COURSE, MORE BEER.
PAW'S PLACE
I REMAINED ON THE BUS.
LAWTON
1966
SCENICRUISER
GREYH
OFFICERS ARE NOT SUPPOSED TO "FRATERNIZE" WITH THE MEN.

ONCE BACK ON THE ROAD, SOME GUY IN THE BACK STARTED BLASTING HIS TRANSISTOR RADIO, AND EVERYONE JOINED VOICES IN A DRUNKEN CHORUS OF "HEY JUDE"... I COULDN'T REALLY BLAME THEM FOR WANTING TO LET OFF SOME STEAM AFTER WHAT THEY HAD JUST BEEN THROUGH-- AND PRIVATE HIGGINS WOULD NO DOUBT HAVE APPROVED.
WE CAN FORGET ABOUT GETTING ANY SLEEP!
NA-NA-NA-NANANANA
WE ARRIVED BACK AT FORT SILL AROUND MIDNIGHT. SEVERAL OF THE MEN HAD TO BE CARRIED OFF THE BUS, WHICH NOW REEKED OF CIGARETTE SMOKE AND VOMIT.
WHAARWFF!
I'M REALLY SORRY ABOUT THE MESS...
SNIFF SNIFF
I THANKED THE BUS DRIVER AND WALKED BACK TO THE MOTOR POOL--AND MY CAR--
LAWTON
--IN THE DARKNESS.

7
GETTING OUT

AT LONG LAST, THE DAY I'D BEEN WAITING FOR HAD FINALLY COME.
6:00
I HAD PICKED UP MY DISCHARGE PAPERS THE PREVIOUS AFTERNOON, AND TURNED IN MY PONCHO, PISTOL BELT, AND CANTEEN.
YOU CAN KEEP YOUR UNIFORMS AN' BOOTS.
AFTER A QUICK BREAKFAST OF EGGS, BACON, AND BLACK COFFEE WITH MR. BROOKS-- I JAMMED MY UNIFORMS AND BOOTS INTO MY DUFFEL BAG-- ALONG WITH THE TEN THOUSAND DOLLARS IN CASH I'D SAVED UP, AND LOCKED IT IN THE TRUNK OF MY '62 CHEVY.
THE WAY I ENVISIONED IT, IN A FEW DAYS I'D BE RIDING MY MOTORCYCLE UP AND DOWN THOSE HILLS IN 'FRISCO WITH ONE OF THOSE GIRLS ON THE BACK WITH FLOWERS IN HER HAIR!
I WAS JUST ABOUT TO GO BACK INTO THE HOUSE TO SAY GOODBYE WHEN MR. BROOKS SUDDENLY APPEARED IN THE DOORWAY...
?
OH, DICK--
DICK...
...THERE'S A "DON" ON THE PHONE FOR YOU.
DON WAS AN ENLISTED MAN IN MY UNIT.

HELLO...
SIR...I'M REALLY SORRY TO BOTHER YOU NOW, BUT MARGIE AND I ARE SPLITTING UP.
I'M REALLY SORRY, DON...
I HATE TO ASK YOU THIS... BUT IS THERE ANY WAY YOU CAN GIVE HER AND THE BABY A RIDE WITH YOU TO CALIFORNIA...?
SHE HAS A FRIEND SHE CAN STAY WITH OUT THERE...
BUT, DON... I'M LEAVING HERE IN HALF AN HOUR!
THAT'S OKAY...I CAN BE THERE IN FIFTEEN MINUTES...

MARGIE EMERGED FROM DON'S CAR HOLDING THEIR BABY. SHE HAD OBVIOUSLY BEEN CRYING.
DON OPENED THE TRUNK OF HIS CAR AND TOOK OUT THREE LARGE SUITCASES AND PLACED THEM ON THE BACK SEAT OF MY CAR.
MR. BROOKS AND I WATCHED FROM AFAR AS THEY SAID THEIR GOODBYES.
THEN SHE AND THE BABY GOT INTO THE FRONT SEAT OF MY CAR.
I JUST WANT TO SAY THANK YOU...
...AND GOOD LUCK IN YOUR NEW LIFE...
AT THAT, HE CALMLY WALKED BACK TO HIS CAR, GOT IN-- AND DROVE AWAY.
I GAVE MR. BROOKS A HUG AND THANKED HIM FOR HIS MANY KINDNESSES, THEN GOT BEHIND THE WHEEL OF MY CAR AND BACKED CAREFULLY OUT OF THEIR DRIVEWAY SO AS TO NOT DISTURB THE BABY, WHO HAD FALLEN ASLEEP IN HER MOTHER'S ARMS.
I WAVED ONE LAST GOODBYE TO THE BROOKSES, WHO HAD TREATED ME MORE LIKE A SON THAN A LODGER.
SUDDENLY I FELT A LUMP IN MY THROAT...
...AS I REALIZED I WOULD NEVER SEE THEM AGAIN.

AS I DROVE ALONG, MARGIE HAD HER FACE TURNED AWAY, BUT I COULD SEE SHE WAS STARTING TO CRY. I GUESS SHE WAS TRYING NOT TO SPOIL MY NEW SENSE OF FREEDOM.
GULF
I'D BEEN LOOKING FORWARD TO FEELING LIKE A FREE MAN--
--OR AT LEAST TO WHAT I THOUGHT A FREE MAN SHOULD FEEL LIKE.
I REALLY DIDN'T KNOW WHAT TO SAY--
--SO I SAID NOTHING.
BUT EVERY TIME I LOOKED OVER AT HER, SHE JUST LOOKED SO SAD.
I FELT BAD FOR HER.
JUST THEN A TEAR ROLLED DOWN HER CHEEK AND LANDED ON THE BABY'S FACE.
I FELT SORRY FOR THE BABY, WHO WAS JUST NOW BEGINNING TO WAKE UP.
SHE WAS GOING TO HAVE TO GROW UP WITHOUT A FATHER.
TO BREAK THE SILENCE, I TURNED ON THE RADIO-- IT WAS PLAYING "SKIP A ROPE" BY HENSON CARGILL.
KLIK
I TURNED IT BACK OFF.

AT THE BOTTOM OF MY WINDSHIELD, THE SKY ON THE EDGE OF THE HORIZON WAS SLOWLY TURNING FROM FIERY ORANGE TO A VELVETY PURPLE.
WE CONTINUED ON IN SILENCE FOR ANOTHER HOUR OR SO.
I COULD SEE A LITTLE GAS STATION UP AHEAD.
GAS
GAS
E..... F
I CHECKED THE GAS GAUGE AND THE TANK WAS ALMOST EMPTY.
FIRST, I WENT INTO THE RESTROOM TO TAKE A LEAK.
WHEN I CAME OUT, MARGIE WAS STANDING BY THE DESK IN THE OFFICE.
DICK--DON IS ON THE PHONE--HE WANTS TO TALK TO YOU.
OIL
OIL
YES, DON...?
SIR.... I'M REALLY SORRY...
...BUT I'VE MADE A TERRIBLE MISTAKE...
...CAN YOU BRING HER BACK?

RATHER THAN FEEL ANNOYED--I WAS HAPPY FOR THE FIRST TIME ALL DAY! I WAS MORE RELIEVED THAN MARGIE WAS.
I SWUNG THE CAR AROUND AND HEADED EAST--BACK TOWARD LAWTON.
GAS
GAS
UNLESS I GOT A FLAT TIRE, I COULD HAVE HER BACK HOME IN ABOUT TWO HOURS.
THE BABY'S HUNGRY--IF I DON'T FEED HER SHE'LL START CRYING...
...SO...
DO YOU MIND IF I FEED HER?
I THOUGHT IT A RATHER STRANGE QUESTION.
NO... OF COURSE NOT.
WHY WOULD I POSSIBLY 'MIND'?
SHE THEN PULLED DOWN HER DRESS AND BEGAN NURSING THE BABY.
I WILL ADMIT... I FOUND THAT A BIT JARRING.
DICK... YOU'RE REALLY A NICE GUY, YOU KNOW THAT?
I WISH THERE WAS SOME WAY I COULD SHOW MY APPRECIATION.

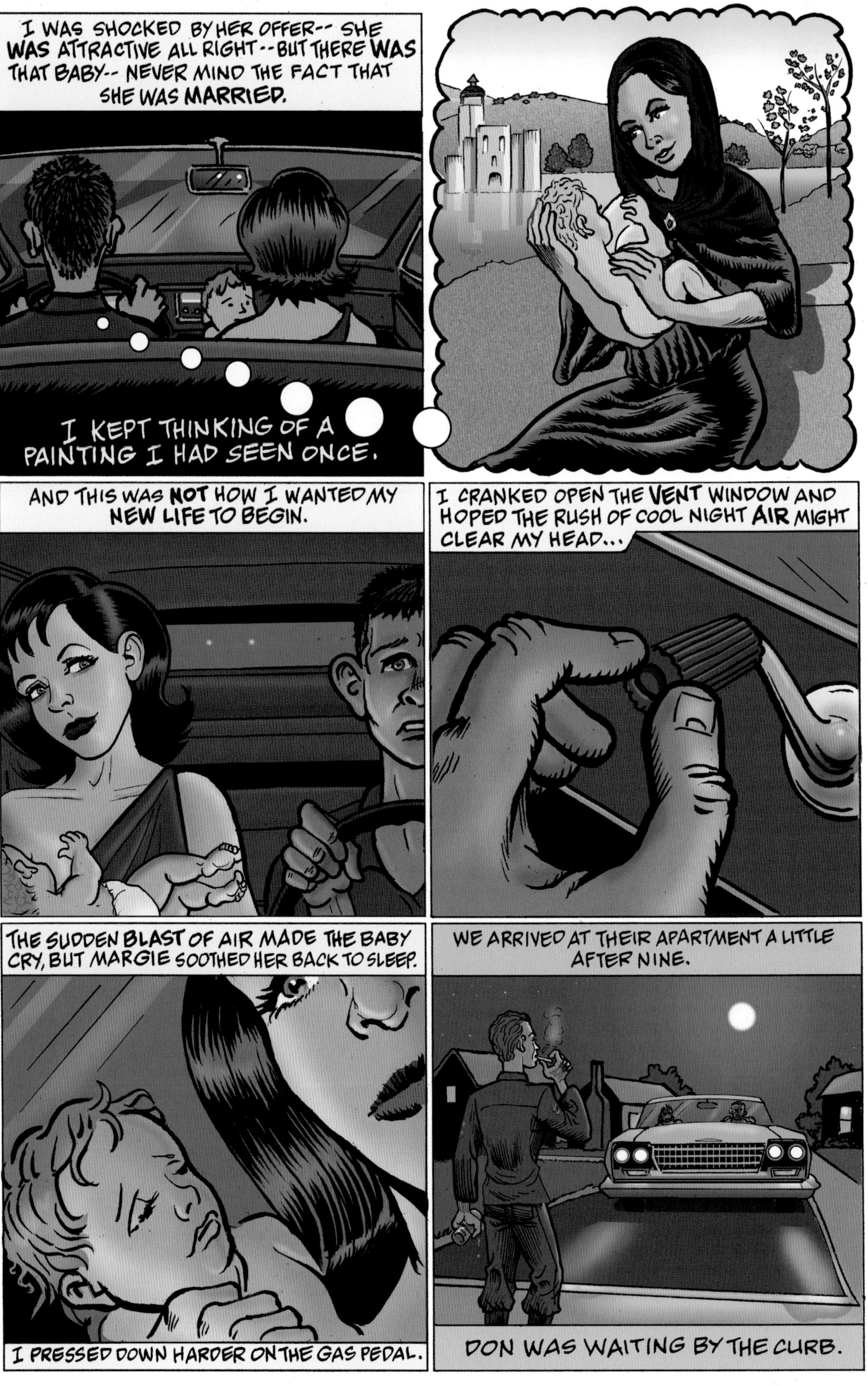
I WAS SHOCKED BY HER OFFER-- SHE WAS ATTRACTIVE ALL RIGHT--BUT THERE WAS THAT BABY-- NEVER MIND THE FACT THAT SHE WAS MARRIED.
I KEPT THINKING OF A PAINTING I HAD SEEN ONCE.
AND THIS WAS NOT HOW I WANTED MY NEW LIFE TO BEGIN.
I CRANKED OPEN THE VENT WINDOW AND HOPED THE RUSH OF COOL NIGHT AIR MIGHT CLEAR MY HEAD...
THE SUDDEN BLAST OF AIR MADE THE BABY CRY, BUT MARGIE SOOTHED HER BACK TO SLEEP.
I PRESSED DOWN HARDER ON THE GAS PEDAL.
WE ARRIVED AT THEIR APARTMENT A LITTLE AFTER NINE.
DON WAS WAITING BY THE CURB.

AS THE CAR ROLLED TO A STOP, MARGIE GRABBED THE BABY, HOPPED OUT, AND THE THREE OF THEM EMBRACED.
I WAS FEELING A TAD "HEROIC"-- AND I GUESS I EXPECTED SOME KIND OF "THANK YOU," OR AT LEAST THE OFFER OF SOMETHING TO EAT...
OH, DON, HONEY...
IT WAS GETTING LATE--AND REALIZING I HAD NO PLACE TO STAY, DON RELUCTANTLY INVITED ME IN.
C'MON, BABY...
LET'S GO HOME.
3A
MARGIE AND THE BABY HAD ALREADY DISAPPEARED INTO THE BEDROOM AS DON SHOWED ME THE CHAIR WHERE I WOULD SLEEP.
YOU CAN SLEEP RIGHT THERE...
...I'VE SLEPT ON IT...
IT'S PRETTY COMFORTABLE, ACTUALLY.
HE TOLD ME TO HELP MYSELF TO SOME BEER HE HAD IN THE REFRIGERATOR.
I GOT MYSELF A CAN OF COORS, LEANED BACK IN THE CHAIR, AND TRIED TO IGNORE THE GROWLING NOISES COMING FROM MY EMPTY STOMACH.
THEY WERE SOON DROWNED OUT BY THE NOISES COMING FROM BEHIND THE BEDROOM DOOR...
GRRROWLL
GRRROWWL
UUH-OOO
MMMMMMOOOO
MAAH-AAH!
THUMPITA
THUMPITA
THUMPITA
I DON'T KNOW HOW THE BABY COULD HAVE SLEPT THROUGH ALL THAT...
...I KNOW I COULDN'T.

THE NEXT MORNING ABOUT 0530 I AWOKE, VAGUELY AWARE OF DON SLIPPING OUT THE FRONT DOOR ON HIS WAY TO REVEILLE.
SGT. MYERS
I SHUT MY EYES AND TRIED TO GO BACK TO SLEEP.
AN HOUR OR SO LATER, THE BEDROOM DOOR OPENED AND MARGIE EMERGED WEARING SOME SORT OF SEE-THROUGH NEGLIGEÉ.
I QUICKLY SAT UP.
SOON...
HOW 'BOUT A LITTLE JAVA?
SURE...
HOW DO YOU TAKE IT?
JUST BLACK...NO SUGAR.
CAN I FIX YOU SOME SCRAMBLED EGGS AND TOAST...?
YES-- PLEASE! THAT WOULD BE GREAT...
JEEZUS...
I HAD TO GET OUT OF THERE BEFORE I DID SOMETHING I MIGHT COME TO REGRET.
DO YOU THINK YOU MIGHT STAY AROUND THIS AREA FOR A FEW DAYS BEFORE HEADING TO CALIFORNIA?
...MORE COFFEE?
OH, NO... THAT'S OKAY...
...I REALLY SHOULD GET GOING.

WELL... ALL RIGHT...
I THANKED HER FOR THE BREAKFAST, SAID GOODBYE, AND WENT OUT TO MY CAR.
SHE TRAILED AFTER ME AND SASHAYED UP TO THE DRIVER'S-SIDE WINDOW.
DICK...?
... ARE YOU SURE YOU DON'T WANT TO STAY JUST A LITTLE WHILE LONGER?
NO... I'VE REALLY GOT TO GET ON THE ROAD.
SAY GOODBYE TO DON FOR ME.
WEST
80
STO
EAST
I BACKED UP SLOWLY, TURNED ONTO THE STREET, DROVE DOWN TO THE CORNER-- AND PAUSED AT THE STOP SIGN. IT WAS AN EAST/WEST HIGHWAY.
UP TO THAT POINT, MY INTENTION WAS TO RESUME MY JOURNEY TO CALIFORNIA.
BUT SOMETHING INSIDE OF ME SAID, "FUCK IT-- I'VE HAD ENOUGH CRAZINESS-- I JUST WANT TO GO HOME."
WEST
80
EAST

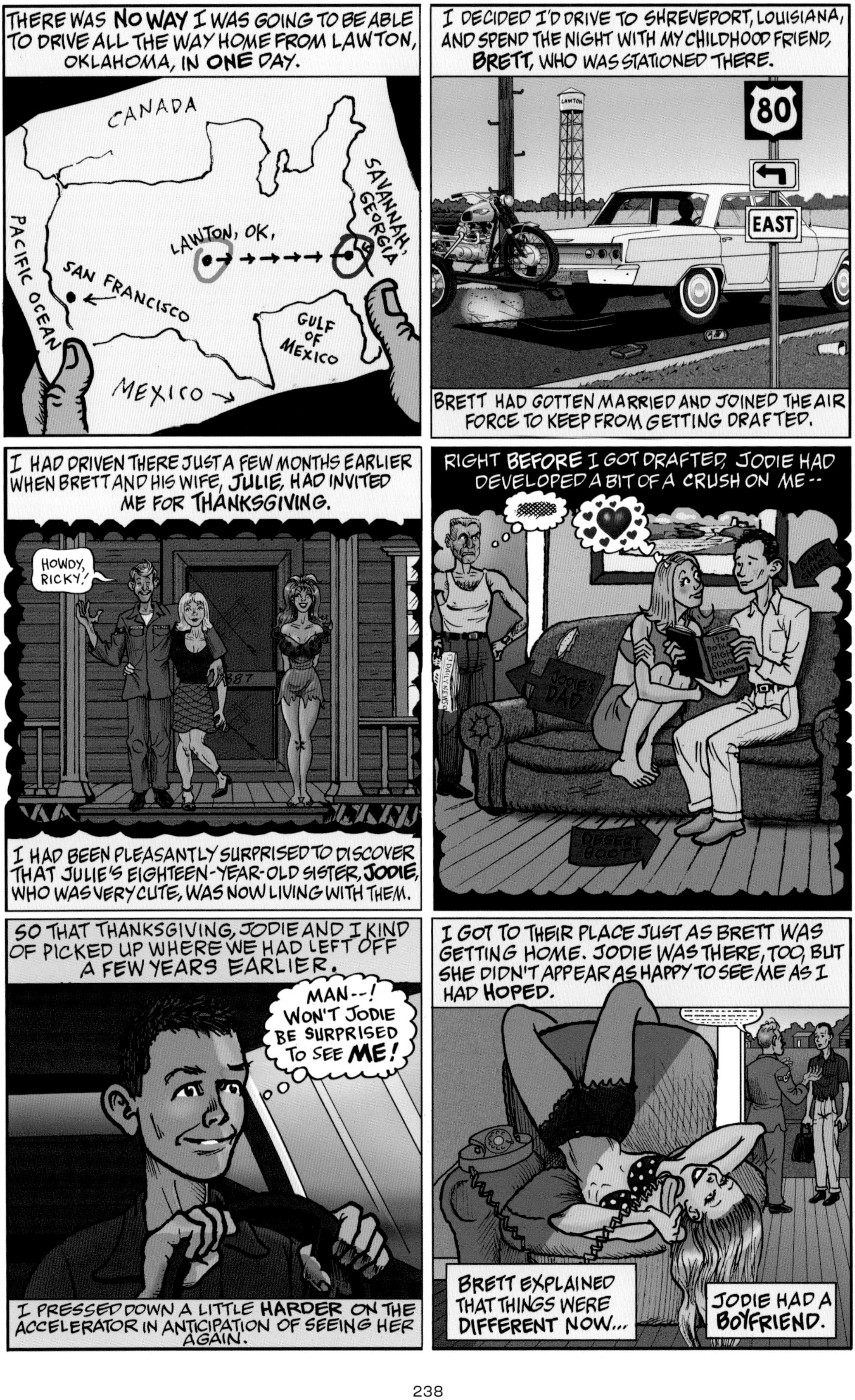
THERE WAS NO WAY I WAS GOING TO BE ABLE TO DRIVE ALL THE WAY HOME FROM LAWTON, OKLAHOMA, IN ONE DAY.
CANADA
PACIFIC OCEAN
SAN FRANCISCO
LAWTON, OK,
SAVANNAH, GEORGIA
GULF OF MEXICO
MEXICO
I DECIDED I'D DRIVE TO SHREVEPORT, LOUISIANA, AND SPEND THE NIGHT WITH MY CHILDHOOD FRIEND, BRETT, WHO WAS STATIONED THERE.
LAWTON
80
EAST
BRETT HAD GOTTEN MARRIED AND JOINED THE AIR FORCE TO KEEP FROM GETTING DRAFTED.
I HAD DRIVEN THERE JUST A FEW MONTHS EARLIER WHEN BRETT AND HIS WIFE, JULIE, HAD INVITED ME FOR THANKSGIVING.
HOWDY, RICKY!
I HAD BEEN PLEASANTLY SURPRISED TO DISCOVER THAT JULIE'S EIGHTEEN-YEAR-OLD SISTER, JODIE, WHO WAS VERY CUTE, WAS NOW LIVING WITH THEM.
RIGHT BEFORE I GOT DRAFTED, JODIE HAD DEVELOPED A BIT OF A CRUSH ON ME--
JODIE'S DAD
DAILY NEWS
1965
DESERT BOOTS
SO THAT THANKSGIVING, JODIE AND I KIND OF PICKED UP WHERE WE HAD LEFT OFF A FEW YEARS EARLIER.
MAN--! WON'T JODIE BE SURPRISED TO SEE ME!
I PRESSED DOWN A LITTLE HARDER ON THE ACCELERATOR IN ANTICIPATION OF SEEING HER AGAIN.
I GOT TO THEIR PLACE JUST AS BRETT WAS GETTING HOME. JODIE WAS THERE, TOO, BUT SHE DIDN'T APPEAR AS HAPPY TO SEE ME AS I HAD HOPED.
BRETT EXPLAINED THAT THINGS WERE DIFFERENT NOW...
JODIE HAD A BOYFRIEND.

I SUGGESTED I TREAT THE THREE OF THEM TO DINNER AT THAT SAME LITTLE RESTAURANT THE FOUR OF US HAD GONE TO AT THANKSGIVING.
BUT JODIE ALREADY HAD "PLANS" AND COULDN'T GO.
FOLLOW ME...
EXIT
WHEN WE GOT BACK, IT WAS STILL TOO EARLY FOR BED, BUT BRETT SAID HE AND JULIE WERE GOING TO TURN IN EARLY.
THEN HE WHISPERED THAT JODIE AND HER BOYFRIEND ROB WERE IN THE OTHER BEDROOM.
BRETT POINTED OUT THE COUCH IN THE LIVING ROOM WHERE I WOULD BE SLEEPING.
JULIE BROUGHT NEITHER SHEET NOR PILLOW.
ALONE NOW IN A SMALL APARTMENT WITH FOUR OTHER PEOPLE, I TOOK OFF MY BOOTS AND LAY DOWN ON THE COUCH... IT WAS LIKE A REPEAT OF THE PREVIOUS EVENING...
AAAAAAHHH...
...OHHHHHH...
OOOOOOO...
MMMMMMM...
...EXCEPT THIS TIME IN STEREO!
AND WITHOUT THE BEER!

THE NEXT MORNING AT BREAKFAST, IT WAS DECIDED THAT I WOULD DRIVE SEVEN HOURS TO ANDALUSIA, ALABAMA, TO SPEND THE NIGHT WITH BRETT'S UNCLE GERRY, A REFINED GENTLEMAN WITH WHOM BRETT AND I HAD SPENT A WEEKEND A FEW YEARS EARLIER.
THOSE BISCUITS SMELL SO GOOD!
PHILCO
YOU SHOULD TRY ONE!
HER GRANNY'S SECRET RECIPE!
I ASSUMED BRETT WOULD CALL HIS UNCLE FOR ME.
HE DIDN'T.
2:15 P.M.
8:30 P.M.
WELCOME TO
ALABAMA
THE BEAUTIFUL
UNFORTUNATELY, BY THE TIME I FOUND HIS HOUSE, IT WAS NEARLY MIDNIGHT-- AND I DIDN'T THINK I SHOULD DISTURB HIM,
HE WAS REALLY NICE... BUT IT HAS BEEN ALMOST FOUR YEARS SINCE I HAVE SEEN HIM.
IT WAS STARTING TO GET COLD...
CRAP!
I GUESS I CAN SLEEP IN MY CAR...
...IN HIS DRIVEWAY.
BUT THE TRUTH IS, IT WAS SO COLD THAT EVEN WITH MY FIELD JACKET ON I WAS FREEZING MY ASS OFF.
THE NEXT MORNING, I WOKE UP BEFORE DAWN AND DROVE AWAY WITHOUT EVER SEEING HIM.

I HEADED EAST ON HIGHWAY 84, PASSING OPP, ELBA, AND ENTERPRISE, AND CROSSED OVER THE CHATTAHOOCHEE RIVER INTO GEORGIA WITH THE BRIGHT MORNING SUN STREAMING THROUGH MY WINDSHIELD. I TURNED ON THE RADIO.
...THE OLD SOLDIER EVERYONE CALLED "IKE" IS GONE... NO MATTER WHAT THEIR POLITICS, EVERYONE LOVED THEIR MOST FAMOUS SOLDIER... HIS BODY WILL BE TAKEN TO NATIONAL CATHEDRAL, WHERE IT WILL LIE IN REPOSE UNTIL TOMORROW AFTERNOON... GENERAL EISENHOWER WAS A MAN OF VICTORY, SUPREME COMMANDER OF THE ALLIED FORCES, WHICH RELAIMED EUROPE FROM THE NAZIS... PRESIDENT OF THE UNITED STATES...
WHAT A COINCIDENCE! IKE AND I GOT OUT ON THE SAME DAY!
SOON I PASSED THROUGH QUITMAN, VALDOSTA, AND HOMERVILLE--LITTLE COUNTRY TOWNS THAT DOTTED THE ROADS OF MY CHILDHOOD.
I WONDER WHAT MY NEW LIFE IS GONNA BE LIKE?
THESE PAST THREE YEARS HAVE BEEN SURREAL!
MELONS
I GUESS I'M GONNA HAVE TO WRITE A BOOK ABOUT IT ALL SOME DAY.
I STOPPED IN WAYCROSS TO GAS-UP, AND BOUGHT A COKE AND SOME CRACKERS.
TEXACO
FIRE-CHIEF
JUST LIKE MY DAD HAD ALWAYS DONE WHEN WE WOULD DRIVE TO FLORIDA TO VISIT MY GRANDMA.
I CALLED MY MOM COLLECT.
I SHOULD BE HOME IN ABOUT AN HOUR...
THAT'S SO NICE, RICKY.
IN TYPICAL FASHION, I HAD NOT INFORMED HER OF MY PLANS FOR CALIFORNIA--AND SHE SEEMED DELIGHTED THAT I WAS COMING HOME.
HIGHWAY 84 DEAD-ENDS JUST SOUTH OF BRUNSWICK, SO I PICKED UP US 17 NORTH, A ROAD I HAD COME TO KNOW WELL AS A BOY.
DAD--! BACK THERE IS WHERE WE SAW THE DEAD ALLIGATOR!
AND RIGHT HERE IS WHERE I ALMOST GOT US KILLED LAST TRIP TRYING TO RUN OVER A SNAKE...
I PASSED THE DUTCH MILL AND THE DIXIE JUNGLE--AND ALL THOSE LITTLE FIREWORKS STANDS WHERE MY FATHER ALWAYS REFUSED TO STOP, NO MATTER HOW MUCH I BEGGED.
I DIDN'T STOP EITHER.
FIREWORKS
TNT'S
BOMBS

WHEN I TURNED OFF THE HIGHWAY ON THE OUTSKIRTS OF SAVANNAH, AND DROVE UP 51ST STREET TOWARD HOME, I COULD FEEL SOMETHING INSIDE MYSELF RECALIBRATING.
L719 A OKLAHOMA
IT WAS A GORGEOUS SPRING DAY.
I PULLED UP IN FRONT OF THE HOUSE AND BOUNDED UP THE STEPS.
THE FRONT DOOR WAS WIDE OPEN.
MY MOTHER WAS SEATED IN HER FAVORITE CHAIR FACING THE DOOR.
I STOOD IN THE DOORWAY FOR A MINUTE, JUST SOAKING IT ALL IN.
THERE WAS A GLASS OF SPARKLING BURGUNDY IN HER HAND AND AN EMPTY GLASS FOR ME NEXT TO THE BOTTLE CHILLING ON THE TABLE.
SHE SAID HER KNEES HURT AND APOLOGIZED FOR NOT GETTING UP.
SMEK
AS I APPROACHED AND GAVE HER THE CUSTOMARY KISS ON THE CHEEK, HER DOG, PEPÉ, WHICH SHE HAD GOTTEN TO COMFORT HER IN MY ABSENCE, SKITTERED AWAY.
HE NEVER WARMED UP TO ME...

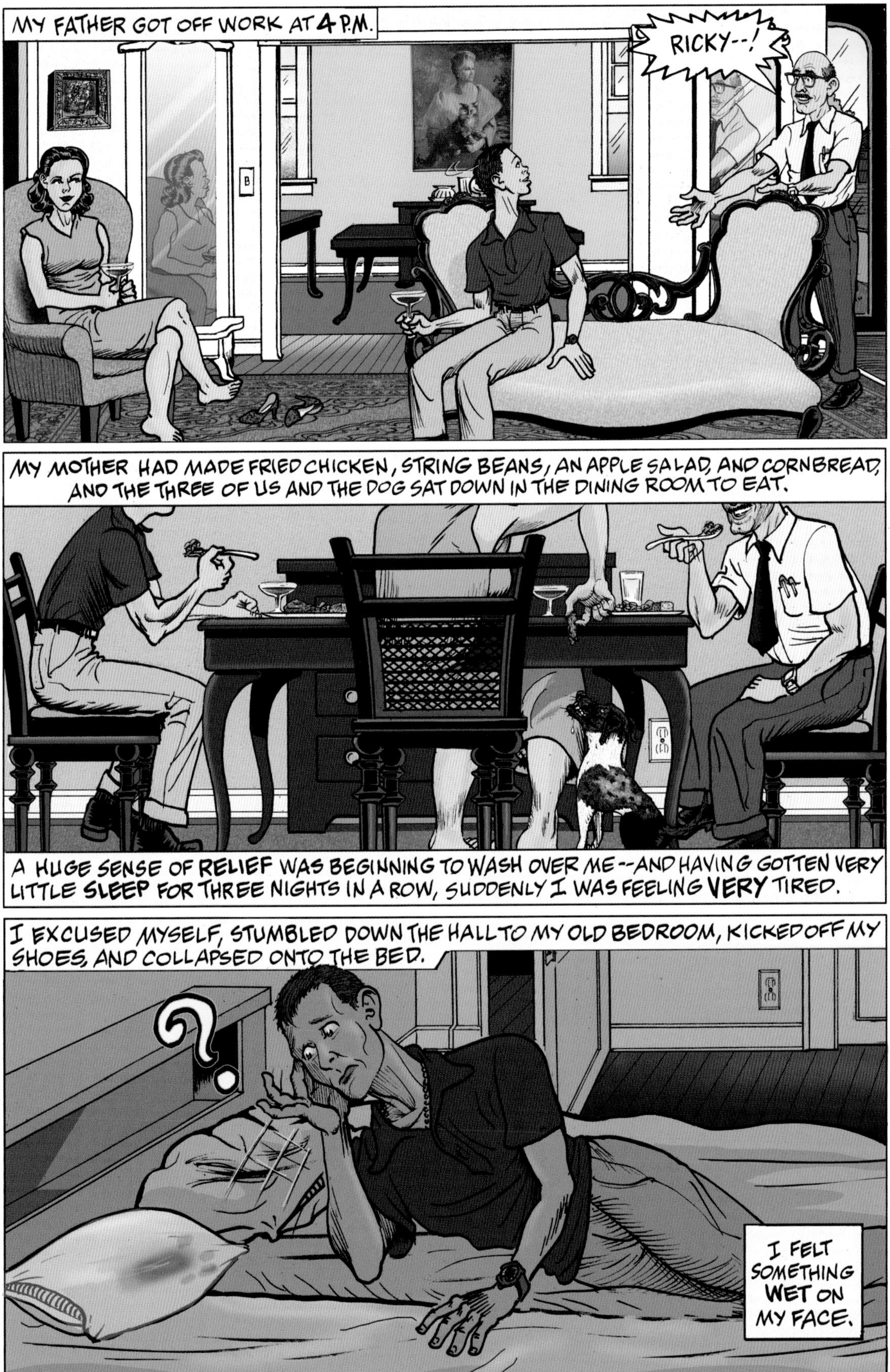
MY FATHER GOT OFF WORK AT 4 P.M.
RICKY--!
MY MOTHER HAD MADE FRIED CHICKEN, STRING BEANS, AN APPLE SALAD, AND CORNBREAD, AND THE THREE OF US AND THE DOG SAT DOWN IN THE DINING ROOM TO EAT.
A HUGE SENSE OF RELIEF WAS BEGINNING TO WASH OVER ME--AND HAVING GOTTEN VERY LITTLE SLEEP FOR THREE NIGHTS IN A ROW, SUDDENLY I WAS FEELING VERY TIRED.
I EXCUSED MYSELF, STUMBLED DOWN THE HALL TO MY OLD BEDROOM, KICKED OFF MY SHOES, AND COLLAPSED ONTO THE BED.
?
I FELT SOMETHING WET ON MY FACE.

MY MOTHER'S DOG HAD PEED ON MY PILLOW!
SLURP
SLURP
TOO TIRED TO CARE, I KICKED THE DOOR SHUT WITH MY FOOT, FLIPPED THE PILLOW OVER, AND PUT MY HEAD DOWN ON THE DRY SIDE.
THE LATE MARCH AFTERNOON SUN WAS FILTERING THROUGH THE STILL-BARE LIMBS OF THE PECAN TREE OUT IN THE BACKYARD.
ITS BRIGHT LIGHT CAST A WARM, ORANGE GLOW ON THE FOLDS OF THE BEIGE CURTAINS BY THE WINDOW.

AS MY EYES WERE CLOSING, I NOTICED THE PECAN TREE WAS JUST BEGINNING TO BUD...

A FEW THOUGHTS

Although I have worked as an artist for Marvel Comics and other companies in collaboration with writers for nearly fifty years, this is the first work of any significant length that I have both illustrated *and* written.

I first began to think of telling this story in book form as it was actually happening to me, when I was a soldier from 1966 to 1969. There were many times during my three years, one month, and five days of military service when I said to myself, "This is *unbelievable* . . . I've got to *tell* somebody about this someday!"

As an only child growing up in the South in the 1950s, who never felt like I "fit in" or "belonged," I often longed to be a part of something.

Joining the Boy Scouts helped.

But it wasn't until I found myself in the U.S. Army a few years later, at nineteen, that I began to have a set of highly intense, shared experiences with others. In the process, especially when being pushed to the limit, I began to learn more about myself, and my fellow human beings.

Drafted is not only my story, but theirs. Private Evatt, Sergeant Allen, Captain O'Connor, and all the others will forever be a part of me. Their names have been changed and situations adjusted for narrative purposes—but the story is true.

I, Rick Parker, do solemnly swear . . .

R.P.
February 2024
Maine

FOR MORE RICK PARKER ONLINE

rickparkerartist.com

facebook.com/rick.parker.artist/photos_albums

Many Are Called, Few Are Chosen
(autobiographyofaformerzygote.com)

Finding Humor in Art: Artist Rick Parker
by Catherine Stratton (vimeo.com/23800789)

Rick Parker, I'm Afraid
by Shannon Meserve (vimeo.com/571295673)

GLOSSARY

The mind of Rick Parker is the source for these glossary definitions. Use at your own peril. Please note: Some terms have been modernized to be more inclusive, but not all, because of the time period in which the story takes place.

about face: A drill command directing a soldier or soldiers, standing at attention, to turn and face in the opposite direction in one movement. Other face commands include right face and left face.

adjutant: A high-ranking, field-grade officer (above a captain) who acts as an assistant to a higher-ranking commanding officer. As in, "The colonel's adjutant arrived early."

advanced individual training (A.I.T.): An eight-week program following basic training where soldiers get specialized instruction and preparation to perform a job.

artist: A person involved in the creative arts, such as drawing and painting.

assistant gunners: The two lower-classmen seated on either side of the gunner, who follow the gunner's orders. Their tasks include emptying uneaten food onto a large platter; stacking up plates, cups, glasses, and flatware; carrying uneaten food to garbage cans and dumping it; and returning dirty plates to the rear of the mess hall.

attention: A military command ordering a soldier or soldiers to straighten up and stand still with heels together and feet at a 60-degree angle.

barracks: A building where soldiers sleep at night and keep their clothing and personal belongings. It includes beds, lockers, and a latrine.

base, a.k.a. military base: Land and buildings owned by the military where personnel are trained, reside, and work; equipment is housed; and operations are conducted.

basic training, a.k.a. basic combat training: A challenging eight-week course designed to turn civilians into combat soldiers.

blanks: Ammunition containing gunpowder but no bullets or projectiles.

boot camp: See *basic training.*

bunk: A narrow bed, often stacked one upon another.

canteen: A metal or plastic container carried by an individual soldier who stores his or her water supply there. It sometimes incorporates a drinking cup.

chain of command: The hierarchy of rank giving authority to higher-ranking individuals over lower-ranking individuals. In this power structure, leaders range from squad leader to platoon leader to company commander to battalion commander to group commander to general of the army to commander in chief, a.k.a. President of the United States.

classman (upperclassman, middle-classman, lower-classman): Officer candidates at various stages of the six-month officer candidate school program.

collect call: A telephone call paid for by the recipient rather than caller. Most were made on landlines, using operators to manage the call.

commissioned officer (C.O.): A military leader with a college degree who completed either additional training, such as officer candidate school (O.C.S.) during their term of service, or Reserve Officers' Training Corps (R.O.T.C.) during college. Another pathway is to enter with a degree from one of the nation's military academies. During the Vietnam War, a soldier who did not have a college degree could qualify for O.C.S. by scoring well on a standardized test.

cubicle: A small area inside an army barracks containing a soldier's bunk, footlocker, wall locker, and sometimes a small table, chair, and lamp.

demerit slips: Small, printed forms issued to officer candidates for violations, such as, "shoes N.S.S. (not sufficiently shined)," "late to formation," "out of uniform." Officer candidates are given punishments when enough demerits, or demerit slips, have accrued. Punishments include being restricted to battery area while others are free to leave, and being assigned physically arduous tasks (see *jarks*).

detail: A military duty assigned to a small group of soldiers, such as flag detail, funeral detail, and guard duty.

deuce-and-a-half: A two-and-a-half-ton truck used for transporting troops or cargo from one place to another.

dog-eyeing: Looking around rather than keeping eyes focused on whatever is directly in front of you. In the mess hall, an officer candidate's focus is expected to remain on the name tag of the officer candidate seated directly across the table.

double-timing: Running, as opposed to walking.

dress uniform, a.k.a. "Class A" uniform: Clothing that a soldier wears on special occasions, such as traveling on public transportation or attending an important ceremony. It consists of more formal pants, shirt, tie, jacket with brass buttons, cap, and shoes (see *low-quarters*).

enlisted men and women: Soldiers ranging from privates to sergeants, but not officers.

expiration term of service (E.T.S.): A soldier's discharge date.

fatigues: The everyday olive drab work uniform of an officer or enlisted man or woman consisting of pants, pistol belt, shirt, jacket, boots, and baseball cap.

field exercise: A training operation in which soldiers perform various military duties in the outdoors, such as setting up a camp, building a perimeter around an encampment, and familiarization firing of various weapons.

field telephone: A device attached by a wire to a similar device some distance away, used by military personnel for back-and-forth, immediate communication. A field telephone is different than a wireless walkie-talkie or radio.

formation: The arrangement of soldiers standing or marching in groups.

gross bite: Putting food into your mouth larger than the size of a human thumbnail.

gunner: A middle-classman who outranks the other six classmen at their dining table in the mess hall and assists the table commandant (T.C.). The gunner sits at the opposite end of the table from the T.C.

harch: A drill and ceremonies command directing soldiers to move forward, left foot first.

headquarters: A gathering place for officers in charge of a military unit, such as battalion headquarters. It can be a building, tent, or armored vehicle.

helmet liner: Plastic headgear that fits inside the outer helmet (see *steel pot*) and has an adjustable headband designed to make the helmet fit properly, providing better protection.

hippie: A free-spirited person who marches to the beat of his/her/their own drum, usually with long hair and unconventional clothing.

hit a brace: To assume a bolt-upright, stiff, sitting position with eyes directed to the name tag of the officer candidate seated directly opposite. It is a command given in the mess hall.

induction station: An army facility where new recruits are processed into the U.S. Army and Marine Corps.

jark: A strenuous, fast-paced march, somewhere between a walk and a run, of several miles up a small mountain. The soldier performs the march while carrying a rifle and full canteen of water. It is part of officer candidate school and is usually given (up to two times a week) as punishment for accruing too many demerit slips.

latrine: A place with toilets, sinks, and showers for washing up.

leave: A period of time when a soldier is not on duty, as in, "We were given three days' leave between A.I.T. and reporting to O.C.S."

low-quarters: Black dress shoes with laces as opposed to combat boots. They are worn as part of the dress uniform.

mess hall: A building with tables and chairs where soldiers are provided food.

non-commissioned officer (N.C.O.): A military leader who enlists with a high school degree or the equivalent, but does not have a college degree, and earns the rank of sergeant by additional formal training. Although they often have more experience than commissioned officers, non-commissioned officers are lower ranking.

officer: A soldier whose rank ranges anywhere from second lieutenant to general. An officer outranks all enlisted men and women.

officer's club: A building or tent that houses a cafeteria, bar, or lounge with comfortable seating, where only officers can gather and relax when off duty. Enlisted soldiers are not allowed in, unless they are signed in as guests, which is unusual.

partisan point: A place where friendly civilians provide rest, food, shelter, and comfort to non-enemy soldiers who are going from one location to another in a war.

physical training (P.T.): Exercises that strengthen the human body, including push-ups, sit-ups, squat thrusts, and side-straddle hops.

pistol belt: A band designed to be worn around the waist, which has small holes for attaching a canteen, pistol, medicine, and an ammunition pouch.

police call: A military duty requiring soldiers to pick up and dispose of litter.

poncho: A kind of loose, waterproof item of clothing designed to drape over fatigues during rainstorms. It can be made of olive drab canvas, rolled up, and attached to a soldier's pistol belt.

post: The location assigned to a soldier on guard duty. More generally, it refers to an army fort. For example, Fort Jackson, Fort Bliss, or Fort Sill are posts, and a soldier may say he is "posted" to Fort Jackson, Fort Bliss, or Fort Sill.

primary load list van (PLL): A vehicle used to transport communication equipment, a.k.a. "commo van," or to pull a trailer full of spare parts.

private E-1: Lowest ranking enlisted man, below private first class, a.k.a. "private E-nothing."

privately owned vehicle (P.O.V.): A truck, car, or motorcycle owned by a soldier for personal use.

ranks: Members of the military who are not officers.

recruit: A person being inducted into military service.

Reserve Officers' Training Corps (R.O.T.C.): Military training for high school or college students conducted by active-duty military personnel.

reveille: Early morning music played by a bugler, or by a soldier playing a bugle, to wake the troops. It is also a ceremony at the beginning of each day when soldiers gather, in formation, to witness the raising of the flag while a bugle call is played either live or pre-recorded.

reverse march: A movement in which a soldier turns around and reverses direction when marching.

round: A single shot fired from a pistol, rifle, machine gun, or cannon.

shoot: A training exercise in the field in which officer candidates practice directing artillery fire onto established targets, such as old car bodies that have been painted red.

speed: A slang term for illegal drugs, such as amphetamines, or "uppers."

spinal meningitis: An infection of the fluid and membrane surrounding the spinal cord and brain that causes inflammation, and sometimes brain damage and death. Depending on the cause of the infection, it can be highly contagious.

squad: The smallest unit in an infantry battalion. With approximately seven soldiers, it is smaller than a platoon.

steel pot: A soldier's helmet.

table commandant (T.C.): An upperclassman, who sits at the head of the table in the mess hall. He supervises and gives orders concerning the meal to the seven other officer candidates at the table.

tactical officer (T.A.C.): An upperclassman in O.C.S., temporarily in charge of lower-ranking officer candidates.

taps: A bugle call, or song, played at the end of each day during the lowering of the flag.

top: A casual, but respectful, term referring to the highest-ranking enlisted man in a unit, usually a master sergeant. Enlisted men are required to salute officers, but they may greet higher ranking enlisted men, including non-commissioned officers, less-formally, as in, "Mornin', top!" A master sergeant is a non-commissioned officer.

volley: Shots fired at exactly the same time from a group of weapons, as in a "21-gun salute."

RECOMMENDED READING AND VIEWING

THE VIETNAM WAR

Atwood, Kathryn J. *Courageous Women of the Vietnam War: Medics, Journalists, Survivors, and More.* Chicago, IL: Chicago Review Press, 2018.

Bowden, Mark. *Huế 1968: A Turning Point of the American War in Vietnam.* New York: Atlantic Monthly Press, 2017.

Ellsberg, Daniel. *Secrets: A Memoir of Vietnam and the Pentagon Papers.* New York: Penguin Books, 2003.

Evans, Diane Carlson, and Bob Welch. *Healing Wounds: A Vietnam War Combat Nurse's 10-Year Fight to Win Women a Place of Honor in Washington, D.C.* Brentwood, TN: Permuted Press, 2020.

Hastings, Max. *Vietnam: An Epic Tragedy, 1945–1975.* New York: Harper Perennial, 2019.

Hayslip, Le Ly, and Jay Wurts. *When Heaven and Earth Changed Places.* New York: Doubleday, 1989.

Johnson, Tom A. *To the Limit: An Air Cav Huey Pilot in Vietnam.* Sterling, VA: Potomac Books, 2006.

Karnow, Stanley. *Vietnam: A History.* New York: Penguin Books, 1997.

Logevall, Fredrik. *Embers of War: The Fall of an Empire and the Making of America's Vietnam.* New York: Random House, 2012.

Mason, Robert. *Chickenhawk.* New York: Penguin Books, 2005.

Moore, Harold G., and Joseph L. Galloway. *We Were Soldiers Once . . . and Young.* New York: Random House, 1992.

Morgan, Ted. *Valley of Death: The Tragedy at Dien Bien Phu that Led America into the Vietnam War.* New York: Random House, 2010.

O'Brien, Tim. *The Things They Carried.* New York: Mariner Books, 2009.

Sheinkin, Steve. *Most Dangerous: Daniel Ellsberg and the Secret History of the Vietnam War.* New York: Roaring Brook Press, 2015.

Terry, Wallace. *Bloods: Black Veterans of the Vietnam War: An Oral History.* New York, Presidio Press, 1985.

COMICS

Barks, Carl. *The Complete Carl Barks Disney Library.* Seattle, WA: Fantagraphics, 2014–2023.

Kelly, Walt. *Pogo: The Complete Daily & Sunday Comic Strips.* Seattle, WA: Fantagraphics, 2011–2024.

Reidelbach, Maria. *Completely MAD: A History of the Comic Book and Magazine.* Boston, MA: Little Brown & Co., 1992.

CIVIL RIGHTS AND SCHOOL DESEGREGATION

Bass, Jack. *Taming the Storm.* New York: Doubleday, 1992.

Daniels, Maurice C. *Ground Crew: The Fight to End Segregation at Georgia State.* Athens, GA: University of Georgia Press, 2019.

Dartt, Rebecca H. *Women Activists in the Fight for Georgia School Desegregation, 1958–1961.* Jefferson, NC: McFarland, 2012.

Gibson, Larry S. *Young Thurgood: The Making of a Supreme Court Justice.* Buffalo, NY: Prometheus, 2012.

Haygood, Wil. *Showdown: Thurgood Marshall and the Supreme Court Nomination That Changed America.* New York: Knopf, 2015.

King, Jr., Martin Luther. *The Autobiography of Martin Luther King, Jr.* Edited by Clayborne Carson. New York: Warner Books, 2001.

Kluger, Richard. *Simple Justice: The History of Brown v. Board of Education and Black America's Struggle for Equality.* New York: Vintage, Revised Edition, 2004.

Ricks, Thomas E. *Waging a Good War: A Military History of the Civil Rights Movement, 1954–1968.* New York: Farrar, Straus and Giroux, 2022.

Trillin, Calvin. *An Education in Georgia.* Athens, GA: University of Georgia Press, 1991.

PRESIDENT JOHN F. KENNEDY

Doyle, William. *PT 109: An American Epic of War, Survival, and the Destiny of John F. Kennedy.* New York: William Morrow, 2015.

Sorensen, Ted. *Kennedy: The Classic Biography.* New York: Harper Perennial, 2013.

U.S. HISTORY

Lepore, Jill. *These Truths: A History of the United States.* New York: W. W. Norton & Company, 2018.

Zinn, Howard. *A Young People's History of the United States.* Adapted by Rebecca Stefoff. New York: Triangle Square, 2009.

Zinn, Howard. *A People's History of the United States: 1492–Present.* Revised and Updated. New York: Harper, 2017.

DOCUMENTARIES

Eyes on the Prize: America's Civil Rights Years 1954–1965. Episode 2: "Fighting Back (1957–1962)." Directed by Judith Vecchione, written by Steve Fayer, Blackside, January 28, 1987.

Little Rock Central: 50 Years Later. Directed by Brent Renaud and Craig Renaud, HBO, 2007.

Nine from Little Rock: Pioneers of Desegregation. Directed by Charles Guggenheim, written by Charles Guggenheim and Shelby Storck, 1965.

The Vietnam War. A ten-part documentary series directed by Ken Burns and Lynn Novick, Florentine Films, WETA-TV, 2017.

Also of interest from Abrams ComicArts—

The Best We Could Do by Thi Bui

The Bomb: The Weapon That Changed the World by Didier Alcante, Laurent-Frédéric Bollée, and Denis Rodier

Commute: An Illustrated Memoir of Shame by Erin Williams

Drawing the Vote by Tommy Jenkins and Katie Lacker

Economix by Michael Goodwin and Dan E. Burr

Fire on the Water by Scott MacGregor and Gary Dumm

Guantanamo Voices: True Accounts from the World's Most Infamous Prison by Sarah Mirk

Kent State: Four Dead in Ohio by Derf Backderf

Mom's Cancer by Brian Fies

Nat Turner by Kyle Baker

Run: Book One by John Lewis, Andrew Aydin, L. Fury, and Nate Powell

Save It for Later: Promises, Parenthood, and the Urgency of Protest by Nate Powell

Showtime at the Apollo: The Epic Tale of Harlem's Legendary Theater by Ted Fox and James Otis Smith

Uncle Sam: Special Election Edition by Steve Darnall and Alex Ross

We Are Not Strangers by Josh Tuininga

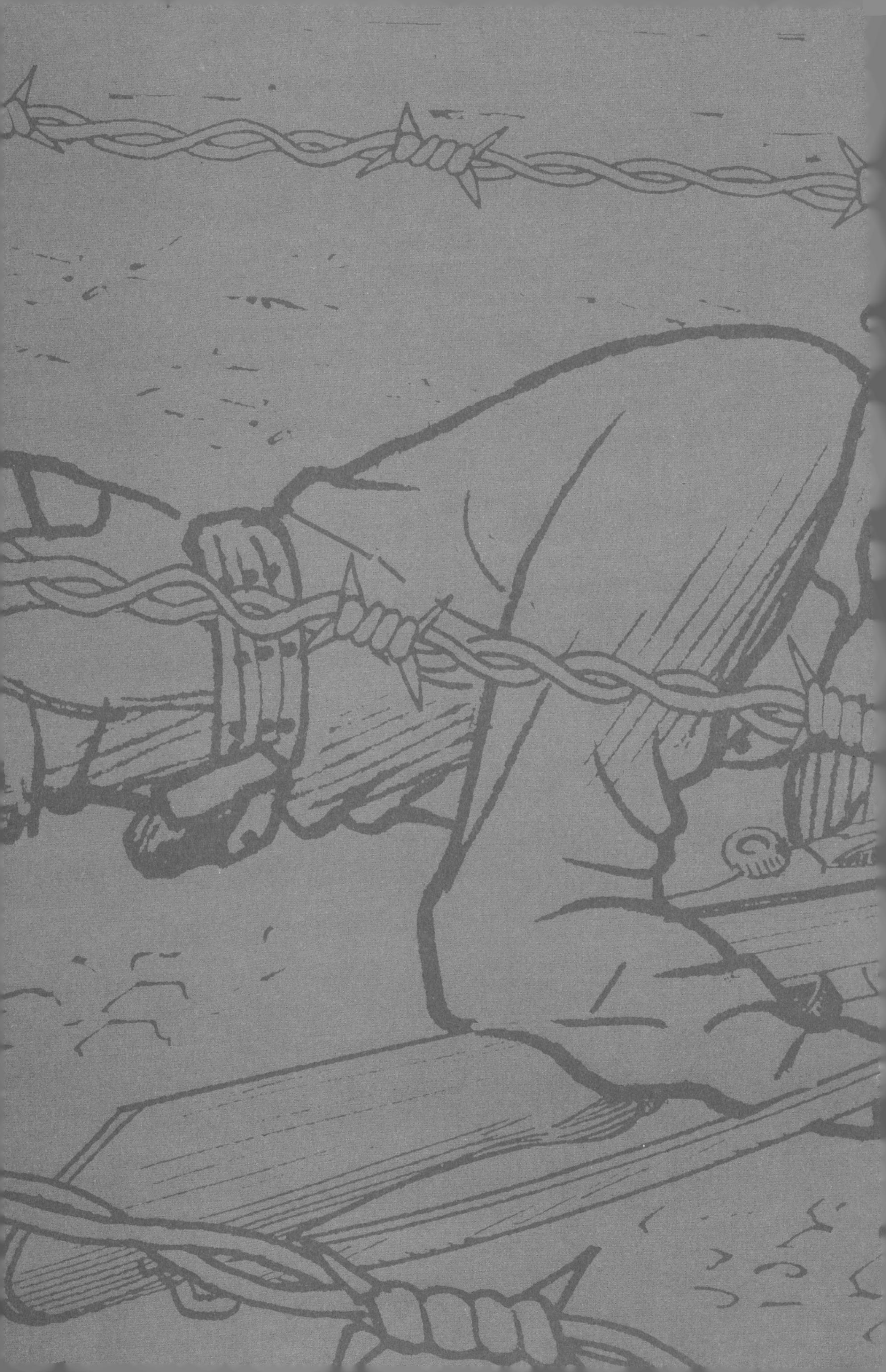